A
AUCKLAND ELECTRIC TRAMS.
QUEEN ST.—PONSONBY

QUEEN ST and Cor Pitt St & Karangahape R	1d To Ponsonby
Cor Pitt St and Karangahape R and Three Lamps	
Three Lamps and Ponsonby Term	
Queen Street via College Hill and Cor Patteson and Drake Sts	
Cor Patteson and Drake Sts and Three Lamps	

Please destroy this Ticket on leaving Car

1d To Queen Street

This Ticket must be shown when demanded or another Fare will be charged. Good only for car and trip issued.

NOT TRANSFERABLE.

The points between which the Passenger is entitled to travel will be punched out. Passengers are requested to immediately verify that the proper portion has been punched out.

FARE 1/2 HALF
THE AUCKLAND ELECTRIC
B6199
TRAMWAYS Co Ltd
PENNY

FARE 1D ONE
AUCKLAND · CITY
· TRAMWAYS ·
PENNY

1D AUCKLAND · CITY 1D
GOVERNMENT AND
37
CORPORATION SERVANTS ONLY
1D TRAMWAYS 1D

Issued subject to City Tramway By-laws. Good only for car and trip on which issued.

	1		4
1		4	3
2			2
3	City Tramways		1
4			
5			
6	CHILDREN		
7	B Must be shown or given-up on demand or another fare paid (Not Transferable.)		

295336

	1		3
4			2
5	CASH		1
6	A Must be shown or given up on demand or another fare paid. (Not Transferable.)		
7			

934137

VICTORIA
D 5252 A.C.T. CASH 1D Must be shown or given up on demand or another fare paid. (Not Transferable.) Issued subject to City Tram-way By-laws. Good only for car and trip on which issued.
AVENUE

6	5	4	3	2	1	IN

Wanganui Corporation Tramways.
Good only for car and trip issued. **1D** This ticket must be shown on demand or another fare will be charged. Please destroy on alighting.

NOT TRANSFERABLE

OUT	1	2	3	4	5	6

110063

NEW PLYMOUTH TRAMWAYS.
Must be shown on demand or another fare paid. Issued subject to Tramways By-laws and Regulations

1d		OUT					
	1	2	3	4	5	6	7
			IN				

Available for trip of issue only and for section punched Not transferable. PLEASE DESTROY ON ALIGHTING

Y62404

GISBORNE
Corporation Tramways

1D NOT TRANSFERABLE.

Good only for car and trip issued.

This ticket must be shown when demanded or another fare will be charged.

Please destroy on leaving.

NAPIER MUNICIPAL TRAMWAYS
BETWEEN G.P.O. & BATTERY ROAD. Please destroy on alighting. 1D No 2734

NOT TRANSFERABLE.

Available for trip of issue only Must be shown on demand or another fare paid. Issued subject to the Tramways By laws and Regulations.

TURNBULL, HICKSON & SODGER, PRINTERS

WELLINGTON CORPORATION TRAMWAYS
PLEASE DESTROY ON ALIGHTING 1D C 31204 1ST B SECTION

NOT TRANSFERABLE.

Available for trip of issue only. Must be shown on demand or another fare paid. Issued subject to the Tramways By-laws and Regulations.

TURNBULL, HICKSON & SODGER, PRINTERS.

KARORI BOROUGH COUNCIL
TRAMWAYS 1D A PLEASE DESTROY ON ALIGHTING 1ST SECTION A 4400

NOT TRANSFERABLE.

Available for trip of issue only. Must be shown on demand or another fare paid. Issued subject to the Tramways By-laws and Regulations.

TURNBULL, HICKSON & SODGER, PRINTERS

MIRAMAR BOROUGH COUNCIL
1D K 9464 BETWEEN MIRAMAR NORTH AND CITY BOUNDARY. PLEASE DESTROY ON ALIGHTING

Must be shown on demand or another fare paid. Issued subject to the Tramways By-laws and Regulations.

TURNBULL, HICKSON & SODGER, PRINTERS

Christchurch Tramway Board.

5	6	7	8
	DOWN		
The passenger is requested to assist Conductor by holding ticket so that it can be easily seen. Another fare must be paid if ticket is not produced for inspection when demanded. Good only for trip issued.			
	DOWN		
1	2	3	4

A 54802

5	6	7	8
	UP		
The ticket ought to be torn from block and punched in presence of passenger. Please destroy it on leaving car. Not Transferable.			1D.
	UP		
1	2	3	4

Invercargill Tramways
Good for One Section Only Not available Sats., Suns., Issued subject to By-laws and Regulations. 7204

Invercargill Tramways
Good for One Section Only Not available Sats., Suns., Issued subject to By-laws and Regulations. 7204

DUNEDIN CITY CORPORATION TRAMWAYS
This Ticket must be shown when demanded, or another Fare will be charged. Good only for trip issued. Not Transferable. 1d.

JOHN McINDOE, PRINTER

No 75211 L

		IN			OUT	
1	2	3	1	2	3

Invercargill Tramways
Good for One Section Only Not available Sats., Suns., Issued subject to By-laws and Regulations. 7204

Invercargill Tramways
Good for One Section Only Not available Sats., Suns., Issued subject to By-laws and Regulations. 7204

THE END OF THE PENNY SECTION

TOP: A restored New Brighton four-wheeled double-decker horse-tram of the 1890s carrying visitors at the Ferrymead Historic Park, Christchurch. *Bruce Dale* LOWER: The last tram to run in New Zealand. Wellingtonians listening to farewell speeches at Thorndon, before the final journey by No. 252 through the streets of Wellington on 2 May 1964. *Graham Stewart*

THE END OF THE PENNY SECTION

When Trams Ruled the Streets of New Zealand

Graham Stewart

Grantham House

New Zealand

By the same author

Tangiwai Disaster
When Trams were Trumps in New Zealand
Tragedy on the Track (with Geoff Conly)

PREVIOUS PAGE, TOP: Looking up Queen
Street, Auckland, from Quay Street in the
1950s. *Reginald McGovern* BOTTOM:
Double-saloon trams in Willis Street,
Wellington, in the 1960s. *W.W. Stewart*

First published by A.H. & A.W. Reed 1973
Limpbound edition published by Collins 1975
Revised enlarged edition published 1993

GRANTHAM HOUSE PUBLISHING
P.O. Box 17–256
Wellington 5
New Zealand

ISBN 1 86934 037 X

Edited by Anna Rogers
Typeset by Setrite Typesetters, Hong Kong
Designed by Bookprint Consultants Limited,
Wellington
Printed by Kings Time Printing Press of Hong Kong
in association with Bookprint Consultants Limited,
Wellington

PRESERVED FOR FUTURE GENERATIONS PREVIOUS PAGE, TOP: The restored Baldwin steam-tram from Wanganui which was built in 1891, seen on a demonstration run at Motat, Auckland, before the line to the Auckland Zoo was electrified. *Les Stewart* BELOW: The Tramway Historical Society's 1881 Kitson steam-tram with steam up at Ferrymead Historic Park. *Bruce Maffey*

THIS PAGE, TOP: A period piece photograph at the Ferrymead Historic Park featuring Dunedin combination tram No. 22 in the created historic Bowman Street. *Bruce Dale* MIDDLE: A Wellington double-saloon tram restored to original 1920s condition, running at Motat, Auckland. *Albert Chan* BOTTOM: The Wellington Tramway Museum's line at Queen Elizabeth Park, Paekakariki. A scenic view looking toward Whareroa Beach with Kapiti Island in the distance. Wellington *Fiducia* No. 239 and Wellington double-saloon No. 151 in the foreground. *Les Stewart*

Contents

The first edition of this book was launched by Lord Montagu of Beaulieu. 400 guests were carried by special museum trams to the function held at the Museum of Transport and Technology, Auckland, on 30 January 1973.

TOP: Dunedin's Maryhill Cable tram descending reputedly the steepest cable tramway gradient in the world in the 1950s. *Reginald McGovern* BOTTOM: Wellington's original Kelburn cable car system which operated for 76 years. *W.W. Stewart*

BELOW: Final journey — the sun rises over the Arapaoa River on the Kaipara Harbour at Matakohe in 1957 as a low-loader transporter heads north carrying a former Auckland tram. Having carried thousands of Auckland commuters over many years, the tram was being taken to its last destination to be used as a holiday home. *Mervyn Sterling*

The last Christmas with trams on the streets of Auckland — December 1956. Two views of Queen Street when everyone came to town for 'late night' shopping on a Friday. ABOVE: Looking down Queen Street from the Victoria Street intersection. LOWER RIGHT: A view from Shortland Street, looking up Queen Street. *Graham Stewart*

Preface

Our cities, like human beings, are growing and altering all the time, the changes so gradual that it is only when we look back at historical photographs that we suddenly realise how different the streets are compared with a few short years ago.

This book not only records the changing modes of passenger transport vehicles, but also gives an insight into the street furniture of each decade, the lamp standards, the style of cars and trucks, the fashions and behaviour of the people, the trees on the footpaths, the gardens, the advertising signs.

I acknowledge again with gratitude all those who assisted me with the original 1973 edition. For their help with this revised and enlarged 1993 edition, I would like to thank Ron Alexander, Sharyn Black, John Bettle, Henry Brittain, Eric Brockie, Albert Chan, Bruce Dale, Gerald Ditchfield, Keith Douglas, George Emerson, Mike Flynn, Richard Gray, Dave Hinman, Alan Lang, Keith McGavin, Reginald McGovern, Bruce Maffey, Dayle Maffey, Lynda Pike, Ian Stewart, Les Stewart, John Timmins and John Wolf.

My special appreciation and gratitude to Bruce Gamble for his research and detailed work with the tramway route maps of each city which feature in the appendices.

Just on 30 years have passed since the trams' demise in New Zealand and it is 20 years since the first edition of this book was published. This story does not extend past the tramway era in New Zealand but, as we approach the 21st century, light rail vehicles, the modern, state-of-the-art tram-cars which are making a comeback around the world, are now being advanced by some advocates as the answer to New Zealand's urban transport problems. The call could be, 'Come back tram-car, all is forgiven!'

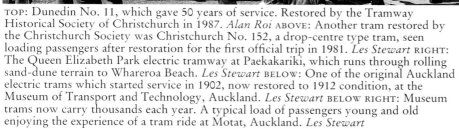

TOP: Dunedin No. 11, which gave 50 years of service. Restored by the Tramway Historical Society of Christchurch in 1987. *Alan Roi* ABOVE: Another tram restored by the Christchurch Society was Christchurch No. 152, a drop-centre type tram, seen loading passengers after restoration for the first official trip in 1981. *Les Stewart* RIGHT: The Queen Elizabeth Park electric tramway at Paekakariki, which runs through rolling sand-dune terrain to Whareroa Beach. *Les Stewart* BELOW: One of the original Auckland electric trams which started service in 1902, now restored to 1912 condition, at the Museum of Transport and Technology, Auckland. *Les Stewart* BELOW RIGHT: Museum trams now carry thousands each year. A typical load of passengers young and old enjoying the experience of a tram ride at Motat, Auckland. *Les Stewart*

Introduction

This book is the story of passenger transport in the urban streets of New Zealand, of the many classic vehicles, the people who manned them and the folk who rode them. Passenger transport gave an essential service which was as important to a city centre as the flow of blood through the veins of a body. These vehicles were never far from people's homes; they passed the corner of the street at regular intervals and became involved in the family life of urban dwellers. The growth and development of the main centres and provincial towns were influenced to a surprising degree by the evolution of transport services.

When the colony was starting to flex its muscles, wagonettes and drags uplifted people from the sidewalks to replace the only known means of locomotion within urban communities—Shanks's pony. Flimsy horse-buses, their compartments perched high above the muddy roads, made local travel an adventure. Then came the steel rail in the streets with the sweating horses and, later, the snorting steam engines. Soon people could settle in outer suburbs that were now within range of employment, with land speculators backing and building lines to the mushrooming estate hamlets. Hills were tamed by the magic cable cars that climbed by invisible power, and electric trams dazzled the populace while housewives were still slaving over coal ranges and lighting was either by gas lamp or candle.

Private and municipal enterprise played a vital role in the expansion of tramways, which brought great benefits and wider horizons to successive generations, opening up new vistas of travel, employment and social activities. They became part of a city's life and led to a considerable raising of land values wherever they ran. The rails were the sole available improvement upon the metal road—dusty in the dry months, muddy in wet weather, rough at all times.

In days of indifferent roads and slow-moving traffic the tramway was a double blessing, moving large numbers of people cheaply and, although it is hard to imagine now, providing smoother travelling for the drivers of other vehicles who followed the tracks.

The tramcar reigned supreme in the streets for longer than any other vehicle and is the mainstay of this story. But early on the scene to challenge the towering streetcars was the gasoline omnibus with solid rubber tyres, ably assisted by the 'Tin Lizzies' and 'Flivvers' when the country first took to personalised wheels on a grand scale. Charabancs and ponderous-looking omnibuses gave a new freedom and flexibility to mass transport. Then came a pioneer trackless tram perched like a jack-in-a-box high on ungainly hard wheels, and oil buses with soft pneumatic tyres introduced a new reign that still rules public transport in New Zealand.

Universal throughout this progression were the weather-beaten drivers holding tight to the reins, grippers, control handles or steering wheels, the athletic and portly conductors, the women who in wartime so ably invaded a man's domain, with the cry of 'Fez Plez'. All served through the years to deliver New Zealanders to their homes, businesses or recreational activities, and New Zealanders in their turn became attached to the vehicles, which became much more than just wood and steel. They were friends who gave everyone freedom in the days before the automobile conquered the highways.

Public transport in urban centres is still a lively topic of discussion and controversy, and as our road communications become increasingly strangled there is a strong possibility that commuters of the future will return to modern forms of mass travel to regain mobility.

For the Festival of Wellington in March 1959, Wellington *Fiducia* tram No. 260 was decorated and illuminated as a travelling advertisement. No. 260 was the last electric tram to be built in New Zealand. *Graham Stewart*

For the Sesqui 1990 celebrations, the Wellington Tramway Museum decorated Wellington double-saloon No. 151, as an illuminated tram. *Les Stewart*

CHAPTER ONE

Frisky Horses and Fiery Steamers

New Zealand Herald

What stories a wine decanter from the Greyhound Hotel in Auckland, now in our sitting room, could tell about the gamble taken by Henry Hardington, who owned the livery and bait stables next door, when he started a horse-coach service to Onehunga in the 1850s. Such a service would never succeed, said the old regulars, who kept the bars flowing with liquor, high spirits and gossip.

The Greyhound, which stood on John Court's corner, was the mecca for seamen and locals who hired Hardington's buggies and saddle horses for a spin in the country, when Newmarket was still a rural settlement. My great-grandmother was born at the hotel when her father was mine host, and now this family heirloom is the only remaining link. From a shelf in the public saloon that old decanter would have fortified many a traveller who rode the Royal Mail coaches to the Manukau. Hardington ran a 'punctual' omnibus during the day, with special coaches meeting each steamer.

Highway travel was hazardous. In Khyber Pass, the breaking of a link chain on a carriage pole rolled a bus down a 5-metre ditch. The fragile conveyance somersaulted twice before coming to rest with shaken and bruised passengers, including four women. Then there was the time when an old lady with a shawl wrapped round her head unintentionally frightened the animals as the jostling vehicle turned from Khyber Pass into Grafton Road one Saturday night. The horses rushed madly off, but were brought to a sudden stop by the coach overturning and pitching the occupants onto the road. The driver, a Mr Gillan, was said to be one of the best and most careful whips on the road.

The demand for transport brought many rival operators into the Auckland horse-bus field. William White flourished for a time, then R. Gilhan ran in opposition to George Cook of the Golden Line Omnibus Company. Other proprietors who bargained for fares to Onehunga included Reid, Kelly and finally Hollis. Crowthers ran Albert cars from the bottom of Shortland Street to Parnell, Newmarket and Remuera, while Frank Quick had a stand outside the Auckland Hotel for Symonds Street, Khyber Pass and Grafton Road, and George Jobson's buses left the Union Bank for Newton and Ponsonby.

On the whole the drivers were a fine bunch who had little leisure time because of their long hours of duty. But, as with all groups of men, there was always the odd

Ponsonby seemed a long way when this horse-tram dominated traffic in Queen Street, Auckland, in 1885. In the centre of the picture is the Greyhound Hotel, on the corner of Victoria Street. Behind the hotel was situated Hardington's Horse and Carriage Bazaar, a favourite meeting place in those years.
Burton Brothers, Author's Collection

When horses dictated the pace of life in our communities, an Auckland horse-bus driver had time for a friendly chat in the middle of Queen Street. This photograph was taken at the Victoria Street intersection in the 1870s. *Burton Brothers, Author's Collection*

individual to give his workmates a bad name. Take, for example, this hair-raising account to a newspaper after a nightmare ride with a drunken driver at the reins:

An omnibus left the Greyhound on Saturday night bound for Onehunga. It was filled with passengers inside and out. The driver was drunk. When in Upper Queen Street he lashed the horses so that the vehicle was jolted violently from side to side. In Karangahape Road he nearly ran into a trap. The man was evidently in a state of fury. He urged the horses at full speed down the Khyber Pass. Opposite Seccombe's Brewery he fouled a milk cart, and smashed it. During the whole journey the vehicle weaved from side to side along the road. Neither the screams of the women inside, nor the remonstrances of the men outside had any avail with this furious driver. Still he lashed his horses, still they jumped and bucked with rage. Going down Queen Street, Onehunga, he fouled a veranda, and carried that away. The excitement and screams of the female passengers inside the omnibus were loud and piteous.

Alarm was expressed when drivers leaving town with theatre crowds started indulging in the dangerous prank of racing. With the horses measuring their strides, passengers sitting on the box seat would hoot and yell at the vehicle being overtaken. This, naturally, was a signal for renewed effort. With drivers laying on the whip, both vehicles would gallop to the head of the road, their iron-shod wheels thundering over the rugged surface.

The well-to-do had their own stables where vehicles of noble origin such as phaetons, victorias, landaus, broughams and gigs were housed. For more humble city dwellers there were wagonettes, drays and horse-buses, until the steel rail conquered the quagmires called roads.

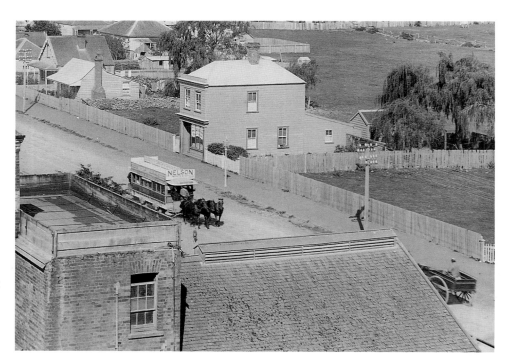

A three-horse team trotting at a steady pace up Khyber Pass Road, Auckland, 1898. Seccombe's Brewery is in the foreground. *Author's Collection*

The Tram-bus at Nelson

On the autumn morning of 7 May 1862, as the clocks chimed in the small colonial town of Nelson to herald nine o'clock, a coach-styled horse-tram was starting on an historic journey. The single horse moved off at a leisurely gait along the 3-foot-wide rails to pioneer 102 years of tramways in New Zealand. Within 20 years horse tramways were to become big business in urban centres throughout the colony, but this was the first passenger street-tramway in New Zealand.

It ran from the corner of Hardy and Trafalgar Streets to the port of Nelson. The line was 1.6 kilometres in length, being the city section of a 22-kilometre tramway built by the Dun Mountain Copper Mining Company to transport horse-drawn wagons carrying chrome ore from mines in the Dun Mountain region to ships at the port of Nelson. With flags and banners waving in salute, the first ore train of eight wagons had opened the line to the mines in February 1862, with the Nelson Brass Band playing patriotic music from a leading wagon. From the Albion Wharf at the port, the line ran via Haven Road, Waimea, Hardy, Alton, Manuka and Brook Streets, across Manuka Road, and on up into the hills to the mines. In return for allowing horse trains from the mines to rumble through the town streets, the town council had insisted that the mining company provide a passenger service to the port.

A tramway carriage, the only capital expenditure involved, was built by Mr Keary, a coach builder of Pitt Street, Sydney, and shipped to Nelson on the steamer *Prince Alfred*. It was similar in construction to the first Australian carriages that had begun running the previous year in Pitt Street, Sydney. In design the early horse-trams were influenced by contemporary vehicles of the period, their appearance revealing a mixture of railway, tramway and stage coach origins. The word 'bus',

The port of Nelson in the mid-1870s showing a horse-drawn tram waiting outside the Ship Hotel in Wakefield Quay. *Bett Collection, Courtesy Nelson Provincial Museum*

New Advertisements.

THE DUN MOUNTAIN RAILWAY OMNIBUS will LEAVE TOWN for the PORT DAILY, at Nine o'clock in the Morning, and LEAVE the PORT for the TOWN at half-past Nine, continuing to run hourly to and fro, until Five, p.m.

Fares—6d. each way. 632

From the *Nelson Examiner* of 7 May 1862, the day the first horse-drawn street tram-car began plodding the streets of New Zealand.

The city terminus of the pioneer Nelson horse-tram service at the corner of Hardy and Trafalgar Streets when the line was owned by Moses Crewdson between 1872 and 1885. *Courtesy Nelson Provincial Museum*

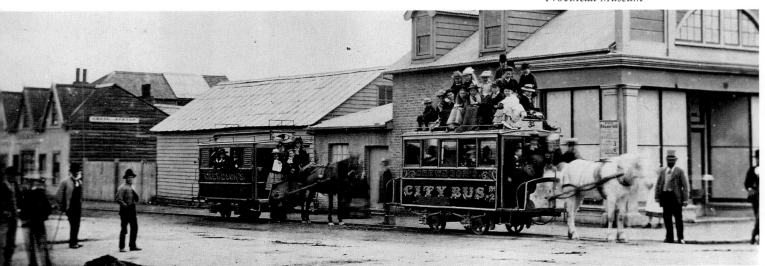

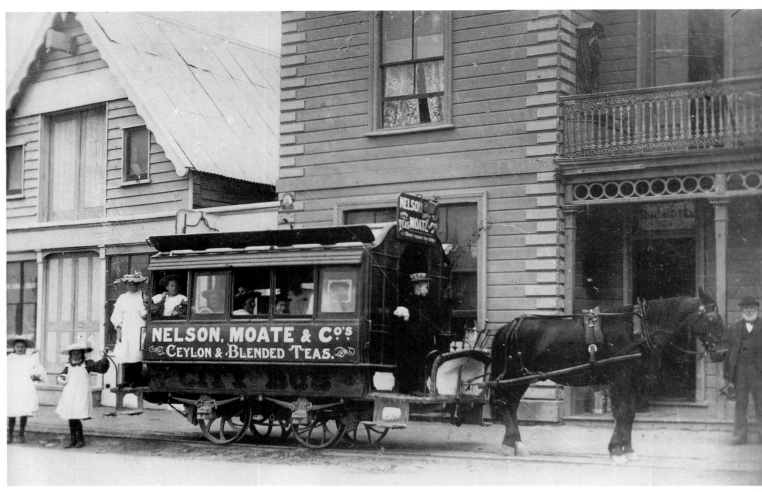

Even in the last century, these young girls with their large-brimmed hats must have been aware of the strength of the sun's rays as they posed by the 'Port Bus' outside the Ship Hotel at Nelson. Was the driver quenching his thirst when the photograph was taken? *Tyree Collection, Nelson Historical Society*

which was painted boldly on the side panels of the Nelson vehicle, may explain why it was always known as the 'city bus', or the 'port bus'. Very seldom was the true description, horse-tram, used by the patrons.

These were the years when 1 horsepower was represented by one horse and everything moved at a slow tempo, the horses plodding along at a walking pace. On arriving at its destination the whole outfit would come to a jolting, swaying halt, with brake shoes screeching in protest, while passengers descended. With a seating capacity for 40, including a back-to-back seat along the pitch of the roof, there was no fear of the poor horse breaking the 6-kilometre-an-hour speed limit. There was no spiral staircase for the roof-top riders, but steel footholds were provided for the more athletic patrons. As there was only a footboard, open to the passing scene, for weary feet, the upstairs passage was strictly for the men. Modesty boards to hide ladies' ankles did not come into vogue on double-deckers until the 1870s.

Initially Mr Nesbit maintained the service for the company, charging sixpence for a single ride, the fare being later reduced to threepence. Pranksters placing stones upon the rails to cause derailments gave the company plenty of headaches in the early days, and forced them publicly to offer a £10 reward for evidence that would lead to identification of the culprits.

In 1872, with mining operations at a standstill, all property and assets of the Dun Mountain Company were auctioned, including the tramway omnibus leased at £3 10s a week. The tramway section became the sole survivor of this pioneer iron road and continued under private enterprise. Over the years ownership of the line changed many times.

Present-day transport executives could no doubt learn a few tips from the various lessees and owners who were full of ingenious ideas when it came to making the line pay. One gentlemen, Mr Crewdson, had his wife sit on the front porch of their home and count the heads each time the tram passed, one pebble for each passenger being placed in a basket. Friends of the driver who frequented the same public house met the challenge by sitting on the floor below window vision on the understanding that the illegal profits would quench thirsts in the evenings. This

When life moved at the speed of a horse, passengers were happy to relax and be photographed while waiting for the 4-mile-an-hour Nelson horse-tram to commence another journey to the port. *Courtesy Nelson Provincial Museum*

woman would have had the dubious honour of being the first tramway inspector in a stationary, unpaid capacity. Other owners, C. and J. Bray, doubled the fare after dark to offset the cost of night running, much to the dismay and expense of young courting couples. A combined concession ticket costing sixpence was introduced in 1887. This ticket entitled the holder to a return tram ride and a swim at the Marine Swimming Baths at the port.

The lone horse was still plodding along the route at a safe and slow pace at the turn of the century, with the track now worn and pot holes prominent after 39 years of service. In 1901 the council decided to widen Haven Road and announced its desire to purchase and dismantle the tramway. Not wishing to lose their beloved tram-bus, irate citizens opposed the poll to sanction a loan of £1,250 to buy the tramway from the owner, Mr Harle. Amid strong demands for electrification by the town's tramway advocates, the loan was carried by a good majority of ratepayers. An investigation by the council found the cost of modernisation and electrification well beyond the reach of their meagre coffers.

The expense of dismantling and removing the 1.6-kilometre section of rails in June 1901 cost the princely sum of £19 18s. Nelson, the first city to adopt the street tramway, had become the first to dispense with it.

A lavishly illustrated timetable issued by C. and J.T. Bray in 1867. *Alexander Turnbull Library*

The Nelson 'city bus' in Hardy Street, in later years when it was owned by Jonathan Harle. *Courtesy Nelson Provincial Museum*

A successor of the port tram — a solid-tyred Thornycroft double-decker bus with curtains in the downstairs saloon. Hardy Street, Nelson, in 1908. *Jones Collection, Alexander Turnbull Library*

Wooden Trails on the West Coast

Gold discovery on the West Coast in the 1860s lured men in droves in search of the elusive royal metal. Living conditions were secondary in the race for the gold. Overnight, the eager diggers erected temporary shanties and tents and made for the claims. By the mid-1860s the population on the Coast had passed the 50,000 mark, with Hokitika boasting 99 hotels.

Wooden tramways were laid with similar urgency to keep pace with the sudden demands of the settlements. The wooden track joints were generally keyed and wedged without the use of nails. Westport had a horse-tram service with crudely constructed trolleys on which a back-to-back seat was placed for the passengers. Such refinements as quarterly tickets were available at a slight reduction, but after nightfall travel cost more. In May 1868 the *Westport Times and Charleston Argus* expressed concern about the dangerous state of the tram track in Westport's Gladstone Street. The paper was convinced that somebody would be killed if the line was allowed to remain.

Some of the towns which had horse traction with freight and passenger traffic in this prosperous age were Charleston, Brighton, Kumara, Greymouth, Kaniere, Hokitika and Ross. Although timber and coal represented the life blood of the Charleston lines originally built by Charles Nees in 1867, passengers landing at the beach from a sailing ship were given the luxury of horse-tram transport into Charleston, with their worldly possessions being carried for 5 shillings a ton. A Charleston publican, John Behan, petitioned the Provincial Council in May 1870 for compensation after the rerouting of a wooden tramway along a branch road had removed most of the stalwart drinkers from his tavern.

Further south a swinging cage driven by steam winches transferred travellers across the Taramakau River between connecting rural horse lines, from Greymouth in the north and Kumara in the south. At six o'clock in the morning the horse-cars, each drawn by a single horse, would start their respective journeys from Greymouth and Kumara to rendezvous on opposite banks of the Taramakau River. Commuters of the day allowed a good three hours for the trip. In winter, flapping canvas blinds covered the windows to keep out the weather, while the passengers sat huddled on wooden seats inside. This line, always known to the locals as 'the bush tram',

The Greymouth-Kumara wooden-railed horse tramway known to locals as the 'bush tram'. *James Ring, West Coast Historical Museum*

Loading freight into the aerial cable cage which crossed the Taramakau River. On the right is the horse-tram from Kumara. *Author's Collection*

Another view of the horse-tram terminus on the Kumara side of the Taramakau River. Two trams can be seen at the end of the line. *William F. Heinz Collection*

The proprietor Tom McGuigan and his one horse-tram at the Hokitika and Kanieri Tram Station. *West Coast Historical Museum*

closed with the opening of the railway between Greymouth and Hokitika in 1893.

From Hokitika a 4-foot gauge tramline ran up the coast to Stafford and in 1866 another went east for about 5 kilometres to Kaniere. In the early 1870s a small steam locomotive worked the Stafford section but it proved unsatisfactory and was withdrawn about 1875. For over 40 years the Kaniere track wound through forests and over bridges to outlast most of its contemporary lines in the province. A broad-gauge line of 5 feet 3 inches, owned by the Ross and Hokitika Tramway Company, followed the beach between the two centres, conveying passengers and goods in grand style.

Slowly, as the government railways edged their way around the coast, timber tram roads, now worn and warped, gave way to the little NZR steam locomotives with horsepower that required no grazing or grooming.

The horse-tram which ran from the coast at Awatuna to Pipers Flat for passengers and goods heading for the Goldsborough diggings south of Kumara. The sign across the side of the building in the left background reads 'Pipers Tramway Station'. *West Coast Historical Museum*

GREYMOUTH AND KUMARA
TRAMWAY COMPANY.

NOTICE.

REDUCTION IN FREIGHT.

On and after Monday, the 24th September, AN ALLOWANCE of FIVE SHILLINGS per Ton of 2,000lbs. will be made on HEAVY GOODS and DEAD WEIGHT.
W. HINDMARSH,
Secretary.

The wooden tram rails were laid through forest areas between Greymouth and Kumara. *James Ring, West Coast Historical Museum*

The De Luxe Kauri Carriage at Thames

With the opening of the Thames goldfields in 1867, the Provincial Council constructed horse tramways to carry quartz to the batteries along the Karaka, Waiotahi, Moanataiari and Tararu Creeks. To honour a visit of the Governor, Sir George Bowen, and Lady Bowen to the workings on the Tararu tramway on 13 January 1870, the Provincial Engineer-in-Chief, Charles O'Neill, engaged Mr Elliot of Auckland to build a tramway carriage. Three days before the vice-regal visit the elaborate tram carriage with polished mottled kauri panels was placed on the rails at the foot of the tramway, and fern arches were erected across the line in readiness for the big day.

When His Excellency with Lady Bowen and their children arrived at the tramway, the fine carriage was lying on the brink of the creek, 9 metres below the line. A final trial run that morning had nearly ended in disaster. Fortunately the 20 passengers, including a few women, scrambled through the broken windows, suffering only cuts from glass. At a speed of 3 to 4 kilometres an hour, the tram had rounded a curve on the downward journey to find a branch lying across the rails. The carriage was thrown off the line and crashed through a plankway intended only for pedestrians, dragging the horse over an embankment about 9 metres above the creek. A tree halfway down the bank prevented the carriage from turning over and so saved the lives of the occupants. Had the car travelled only a metre or so farther down the line, it would have been hurled into the creek below. Help was soon at hand and after the felling of a few trees, the carriage was lowered to the foot of the bank. Damage was slight considering the drop sustained, truly a testimonial to the builder. The Governor and Lady Bowen seemed, apart from the fact of the accident, not at all disappointed at having to walk up the tramway. They stopped at the scene to have the situation explained, before moving on to the mining sites.

Later in the month members of the Provincial Council questioned the expenditure on such an elaborate vehicle, and asked for an inquiry. A report to the council in February 1870 gave the cost of the carriage as £166 9s 6d, and the shed to house the vehicle as £60. Newspapers were now referring to the tram as 'the celebrated mottled kauri carriage'.

In September 1871 60 men started work on a track along the beach above high-water level for the Grahamstown and Tararu Tramway Company. The company had been formed to exploit the abundance of traffic offering on the coast. From Curtis Wharf, at the foot of Albert Street in Grahamstown, the line ran north-west to the deep-sea wharf at Tararu Point. A four-wheeled steam locomotive with a vertical boiler was bought from the Bay of Islands Coal Company at Kawakawa and shipped to the Phoenix Foundry in Auckland for overhaul.

On St Andrew's Day, all the gigs, traps and horses in the district were taxed to the limit conveying people to the Caledonian sports at Tararu. Taking advantage of

New Zealand Herald

GRAHAMSTOWN AND TARARU TRAMWAY.

TENDERS will be received up to TUESDAY, the 15th instant, for the CONSTRUCTION of a TRAM-WAY between Grahamstown and Tararu. The Engineer will be in attendance at 9 a.m., on TUES-DAY, the 8th instant, to point out the route, after which date, plans and specifications can be seen at the office of Messrs. DANIEL SIMPSON AND SON, Civil Engineers, Owen-street, Grahamstown.

The original drawing of the borough of Thames coat of arms, designed by F.A. Pulleine, who won a prize of £5 in a competition conducted by the borough to select a suitable emblem in May 1874. Prominent in the centre is the 'coffee pot' locomotive and mottled kauri tram carriage which ran on the Grahamstown-Tararu tramway. *A.E. Espiner*

the gala occasion, the tramway company opened its new line by using horses for locomotion. Locals crowded the trucks fitted up for passenger accommodation, and the mottled kauri carriage, which had passed from the possession of the Provincial Government to the private company, carried anyone who could pay sixpence. Directors of the tramway company had threatened to put their engine on the line, but the Highway Board opposed the move because there would be so much horse traffic on the road.

Two days later the little Chaplin locomotive made a trial trip to Tararu and back at a good pace with the handsome mottled kauri carriage attached. The *New Zealand Herald* of 4 December 1871 said in a report from Thames:

> TARARU TRAMWAY: The formal opening of this line could not be said to have taken place until today (Saturday, December 2), in consequence of the absence of the steam engine, which was landed today from the vessel, and at once placed on the line, and is now running from Grahamstown to Tararu, much to the delight of troops of urchins, who were trying their powers of endurance against that of steam. The engine worked beautifully on its maiden trip, going at the rate of from 6 to 8 miles per hour, under the charge of Mr Fraser, who has had the repairing and overhauling of it since it was sent from the Bay of Islands.

Every hour from nine in the morning until five at night this forerunner of New Zealand steam trams would puff away from Tararu with its kauri charge in tow. From Grahamstown the iron horse would leave on the half-hour from 9.30 am until 5.30 pm. Regular damage to the Tararu Wharf and beach by the heavy seas that lashed the coast in storms brought about the abandonment of both wharf and tramway after a few years. On the last day of May 1874, a heavy gale partly destroyed the Tararu Wharf, and a large section of the tramway between the goods wharf and the Marine Hotel was washed away.

The *Thames Star* reported the closure on 11 November 1874: 'The Tararu tramway closed yesterday on account of there not being sufficient traffic to make it pay now the daily passenger trade to Tararu has ceased through the sale of the "Golden Crown" steamer. The steamers at present in the trade are generally able to bring passengers to Grahamstown and Shortland on account of their light draught.'

It was fitting that one of the earliest locally built tram carriages had been made with the most famous of New Zealand timbers, the kauri.

The coat of arms as used on council correspondence for many years.

ALL CORRESPONDENCE
TO BE ADDRESSED TO
"TOWN CLERK"
THAMES.

Steam Monsters

Camouflaged with a false body of a carriage to disguise their identity from temperamental horses, the pint-sized, snorting steam-tram locomotives were first introduced to Wellington, Christchurch and Dunedin.

The steam-tram was commonly known as a 'dummy' because it carried no passengers, took the place of a horse and in outward appearance looked like a horse-tram. These diminutive locomotives were despised by cabbies and feared by horses as they chuffed through the city streets with tram-trailers in tow under the watchful eye of driver and guard. Much thought had been given to making the steam-tram, a dignified coke burner, as inconspicuous as possible. Covers hid the flashing piston rods from gaze, and water condensers were provided to reduce the emission of steam and to conserve water. Coke was used as fuel to eliminate, as far as was possible, the smoke and soot nuisance.

Wellington, with a population of only 19,000 people, launched its steam-trams in August 1878 with the Governor, the Marquis of Normanby, riding in style on the first car at the exhilarating speed of 10 kilometres an hour. All along the route, which was gaily decorated with streamers, crowds gathered to witness the marvel — Look, no horses out front! From the Government Buildings in Lambton Quay, the vice-regal party rode along Willis Street, Manners Street, Cuba Street, Vivian Street, Cambridge Terrace, around the Basin Reserve and on to the terminus at the Adelaide Road car sheds. Three engines resplendent in a claret livery and gold lining, bearing the names *Zealandia*, *Hibernia* and *Wellington*, each had one trailer attached for the opening procession. Following were three horse-drawn trams, relegated to the rear in this new age of steam locomotion. After the Governor had declared the system open, over 200 guests of the Wellington Tramways Company attended a banquet lit by gaslight specially for the occasion.

It was claimed to be the first steam-worked street rail system in the Southern Hemisphere. Merryweather and Sons of London, the well-known makers of fire engines, had built the engines for £975 each.

One of the promoters who first broached the idea of a tramway in 1873 was the civil engineer, Charles O'Neill, who had been responsible for the Thames goldmining tram-roads and the building of the kauri carriage at Tararu. A former Prime

Ready to uplift the citizens of Wellington — the Merryweather steam-tram locomotives *Florence* and *Hibernia* with their trailers at Adelaide Road Depot on the corner of King Street on opening day, 24 August 1878. *James Bragge*, National Museum

'Trams only stop at street corners' said a message to Wellingtonians on the panel under the trailer windows. The Merryweather locomotive is *Zealandia*. This picture was taken out in the 'country' at Newtown. The conductor, leaning on the engine below the driver, wears a straw boater. *P.C. Sorrell, Author's Collection*

Minister, Sir Julius Vogel, always referred to him as the 'Father of New Zealand Tramways'.

Jibbing and restive horses soon brought the steamers into displeasure with the public. Citizens had been advised to have their grooms walk the horses quietly down to the tramline to get them accustomed to the snorting puffer. A newspaper account of a private trial a few days before the grand opening with the Mayor of Wellington, Mr Dransfield, on board, was typical of the attitude taken by our four-legged friends. As the engine was shunting by the Opera House in Manners Street, the *Evening Post* had this to say:

> Here was afforded a good opportunity of observing the demeanour of horses as to the engine and car for a continuous stream of carriages, cabs, expresses, carts and buggies passed during the stoppage in Manners St. A few of the horses showed slight signs of surprise at the novelty, but only two proved at all seriously obstreperous, one insisting on executing a polka (arranged as a solo for four feet) on the footpath, while the other, evidently a confirmed jibber, was equally resolute in performing a war dance in front of the engine and, after passing it, making vicious efforts to rap double knocks at the door of the engine cab with his heels. In fact, after passing the engine by fully 20 yards, this unamiable steed suddenly made a violent strategic movement to the rear with the obvious intention of dashing the buggy against the locomotive. This kind intention was frustrated by about a dozen men seizing the buggy and shoving it and the horse bodily forward, but even then the animal succeeded in hoisting the vehicle high in the air. At length the equine nuisance was got rid of and no other difficulty ensued.

The *Post* went on to comment on the glaring exterior colour of the carriages which, like a red rag to a bull, would have to be rectified:

> It was manifest throughout that what startled the horses was not the engine, but the car which most foolishly has been painted a glaring scarlet, picked out in gold. This was proved by the fact that while the horses took hardly any notice of the dark claret engines when running alone, they exhibited much repugnance to a car which was standing separately. What effect the scarlet hue would have on a herd of cattle we need not conjecture, as it is not probable the juncture will arise.

More accidents followed because drivers were unable to control the reaction of their horses to the steam-trams.

During their first week of operation an irate young mechanic wrote to the editor of the newspaper complaining that he had been refused a seat because of his working clothes. 'Too dirty, can't have a seat,' the conductor had coolly remarked. In January the first fatal accident happened when Mr Luhning, a tobacconist in Lambton Quay, jumped off a moving tram in Cuba Street. He fell under the wheels of the second carriage and was killed instantly. Vivid newspaper reports described the fatality in grim detail, recording that 'blood was pouring forth like a slaughter yard'.

Steam, horse and electric transport passing the largest wooden building in the Southern Hemisphere in Lambton Quay, Wellington — the 1880s, 1890s and 1961. Only the 22 chimneys have gone, removed as a precaution against earthquakes. *Alexander Turnbull Library* The electric tram, No. 260, was the last built in New Zealand. It is now preserved by the Wellington Tramway Museum at Queen Elizabeth Park, Paekakariki. *Graham Stewart*

TOP: The camera could not freeze the 6-miles-an-hour pace of this Wellington Palace-type horse-tram prancing along Lambton Quay by Ballance Street. *Author's Collection*
BOTTOM: A similar view of Lambton Quay after the arrival of electric trams in 1905. *Muir & Moodie*

Cabmen no longer had supreme control of the urban transportation business and started obstruction tactics by driving two and three abreast in front of an engine, or cutting across the track in order to make the driver pull up. They presented a petition to the Governor 'praying that the Wellington Tramways Company be compelled to discontinue the use of steam and substitute horse power'. His Excellency gave them a sympathetic hearing, stating in reply that he thought the escape of steam from the tramway engines was very objectionable, especially as the streets were so narrow. It had made him very chary, he said, about driving through the streets of the town, and for that reason he had been about very little of late.

An embarrassing accident occurred in Lambton Quay in January 1880, when the daughter of Dr M.S. Grace, chairman of the tramways company, was driving her father in a buggy on his rounds. The mare became alarmed as the puffing steam engine came in sight. The daughter, being a learner-driver, pulled at the reins with fright, instead of gently touching the animal with the whip, making the horse shy backwards. One of the shafts broke off as a wheel came into violent contact with the kerbstone. Dr Grace and his daughter escaped without injury, and the doctor continued his calls on foot. The press, tongue in cheek, said: 'It is curious that such an accident should have happened to the chairman of the tramways company. It is rumoured that Wellington cabmen intend to present him with an address of condolence.'

Shying and bolting horses became less frequent, but the tramways' noisy cinder-spraying machines were never really accepted by Wellingtonians.

David Proudfoot of Dunedin

In 1879 an enterprising land speculator named David Proudfoot started steam and horse-drawn services in Dunedin. On 7 July 1879 the *Evening Star* published this announcement:

> The tramways were in partial operation today and were largely patronised, free trams being run. Until more powerful engines are obtained traffic will be confined to the Castle Street route, the present engines not being able to take cars up the steep rise to the Octagon. The journey from Cargill's Monument to Water of Leith, nearly two miles in length was done in ten minutes including stopping. The trams run very smoothly.

One steam puffer, a combined steam carriage named *Washington*, with accommodation at the rear for 20 passengers, had a very brief and stormy career. First the passengers viewed with disdain the flimsy partition separating the boiler from the saloon. It made them uneasy when sitting by a power plant with a reputation for being prone to exploding. Then, with no turning loops at the terminals, the driver who sat up front on the outward trip had to reverse all the way back to town with little vision in this direction. This dangerous practice on a city thoroughfare that had seen many accidents lasted only 16 days. While reversing in Castle Street, the *Washington* knocked down and killed a man, and was banned from the streets. From the back platform the conductor was supposed to pilot the car in reverse, but on this occasion he had not been able to communicate with the driver in time.

In September several trackmen were charged in court under an Act of Charles II with working on the city tramways on a Sunday. Mark Hind, foreman of the gang, explained that rain on the Saturday evening had stopped work on a curve at the corner of King and Albany Streets. The judge ruled it a work of necessity to complete the task and clear the street of obstruction, so the workers left the court free men. The curve had been relaid at the insistence of the publican on the corner, who had complained that the vibration from steam-trams was so great that it spoiled the beer in his cellar.

After the success of his first line, Proudfoot obtained the right to run tramways to the boroughs of North-east Valley, St Kilda, South Dunedin and Caversham. Besides being a boon to the residents, this was a great inducement to purchase land that largely increased in value once the improved service was running. Some lucky travellers found travel with Proudfoot profitable, as this shrewd businessman — in order to boost trade — ran a lottery based on the numbers of the tram tickets. Prizes varied from gold watches to blocks of land served by his trams. But Proudfoot soon encountered opposition from the cabbies who, like their Wellington counterparts, thought they saw their livelihood doomed with the advent of the clanking steam-trams.

Men and their mechanical marvel. A Hughes steam tramway engine and trailer in the Octagon in Dunedin. *Author's Collection*

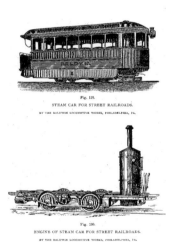

The official sketches by the Baldwin Locomotive Works of Philadelphia of their combined steam carriage. One was imported by David Proudfoot of Dunedin and given the American name *Washington*. *Author's Collection*

Dressed in their Sunday best, the citizens of Dunedin alight from horse-trams in Princes Street for an outing on the Sabbath. A view looking towards the Exchange.
Author's Collection

A penny section token which was issued on the horse-trams after the system was taken over by the Dunedin Corporation.
Author's Collection

At the height of the cabmen's battle in December 1880, the entire plant of 34 cars, seven engines and one wagon was destroyed by fire. Over 3000 bushels of oats for the horses helped feed the flames on that fateful Sunday morning. The depot had originally been the first church in Dowling Street and, when bought by the tramways, had been shifted to the foot of Rattray Street, below the old railway station. Only two cars survived the blaze and these, together with two others stored at Ocean Beach, constituted the total fleet of trams in Dunedin for several months. Proudfoot used surplus carts and wagons to maintain a skeleton service while new cars were being built, the steam engines having suffered little damage from the flames. Newspapers later had this to say about the calamity: 'There is little doubt the place was deliberately set on fire, but although Mr Proudfoot offered a reward of £400 for information that would lead to the discovery of the incendiary, no clue was obtained.'

One bright spot for Proudfoot at this time was the success of his St Kilda line, which was in opposition to the established Dunedin, Peninsula and Ocean Beach Railway Company. In 1876 this company had opened a line to Ocean Beach (St Kilda) and along the foreshore to Musselburgh, where it branched off to the right along Royal Crescent and Victoria Road to a point near the Forbury Park Racecourse. Another branch skirted the cliffs to the Andersons Bay area. In a bid to win back patrons now using Proudfoot's trams, the Dunedin, Peninsula and Ocean Beach Railway Company extended its line up Crawford Street to the city centre and bought two second-hand steam-trams, the *Scotia* and *Anglia*, together with four trailers, from the Wellington Tramways Company. Proudfoot ultimately won the battle, but his steamers on the streets were still in disgrace.

As the months passed the steam-trams were the cause of many accidents and became an intolerable nuisance because of the deposits of ash that lay about on city buildings and on the clothes of pedestrians. Much maligned as the trams seemed to have been at this period, the fashionable marriage in Dunedin, in July 1883, of the eldest daughter of Captain Baldwin to the Hon. E. Parker, son of the Earl of Macclesfield, and nephew of the Duke of Westminster, saw the city tram-cars trundling to and fro with decorations and flags flying in honour of the event. They were at least accepted by some members of the community.

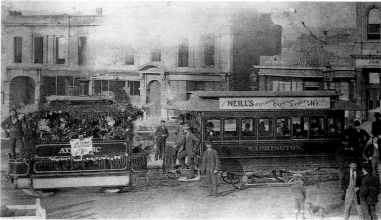

Proudfoot was prosecuted on a number of occasions for the disturbance caused by smoke and steam, but legal technicalities always proved him innocent. Then, in the January of 1883, he was again prosecuted in the Magistrate's Court for using motors 'so as to be a nuisance and annoyance to the public'. Great sympathy was shown for the proprietor, who undoubtedly had the right under his agreement with the council to use steam power if he pleased. The judgement of the court, which went entirely in his favour, was received with acclamation.

Later in 1883 Proudfoot sold his interests to the Dunedin City and Suburban Tramway Company but the council stipulated that the steam-trams must be phased out within 12 months or else altered to comply with the regulations. Otherwise it would not transfer Proudfoot's rights to run the services. Finally the engines were removed from the streets in March 1884, after Oliver Wakefield, a nephew of Edward Gibbon Wakefield, was killed under an engine in Princes Street.

So the steam monsters faded from the scene, and faithful old dobbin plodded on through the 1880s pulling the masses in Dunedin.

Flags and greenery adorned the Dunedin steam-trams *Grand Pacific* and *Atlantic* and trailers when David Proudfoot celebrated the first year of service in 1880. *Author's Collection*

David Proudfoot. *Otago Early Settlers' Museum*

The Merryweather steam-tram *Anglia* with trailers in Crawford Street, Dunedin. The *Anglia* was bought second-hand by the Dunedin, Peninsula and Ocean Beach Railway Company, from the Wellington Tramways Company. *Author's Collection*

High Street, Dunedin, from Princes Street, showing one of the original Mornington cable-trams and a city horse-tram waiting for customers. *Author's Collection*

Umbrellas on the top deck were there to deflect cinders, not rain. Christchurch No. 1 steam tramway engine leaving Cathedral Square with trailers attached. *Author's Collection*

A Haven for Steam Dummies in Christchurch

An old 'puffing billy' chugging out of Cathedral Square with six double-decker trailers laden with picnic parties bound for the seaside must have been a magnificent sight. In the typical English tradition of Christchurch, a narrative relating to the birth of tramways in the town maintains that it all started, as would be expected, after a cricket match at Hagley Park. A group of townsmen trudging home in their whites along a dusty Riccarton Road first discussed the possibilities of rail conveyances for the growing settlement.

After much planning and several proclamations the Canterbury Tramway Company was formed and on 9 March 1880 began a service from Cathedral Square to meet all passenger trains at the railway station. Two heroic little steam engines paved the way, towing double-decker trailers of 'Emmett' character, with an upper open deck that gave passengers the full blast of the smoky exhaust from the locomotive. To check reckless drivers a governor was fitted to each steam motor, keeping its speed to the 16 kilometres an hour fixed by law.

A lot of research had been undertaken by the makers, Kitson and Company, of Leeds, England, to produce an engine able to mix with horse-drawn street traffic. Original regulations of the 1860s had stipulated that a man carrying a red flag must walk ahead of the engine to ensure that a sober maximum speed of 6 kilometres an hour was not exceeded on a public road. One suggestion to help soothe terrified horses was to build the machine in the shape of a natural animal, bright ideas even including an engine in the shape of a swan with the long neck neatly enclosing the chimney. These Kitson engines were of diminutive proportions, but were capable of drawing anything from six to eight fully loaded trailers. In most respects built on the same principles as their unpopular counterparts in Wellington and Dunedin, they were the prototypes of over 300 standard-model tram engines which the Kitson Company later built for tramway companies throughout the world.

The broad streets of Christchurch made for less congestion and, together with the absence of any gradients, proved ideal for the steam dummies which were duly accepted by the public. Rapid progress by contractors saw the nucleus of the system put in place, with lines to Papanui, Sydenham, Addington and to Woolston opened by the December. Tramways in Christchurch became a popular business in the 1880s with two private companies competing for trade.

Along a 20-metre-wide private right-of-way the New Brighton Tramway Company built a line to the beach in 1886, adjacent residents being given an easement over the lane for access purposes. A Mrs Knight who had a grievance against the company, persisted in leisurely driving a horse and cart along the track in front of the morning tram loaded with businessmen, who were forced to follow impatiently at a sedate pace. To further exercise her right-of-way concession, Mrs Knight chose one moonlit night to barricade the road with the help of her sons. With the tram held up, the warlike lady put a gorse stick to her shoulder so effectively that the outside

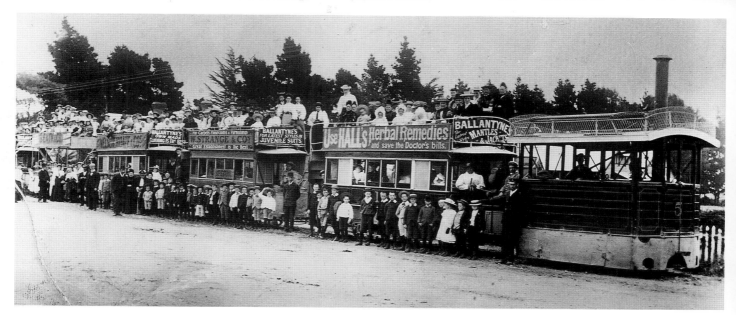

tram passengers sought cover with haste. The clerk of the Magistrate's Court crouched under the tram stairway, while a leading customs agent of the day dived headlong into the nearby drain.

Steam was first used as the traction force on the New Brighton line in 1887, with the aid of a locomotive hired from the Canterbury Company, but horses were soon found to be more suitable. On moonlit nights the rhythmical trotting of a spanking two-horse team, harness a-jingling, gave the top-deck passenger — provided he had suitable company — a ride that could not be equalled today.

The third competitor, the City and Suburban Tramway Company, often used open-sided double-decked horse-cars. These were exposed to the full force of Mother Nature, as they ran through Linwood and Richmond to North Beach and along the Esplanade to New Brighton. This company did not have access to Cathedral Square, so ran its trams to North Beach via Cashel Street, from the old clock tower site in Manchester Street.

On a Sunday in November 1886, as a guard walked back to a steam-tram standing outside the Heathcote Arms Hotel in Ferry Road, the tranquil morning air was suddenly shattered when the exploding boiler from the engine hurtled through the air and landed 30 metres away. Fortunately the driver was watching a ploughing match in a field across the road and the two trailers were deserted. Kitson No. 7, with her cab and condensers torn away, was a tangled mass. Also a casualty was the leading trailer, which bore the same number, its splashboard, panelling and windows being blown in by the concussion. This display of fireworks was only the start of a colourful career, for No. 7 outlived all her sisters. When Canterbury Province celebrated its centenary in 1950, this veteran of 1881 paraded through town as a float on a transporter, and then puffed on period-piece runs to Sumner, New Brighton and Riccarton racecourse. Today this steam dummy can be found in full working order at Ferrymead Park with a trailer of her decade in the same state of preservation.

Sunday school picnics were fun — steam-tram 'specials' in Christchurch took children, their families and teachers, to the seaside for an annual outing that was remembered by all for the rest of the year. *Author's Collection*

Kitson steam-tram No. 5 with four fully laden double-decker trailers turning into Cashel Street, bound for the seaside at Sumner, Christchurch. *Author's Collection*

A short-lived bid for one-man operation was made as early as 1887 when an order was placed with a company in New York for a one-man, one-horse tram. Conductors were, however, soon reinstated to catch all the fares.

In the mid-1880s a journey to Sumner involved transferring at the Heathcote Bridge to the steam ferry *Colleen*, owned by the Canterbury Tramway Company. One then had the choice of either an established coach service or a horse-dray belonging to William Hayward, who ran a service in cut-throat opposition to the coaches. Skirting the cliffs around McCormacks Bay and through Redcliffs, then over a wooden bridge at Clifton, the tramline reached the seaside resort of Sumner in the late 1880s. Huffing and puffing, long trains of fragile-looking double-decker trailers would bring hundreds in relative luxury for a day at the beach. Ladies wearing long dresses and large Victorian hats to shade their complexions from the wicked sun, men with straw boaters and the children armed, as today, with buckets and spades—all enjoyed the sunshine and sand. A diverting pastime for the crews while waiting to bring a tram back from the beach was to gather pipis and cook them in the improvised galley of the steam engine.

An old-timer once told me that when he was a conductor on the steam-trams, he was asked to drive while the driver when aloft on the double-decker trailer to talk to his fiancée. His willingness to help ended when the pressure-gauge glass in the cab broke and the couple on top disappeared in clouds of steam. Another described the day the Sumner tram came rattling around the foreshore to find a fisherman having trouble with his drift net on the estuary. Claiming that his net was so full of fish that he could not haul it in, the fisherman asked the driver to oblige by hitching the trawl-line to the tram and thus the catch was landed. A regular passenger was a dog named Casey, who used to board the tram at Sumner every morning, travel to the Square, and return late in the afternoon. Redcliffs was a favourite stop when life was not dominated by timetables, enabling passengers to gather mushrooms. On theatre nights the last tram to Sumner was horse-drawn, and consisted of two cars. Horses were stabled overnight at Sumner and pulled the first tram to the city the next morning.

Josh Lewis, known around town as the 'Gentleman Driver', in the 1890s began a rival service with a two-horse coach on Papanui Road. A shrewd businessman, he began to make serious inroads into the revenue offering, but the Canterbury Company was equal to the problem. By detailing a coach to roam all the side streets and pick up fares just ahead of the gentleman driver, the company succeeded in chasing its competitor off the roads.

In 1891 the Canterbury Company placed an early morning car on the Papanui line especially for those who enjoyed a morning pipe on the way to the office. Businessmen started going home for lunch, and at 12.45 pm two double-decker cars for Papanui would pull out of the Square with a spanking four-horse team.

Low fares resulting from excessive competition for beach traffic brought the Canterbury Tramway Company into liquidation in 1893, to emerge with added capital as the Christchurch Tramway Company, which carried on until the Christchurch Tramway Board took over in 1905. Christchurch, with its flat terrain, became a haven for steam dummies, although within a few years it was found more economical to employ horses on the shorter runs. The steam engines survived early misgivings and lasted until well after electrification.

Kitson steam-tram No. 7 hauling two open double-decker trailers returning from Sumner during the Canterbury Centennial celebrations in 1950. *W.W. Stewart*

Cathedral Square, Christchurch, in the 1880s. Passengers alighting from a train of double-decker trailers, hauled by a Kitson steam-tram. *Author's Collection*

Cathedral Square in the 1950s, with a one-man tram, No. 178, loading for Spreydon. This tram has been restored to running order at the Ferrymead Museum, Christchurch. Behind is a Boon-type tram bound for New Brighton. *Graham Stewart*

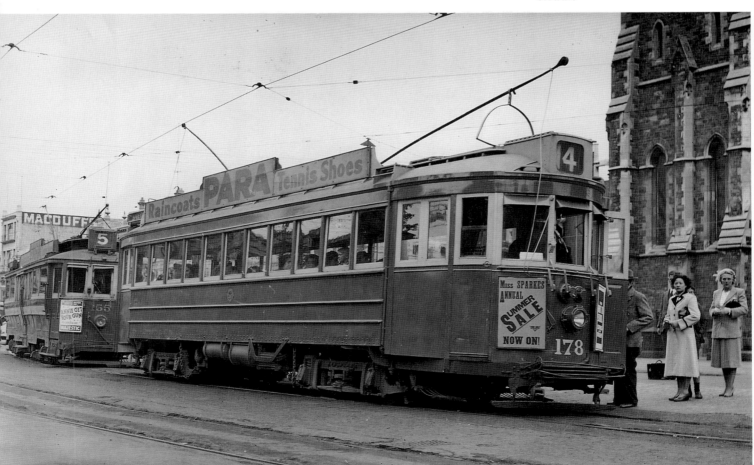

Changing the horsepower. A team of horses being driven to New Brighton Tramway Company trams in Cathedral Square, Christchurch. *Author's Collection*

The southernmost horse-drawn tram in the world. A one-horse-powered car in Dee Street, Invercargill. *Burton Brothers*

CHAPTER TWO

Traction with Four Legs

Invercargill — Most Southern in the World

Built on level country with streets of regal width, Invercargill was the answer to an engineer's dream; there could have been no more suitable locality for tramway. Back in 1876 Frederick Clifton had run a two-horse bus from the Club Hotel to the Gladstone Hotel, four times a day at a 'sober trot', no doubt. After the usual objections and meetings the Southland Tramway Company was formed to run a network of horse-trams to the suburbs. The four-wheel cars were built at Birkenhead, England, by George Starbuck, an associate of George Francis Train, who in August 1860 had introduced the first true horse-drawn street tramway to England, only two years before the Nelson venture. Train, a vain and flamboyant character, had inspired Jules Verne to create Phileas Fogg, after he himself travelled around the world in approximately 80 days.

Loose metal scattered by the feet of horses spoiled the maiden trip to Gladstone in December 1881. At several points the stones got under the wheels and threw the car off the track. Large numbers of citizens took advantage of a free ride when this car made its first appearance on that Saturday afternoon. The car was fitted with all the latest improvements, including conductor's bells, lamps, automatic fare-takers and two horses for locomotion. Once the tracks were cleared and the yoking of the horses adjusted, a single horse was found to be sufficient for haulage. From the Invercargill Post Office the track ran north along Dee Street and North Road to Waikiwi, a distance of 4 kilometres. Halfway between the terminals, at Gladstone, were the stables and horse paddocks.

To cater for the traditional Saturday night on the town, cars ran until 10.45 pm and at first there was no tram service on Sundays. The last car on week nights left town at 8.45 pm. Later, routes were extended to the south and east, but the East Road service was a failure and ceased after about four years.

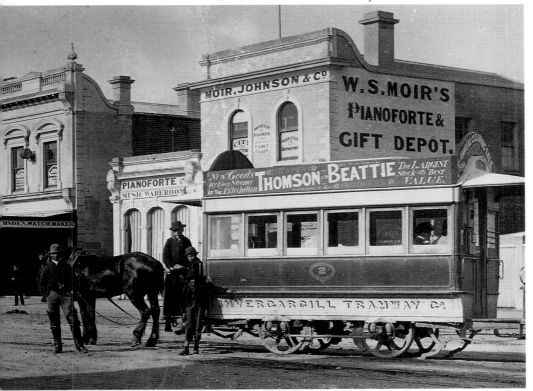

The wages paid to drivers of the horse-cars were £2 a week, and to conductors £1 a week. While all lines were operating, the total staff at its maximum strength comprised a manager, three drivers, four conductors and two stablemen. This meant greater overhead, and wages were reduced to 35 shillings for drivers, 15 shillings for conductors and 30 shillings for stablemen, these being for a week of 12 hours a day and eight hours on Sundays.

A depression hit the town in 1887 and the trams ran empty for days on end. People were too hard up to ride, although every means was used to entice them to save shoe leather. Concession and workers' tickets were issued, but they were coldly ignored, with the result that the revenue at times would not cover the wages bill. A new company, the Invercargill and Suburban Tramway Company took control, but as no major changes were made, the average deficit was some £300 a year, according to one of the old drivers, and the company went into liquidation about three times. However, there was always somebody to keep the wheels turning as the trams slowly pitched with a nauseating roll over the pavements of Dee Street, the rattle of hoofs echoing in the doorways.

In the 1890s J.G. (later Sir Joseph) Ward and Walter Henderson purchased the company, once again in liquidation, and operated it as a private company, although retaining the old name. The cars kept rolling until fire destroyed the stables, barn and horse-trams. This was the final chapter in the story of the southernmost horse-trams in the world.

Eternal Journey — The Tramway Hearse of Christchurch

Designed so that passengers sleeping in eternity could glide quietly over a line on which no bell ever clanged and no rider ever paid a fare, the tramway hearse built by the Christchurch City Council in 1885 had accommodation for four coffins. Painted in dignified black for its solemn task, the hearse had two elliptical windows on each side to enable mourners to pay their last respects, and railings on the low roof to hold the floral tributes.

From the council yards, opposite the Clarendon Hotel, where the Scott Memorial now stands, the line went through Cathedral Square and along Worcester Street to the old public cemetery, continuing along Buckleys Road to Slaughterhouse Road (now Rudds Road), and thence to the council's nightsoil reserve. A branch line for the hearse tram ran down Cemetery Road (now Butterfield Avenue) to the Linwood Cemetery. Dust and rubbish was to be transported to the yard with discretion so that this traffic would neither interfere with nor embarrass a funeral cortege. Apart from cashing in on the undertaking business, the council proposed to establish a crematorium which, it was hoped, would keep the tramway hearse busy, in conjunction with two passenger cars built locally by Booth McDonald.

But the idea never reached reality and the council leased its mortuary line to an opposition company which extended it to New Brighton for patrons who were very much alive, although the council did use the line for the cartage of rubbish. The hearse tram never led a funeral and for many years it reposed on the mudflats near Heathcote Bridge, being used as a powder magazine at Andrews Quarry. Later the hearse was placed on a pontoon and used as a houseboat on the estuary.

Built for the final journey, this Christchurch Corporation tramway hearse never actually carried a corpse. *Canterbury Times*

Hill Boys and Sweating Horses in Auckland

When the first horse-tram appeared in Queen Street, Auckland, on an experimental run in July 1884, one man threw a stone at the car and was arrested on a charge of insulting behaviour. Cab-drivers resented an order to move their stands from the middle of the street, and refused to budge. Much clashing of swords followed, the cabbies parking their hansom cabs along the up track on the eastern side of Queen Street. Fortunately the company only used a single line for the first fortnight and the obstruction was of little inconvenience while the feud lasted.

A company with large property holdings in the town, the St Heliers and Northcote Land Company Limited, had been instrumental in constructing the lines and in August 1884 had opened the first section from the intersection of Customs Street, via Queen Street, Wellesley Street West, Hobson and Pitt Streets to Karangahape Road and thence to the Ponsonby Reservoir. Some experienced conductors were obtained from David Proudfoot's Dunedin tramways, and these men handled close on 500 fares on opening day. Official red tape brought the cars to a halt for four days just as the populace was beginning to understand and appreciate the benefits of tramway travel. It was alleged that Mr Hales, the Public Works Department's District Engineer, had exceeded his authority in giving sanction for the opening, the necessary permission having to come from Wellington.

Tramway horses were very timid in the presence of any form of motive power other than that of their equine brothers. A stranded street-roller in Queen Street created so much doubt and fear in the tram-car horses that it was necessary to erect a hoarding — to shield the monster from their gaze. The fast motor bikes and teenagers' cars that scatter pedestrians in this modern age had predecessors, as the *New Zealand Herald* of 15 November 1886 commented:

> Some steps should be taken to prevent furious driving in Queen Street on Saturday nights when the streets are crowded with people. The tramcars move almost at a walk, with whistles blowing, though confined to the rails, but it is no uncommon thing to see a cabman careering along — driving through long lanes of people at six or seven miles an hour, the only warning being the occasional crack of his whip. On Saturday nights this reckless conduct is most conspicuous and gives the impression that such rapid driving is done out of bravado and pure cussedness, rather than anything else.

Downtown Auckland in the 1890s. A summer horse-tram waits at the foot of Queen Street for passengers from the North Shore arriving on the paddle steamer Britannia, seen berthing in the background.
Alexander Turnbull Library

Straining on the traces. A 'hill boy' on a powerful draughthorse assisting a heavily loaded Auckland horse-tram up the Wellesley Street West grade of 1 in 12. *W.B. Beattie Snr*

Tests found that three horses could take a tram containing 35 passengers up the Wellesley Street West grade. It was discovered, too, that the grade in question was the same as College Hill, namely 1 in 12. A cable tram had been suggested for College Hill, but the cost of £10,000 was a serious item. Clydesdale leader horses with boys astride were used to assist on the steep grades. A 'hill boy' would wait at the bottom, hook a chain to the pole, help the lighter tram horses on the haul, then ride down the grade for the next tram. Sometimes when the cars were packed in the evening peak periods, a tram would come to a stop, then roll backwards down the hill, dragging the three horses with it. Passengers and conductor would jump off and chock the wheels with road metal. Then, with the encouragement of 'Git ups', the horses would bravely struggle up the hill with passengers giving a helping hand to push from the rear. Incidentally, Dunedin also used leader horses and boys on the grade out of the Exchange and up to the Octagon.

By February the Auckland tracks ran to Three Lamps and down Jervois Road to the car sheds and stables at Wallace Street. The inward trip from Three Lamps was done in half an hour, no leisurely journey for the horses, which had to travel at a smart trot.

Jim Divers, who was a conductor on the horse-cars from 1899 to 1902, recalled the excitement that prevailed whenever the firebell clanged in town. Shops emptied, assistants tore off their aprons and smocks as they ran to see the sparkling fire

An inward-bound horse-tram from Newmarket proceeding at a leisurely pace down Queen Street, Auckland, having just passed Fort Street on the left. *Author's Collection*

Auckland at the turn of the century. Looking down Wellesley Street West towards the junction of Queen Street. On the right a 'hill boy' waits on his horse to assist the Ponsonby tram turning out of Queen Street. Below the public library a Newmarket tram, with leader horse attached, plods slowly up the Wellesley Street East incline. *Author's Collection*

Open summer horse-tram No. 32 bound for Newton and Ponsonby, Auckland, passing under a welcome arch erected at the intersection of Queen and Victoria Streets for the visit of the Duke and Duchess of Cornwall and York, in 1901. In the foreground a funeral procession proceeds down Queen Street. *Auckland Weekly News*

The same intersection in the mid-1880s, from the opposite side of Queen Street, showing Victoria Street West on the right. The two-horse tram is inward bound from Ponsonby. *Alexander Turnbull Library*

Auckland horse-tram No. 34 passing old St Matthews in Hobson Street, en route to the then distant suburb of Ponsonby. Wellesley Street West is on the left. *Author's Collection*

engine, or dashed off to the blaze itself. And away would lumber the tram boys on their draught horses. Jim had known a lad to be gone as long as two hours, while the tram he was supposed to be assisting waited patiently at the foot of the incline. About halfway up the slope of Wellesley Street East stood a second-hand shop owned by a woman known to everyone as Ma Lindsay. Ma had two intelligent parrots which sat in their cages and never missed a movement on the sidewalk. It was not long before they became aware of the whistling of the tram conductors and were soon mimicking them. Of course the inevitable happened. As the horses were straining on their collars with a heavy load, a whistle would pierce the air and a cursing conductor would frantically apply the wheel brake, while the passengers leant out the windows and told Ma what she could do with her birds.

In 1886, the St Heliers and Northcote Land Company changed its name to the City of Auckland Tramways and Suburban Land Company Limited, and later, as promoters of the Auckland City and Suburban Tramway Company, extended the iron web. The eastern circuit to Newmarket, and a branch down lower Symonds Street to the Choral Hall for concert traffic, were opened in February and March of 1886 respectively. Outside the Choral Hall and the theatres, opposition bus drivers could be heard at the conclusion of concerts, shouting their destinations. Trams would wait if patrons of the vaudeville or opera houses were late getting out.

Steel rails in Broadway, Newmarket, with a loop line in Remuera Road, were a boon for punters on race days. In Broadway one now alighted from the horse-tram where one of Hollis's buses for Onehunga would be waiting. Within the first week 2000 were using the trams daily to Newmarket. For the two-day Easter race meeting the tramway company ran a brisk shuttle service from Queen Street where the horse-cars, laden with racegoers, were met by a fleet of horse-drawn omnibuses bound for the course. Buggies, victorias and broughams headed in droves for the Ellerslie track. The extension of the horse line to Epsom, which ran by the side of the road, was bordered all the way by arum lilies. In 1888 the City of Auckland Tramway and Suburban Land Company bought the paddock on Epsom Road, known as Potter's Paddock, and on it built stables and car sheds.

To cater for sporting attractions, the land was laid out as a racecourse, with football grounds in the centre. The company built grandstands and other facilities required for agricultural shows and meetings of the Onehunga Racing Club, and also later for trotting meetings. Rugby football, which had been played on Dilworth's property, came to Potter's, together with all the visiting shows. This boosted tram traffic and the company could now count on one or two gatherings each week at the 'paddock'. Locals had named the paddock after William Potter, who bought the land from the Maori. Potter had first resided in the Bay of Islands in 1835, where he owned a hotel until it was destroyed by fire at the outbreak of Hone Heke's war of the 1840s. He then sailed in his own vessel to Auckland and settled at Epsom. After the Duke of Cornwall and York had reviewed troops on the paddock during the Royal tour of 1901, the Auckland Electric Tramway Company — which by then had acquired the property — asked a London director to obtain Royal permission to rename the paddock in commemoration of the visit. Sanction was given and the paddock became Alexandra Park.

At the Ponsonby stables there was one horse which never lay down. The stablemen put a chain across the back of the stall and it sat on that. Another mare known as Blanche hauled the jigger car between the stables and Three Lamps. Blanche had been seen to start with 25 passengers on a wet day, her front legs distinctly bent as she took the strain of the load. No uniforms were supplied to the crews, so every man dressed as he or his wife pleased. Conductors were given a cap and a money bag. Single men could have lodgings for 12/6 a week at a boarding house which the company owned at Epsom, and as a gift when a driver or conductor wed, the company would provide a special tram to take guests to the wedding function and home again.

Steve Heaney, foreman at the tramway stables in Carbine's cup year, 1890, owned a grey called Commodore, winner of the first Auckland Trotting Cup. Commodore was walked all the way back from Epsom to the Ponsonby tram sheds after the race with a tribe of proud Ponsonby boys trailing behind. The old grey finished up as a member of a three-horse team dragging a bus to outer suburbs.

Horse-car design began to specialise, open trams being provided for the dry summer months. These had seats across the full width of the vehicle, and the conductor, who normally stood on a platform at one end, had to edge his way along a running board to collect fares. In summer Queen Street was thick with dust, and in winter the mud was ankle deep. A bell-punch was used to mark and register the tickets sold, which were in coloured ribbon form, and often at the same time the conductor recited J.H. Bromley's well-known verse:

The conductor when he receives a fare
Must punch in the presence of the passenjare
A blue trip slip for an eight cent fare
A buff trip slip for a six cent fare
A pink trip slip for a three cent fare
All in the presence of the passenjare
Punch boys, punch with care
All in the presence of the passenjare.

Thirty-six trams comprised the fleet, many buses ran on various routes and 350 horses were employed. The trams were of two sizes, the larger type being designed to carry 24 passengers seated and 14 standing. Overcrowding was common and as many as 70 people were sometimes packed on board. Football crowds from Potter's Paddock even invaded the roofs. Huge crowds — up to 8000 — took a lot of shifting when only horses' legs trod the ways. Leader horses hauled the masses up Wellesley Street East to the game, then jogged over to Khyber Pass for the haul back. In Khyber Pass Road, the rugby fans had to get out and push at the back while the horses pulled in front.

Competition between bus and tram was spirited but often it had its humorous side. The drivers of buses and trams often engaged in races which provided considerable amusement, particularly on a stretch of single line, when a tram driver saw that if he waited at a loop to pass a sister vehicle, a bus could dash by to secure the next group of waiting passengers. The tram driver would meet the situation by driving his tram off the line and, after passing the opposing tram, drive it on to the rails again, proceeding at the fastest pace his team could master. Generally the tram had the advantage, not always because of superior speed, but because the average person would rather spend twice as long in a vehicle on rails than in a bus rocking along the atrociously rough roads of the day. On the last run to the stables a dozing or inebriated passenger would be deposited right at his doorstep by the crew. Pubs closed at 11 pm and the big night was Saturday, which meant merry passengers as the last car left town with the Waverley Hotel bar trade on board.

S.M. (Mick) Farrelly, a pioneer tramwayman who began as a horse-tram conductor in 1898, recalled that at this period the favourite Sunday outing for residents was a special bus which ran from the Three Lamps to Onehunga. A major reason for its popularity was that in those days people were not allowed to drink at an hotel on Sundays within 5 kilometres of their homes, and a roaring trade was done at Onehunga when the 'tourists' arrived.

Continual competition from horse-buses made for little tramways profit, but the downfall was said to have been land liabilities. Financial difficulties finally placed the assets of the company in the hands of the Bank of New Zealand. The financial slump of the late 1880s and 1890s saw further transfer of ownership. For about 12 months the tramways were leased to Patterson Brothers, a large horse-bus and carrying firm. Then, in 1899, the British Electric Traction Company purchased the undertaking and the Auckland Electric Tramways Company was registered in London.

Two views of the Queen and Wellesley Streets junction, Auckland, showing the public library building. The upper photograph, taken in the 1880s before the library was completed, shows horse-tram No. 11 with a full load, turning into Wellesley Street East while a Mount Roskill horse-bus waits for patrons outside where the Civic Theatre now stands. *Alexander Turnbull Library* The lower photograph, taken in about 1906, shows how the advent of electric tramways brought improved roading to the inner city streets. *Author's Collection*

Looking up Queen Street, Auckland, from the junction of Customs Street. An inward-bound horse-tram can be seen in the foreground of the upper photograph taken at the turn of the century. *Auckland Weekly News* The lower photograph shows the midday rush on a Saturday in the 1920s. *New Zealand Herald*

A line of two-horse trams waiting in Lambton Quay, Wellington, for the evening rush hour in the 1880s. The Government Buildings still look down on transport using the Quay today, but the road surface is now somewhat smoother. *Alexander Turnbull Library*

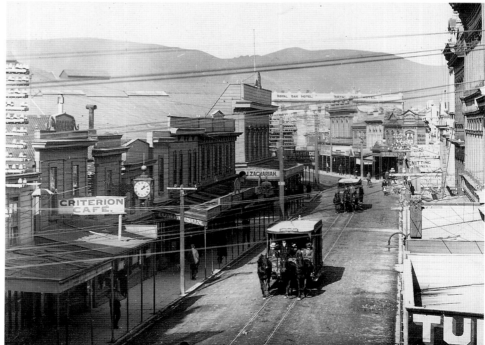

A lunch-hour scene in Manners Street, Wellington, at the turn of the century. Streets were quieter then, with no more than two horse-trams and a couple of bicycles clogging the thoroughfare. *Author's Collection*

Neville Lodge

IN THE NINETIES TRAMS WERE HORSE-DRAWN.

TODAY ELECTRIFICATION HAS SPEEDED THINGS UP CONSIDERABLY.

Wellington Heydays

Heavy street locomotives riding track that was too light to take the pounding led to the eventual downfall of steam traction in Wellington. Hard times came and at an auction in March 1880 the entire stock and plant was sold to E.W. Mills for £19,250. Mills decided to sell the iron beasts and to use three horses harnessed abreast, thus saving major expenditure on the track which the company could not afford.

The clatter of shod hoofs and the shining iron tyres of the carriages ringing on the curves reigned supreme in the narrow thoroughfares by the middle of 1882. Stalls for the horses replaced the engine shed in Adelaide Road. These stables were gradually enlarged to hold 140 animals when Dr Grace, Robert Greenfield and Mr Stewart became the proprietors by 1888. Horses procured from the Wairarapa were said to be of very fine stamp and admirably suited for the work. They were broken in on the premises, one steady old mare called Florrie being kept specially to assist. At night the horses were turned out on to paddocks leased by the company, comprising some 24 hectares of the Town Belt. Ready-cut chaff was obtained from Sanson, and a large corn-crusher, through which all the oats passed, was powered by one of the old steam engines, all the others having been sold. The oats and chaff were mixed in a loft overhead and sent down chutes to convenient bins. No straw was used in the stables, the horses being bedded on sawdust, which was found to be much cleaner and less of a fire risk. In 1888 the average daily cost of keeping each horse was about 1 shilling and a halfpenny. A patent water blast replaced the old-fashioned method of blowing the forges with bellows, which pleased the blacksmiths.

Two imported light horse-buses started running in Thorndon Quay and Tinakori Road in conjunction with the tram-cars and local enterprise received further orders to encourage the coach-building trade. A new line running through Courtenay Place proved a boon, and all guards now wore dark colonial tweed uniforms, braided with black. After a strike lasting many weeks during 1890, the service was leased to Archibald Hall, a coach operator from the West Coast. Eight years later it reverted to the former proprietors. Competition with horse-buses flared and there were frequent clashes between the staff of the rival services. Andrew Young and Company had their fleet of scarlet and gold 'Palace' buses made with wheels gauged to obtain the maximum benefit from the smooth surfaced tram rails. These buses would dash along the tracks, scurry around a labouring tram, then move back on to the tracks again, collecting the cream of the customers.

A Palace-type horse-tram heading for the suburbs in the early 1880s along Lambton Quay, Wellington, towards the intersection of Willis Street. Hunter Street is on the left. Three of these horse-trams were later used as trailers on the Kelburn cable tramway until withdrawn in 1974. *Author's Collection·*

To combat the challenge the tramway company ordered four Palace-type trams of similar design to Young's buses, with rows of seats running across the car as in an English railway carriage. This arrangement made for much quicker pick-up and discharge of passengers. Called the 'flying scudders', these trams would drive ahead of the horse-drawn buses in the five o'clock evening rush and uplift all the waiting passengers. With the help of tramway horse-buses and legislation, the activities of pirate bus men were slowly terminated. Young, who traded as Cobb and Company, had contested a successful court case against the tramway company for building trams to his patent 'Palace' design, but a short time later the tramway company bought the Wellington rights and Young shipped his buses, horses and men south to Dunedin where he reverted to his pirate running on tram rails. The public of Dunedin remained loyal to the local enterprise and Young went bankrupt. Other companies plying to the Wellington suburbs included the Wellington Co-operative Bus Company, the Newtown Co-operative Bus Company and the Lyall Bay Metropolitan Carrying Company. Lads would be seen stealing free rides by kneeling on the back step of the bus, out of the sight of the driver on his high perch up front.

Time moved on at the pace of the horse, with carters and expressmen crowding the quaysides. Four-wheel cabs, hansoms, gigs and buggies were the order of the day. Extra horse-trams catered for the crowds that flocked to the first silent movie in 1893; these were black and white flickering comedies, played to the accompaniment of a piano. Cabbies had realised that folk still required door-to-door personal transport. One of the first forms of private-hire street transport had been the hansom cab, introduced to the streets of the colony in the 1860s. The driver, sitting elevated at the rear of the body, used a trap-door in the ceiling to receive directions from his passengers, always alighting to open the door and assist with luggage in a cheerful manner. For 4 to 5 shillings an hour one could be jostled to the destination of one's choice. A corrugated glass panel for smokers to strike matches, a small hand-bell to call the driver, and at one's elbow the morning paper—these were among the facilities provided. To add colour to the interior, some of the better cabs even sported a vase of freshly picked flowers. A Mr Hansom in England had patented the design in 1834, hence the name.

Even if a loaded dray with a broken axle blocked the tracks, the horse-tram passenger was not a victim of delay. The crew would derail the tram and bypass the offending vehicle, then rejoin the steel road again. The idea of having a postbox attached to a tram, enabling a suburban dweller to pop a letter in the mail for clearance and despatch in town as the vehicle trotted past a street corner, was not a success and the service ceased in 1896.

As the new century dawned, the Wellington City Council completed negotiations with the company, taking over the services on 1 August 1900. The theatre specials that were to become part of after-dark rosters in the 1930s were well patronised when the first American show, *The Belle of New York*, arrived in town. Men were now working 60 hours a week for 35 shillings, and overtime rates were sixpence an hour if they worked on Sundays or holidays.

All change here for the distant suburbs of Miramar and Lyall Bay, Wellington. Workers going home in 1904 after transferring from horse-trams (left) to horse-buses in Cambridge Terrace, opposite St Patrick's College. *Author's Collection*

Animal Power

The trams were served by robust animals that were changed three times a day. But the human material was held to be more durable, and the same driver had to stay on duty throughout the three horse shifts. In Auckland horses were required to walk almost 30 kilometres a day, getting a quarter-hour spell between each trip. Hauling was a fairly heavy task, particularly when the 3-tonne trams were overcrowded. An average of 200 horses were stabled at each depot. The stalls were divided, Yankee fashion, by hanging bars and at times there was great commotion on the cobbled floor when a number of horses, forgetful of tomorrow's toil, would playfully push the bars about. A small stocky type of horse proved the best for the job. Originally large numbers were brought from Wanganui. They were a fine upstanding lot, all possessing good blood and breeding. Later they were supplanted by a breed from the Waikato, until the late 1890s, when suitable horses were imported from Queensland for £1 a head, plus £1 for freight. These fiery untamed animals were shipped in droves and swum ashore at St Heliers to be broken in by the company on their 160-hectare farm. Many a beast bred on the ranges of Waikato and Queensland settled down to a career of steady toil in front of a tram.

One imagines a horse would have chosen a better fate, even though the rations were regular and good. A car will only run a certain distance on the fuel in its tank, and the horse was no exception. Motive power subject to physical fatigue had a limit and needed to eat and drink occasionally. Special departments at the depots prepared the food for the hungry horses. Most companies grew progressive crops to keep up a steady supply of maize, oats and chaff on out-of-town farms. The daily ration for one horse consisted of 4.5 kilograms of oats, 1.3 kilograms of maize, half a kilogram of beans (weighed after crushing), just over 6 kilograms of chaff and 2 kilograms of hay, with 1 kilogram of bran, or an equivalent of green food. Carrots were also included.

Harness was always a costly item, having originally been imported from the United States, but local harness-makers later fulfilled orders. Each groom had a team of horses, ranging from 15 to 20, under his care to feed and keep tidy with glossy coats and manes brushed. Grooms oiled the many sets of harness, made reins pliable and kept collars and traces to a high standard. In the smiths' department stacks of iron shoes for the steeds and iron tyres for the buses reflected the glow from the forge fires. The health and general well-being of the animals were always foremost. A small horse hospital was part of a depot, and veterinary attention was considered as important as maintenance expenditure on the trams. Big money was invested in the horses, each car requiring between seven and eight animals to work the shifts.

Leaning into the collars with ears pricked forward, necks and knees bent, a team would settle into position like a football scrum and appear just as keen. By habit the horses followed the centre line of the tracks and kept the car on the rails. Not only was it their duty to pull the car, but they had to act as a brake on the down grades when the handbrakes were faulty. Large advertising boards added excessive weight and many an unnecessary burden must have been imposed on the hapless horses. The blood of the animals which provided propulsion for a city in those years was the life blood of the city itself.

Dunedin horse-trams stored with no protection against the weather at the small St Kilda suburban depot. *Russell Grigg Collection*

Transferring from one of the new speedy electric trams to a horse-tram for Linwood and North Beach in Manchester Street, Christchurch, in 1905. The clock tower is seen on its original site at the intersection of Manchester and High Streets. *Head Collection, Alexander Turnbull Library*

An Auckland horse-tram conductor complete with the regulation bag that contained tickets and cash, fob watch and whistle. *Author's Collection*

Urban Travel in the 1890s

The horse-tram drivers knew nearly everyone who travelled and should a regular passenger be late over breakfast, the driver occasionally would wait. Schedules were not strictly followed and on the rear platform the conductor would be watching for his regular clientele. In addition to halts at important traffic points, the trams would stop when signalled by the wave of a hand, umbrella or walking stick. It was general practice when the car approached to walk out onto the street and step aboard, the horses slowing momentarily before resuming their 10-kilometre-an-hour pace. Naturally, when a woman or an elderly person required transit, the driver would call the horses to a halt. With the shrill blast of the conductor's whistle and the cheery 'Giddy up' as the driver flicked a whip over the shiny coats of the oats-charged horses, the tram would surge forward and the clip-clop of the horses' hoofs would echo back through the saloon.

On the front platform, exposed to the weather, sat the driver, who had only a small splashboard to shield his legs. His hands firmly held the ribbons that gave him complete command. There were no 'Do not talk to the driver' platform notices to discourage male passengers from exchanging racing tips with the driver as they boarded the car. On entering the small passenger saloon, which had a smell peculiar to the horse-car — heavily scented with kerosene lamps and sweating horses — passengers would sit on one of the two wooden lengthwise benches. The conductor would issue the passenger with a ticket the size of a postage stamp, punch it with a bell-punch for all fellow patrons to hear and then one could relax and enjoy this latest form of suburban travel.

The rails made the ride so smooth that reading was no effort, and the males would spend the journey with their heads buried in the morning paper. Because of the relatively low resistance offered by iron wheels on iron rails the cars could handle bigger loads than the horse-buses. Smoking was definitely not permitted in the presence of women, the back platform being the accepted place for men to enjoy their pipes. From this early ruling must have stemmed the reason for men persisting, through the ensuing years, in gathering on tram platforms, blocking all entrances. Frisky young mares drawing spring carts and placid wagon teams challenged the right of the road at intersections. After thumping over a crossing with

another tramline the car would glide like magic around a curve with the ease of a roller-coaster. At the city terminal the men always doffed their hats to the ladies seated opposite, and then everyone alighted fresh from this new mode of travel. The driver in his weathered clothes unhitched the team and, leaning back on the heavy swingle-tree, piloted the horses to the other end of the tram with trace chains dragging in the dust, while the passengers briskly made their way past a line of hansom cabs to their places of employment.

Three horses pulling a Dunedin-bound tram from St Clair in the 1890s. On the top deck you could have a friendly chat and get a grandstand view without the risk of losing your hat. The tram never exceeded a steady 6 miles an hour. *Author's Collection*

In the 1900s an Auckland cab driver gives this two-horsepower vehicle a drink at a horse trough in Victoria Street East, opposite the original site of the Greyhound Hotel. *A.N. Breckon, Author's Collection*

Stanmore Road Bridge, Christchurch N. Z.

F. T. Series. Nº 74 A.

A four-wheeled double-decker horse-tram crossing the Stanmore Road bridge, Christchurch. *Postcard, John M. Bettle Collection*

WELLINGTON

Hunter Street, Wellington. The upper photograph, taken in the 1880s, shows a small four-wheeled horse-tram (left), in Lambton Quay, bound for Courtenay Place. *Burton Brothers, Alexander Turnbull Library* The lower photograph is of the same scene in the early 1960s. In the foreground is a former freight tram which was used in the later years of trams to grind any corrugations out of the rail surfaces. *Graham Stewart*

38

The cabbies' stand in Victoria Street East, Auckland, about 1909, with the old Central Hotel in the background. *A.N. Breckon, Author's Collection*

Horses Killed While Toiling

Accidents were inevitable when these primitive vehicles and their temperamental horses got out of control. Teddy Crousen, who held the ribbons on the first trot up Queen Street, Auckland, had been killed by a bolting three-horse team in Jervois Road. He was a former coachman with remarkable skill in handling animals, but was a victim of the dangers that all these men faced in their routine daily toil.

In August 1902, only three months before the new, jazzy electrics thundered up the streets of Auckland, a three-horse tram got away down Wellesley Street East. As the inward-bound tram, with driver Michael Hogan holding the reins, was descending Wellesley Street East, the brakes failed to grip the wheels. Hogan at first thought that someone was tampering with the rear brakes. By the time the conductor, John Davis, had found this not to be so, the car had accelerated greatly. The tram careered madly out of control to the bottom of the hill, the crew vainly throwing sacks and gear onto the track in front of the car in the hope of stopping it. Their combined efforts were useless.

Jumping the tracks, the car landed with a deafening crash against one of the steel poles erected in the middle of Queen Street to carry the overhead wires for the electric trams. The horses crashed into the pole, which sent them skidding with snapped traces across to the opposite corner and breaking the hind legs of one poor beast, which had to be destroyed. The force of the impact was terrific, the upright pole penetrating the car for almost a metre and pinning Davis the conductor to the front wall. Fortunately there were few passengers in the car, and these had jumped off and so escaped injury, with the exception of one unknown man, who received a severe bruising. Apart from a bruised knee, the driver escaped practically unhurt, but Davis had his right foot amputated. The front plates of the car were twisted and crumpled like paper, and a couple of the seats and windows were broken, while the metal base of the centre pole was almost completely severed.

In Christchurch a serious head-on collision on the Sumner line took place one evening between a steam-tram and a horse-tram. The steam-tram, chugging along Ferry Road towards Sumner, should have passed the horse-tram at a siding nearing the Caversham Hotel. Because no horse-tram was in sight, the steam-tram went on without waiting. Some 100 metres farther down the line, the driver of the horse-car spotted the puffing billy and trailers heading along the single track at a fair pace towards his team of horses. The horse driver immediately rang his bell continuously to no avail, the engine driver being engaged in stoking his fire. Realising that a collision was imminent, the horse-car driver pulled his team off the line, but one horse received severe injuries and died shortly afterwards. Five passengers were injured as the poor animals entangled in harness battled to free themselves from the snorting iron horse which blindly engulfed them with steam.

A contemporary newspaper artist's impression of the runaway horse-tram hitting the newly erected steel pole for the electric trams at the intersection of Queen and Wellesley Streets, Auckland. *Author's Collection*

On a nice day a voyage across the Waitemata Harbour on the promenade deck could be very pleasant. The paddle steamer *Takapuna* leaving Auckland for the North Shore. *Price, Author's Collection*

Paddle Wheels

Before direct road communication, wherries and ferries dependent on favourable weather conditions were the only form of communication for many infant settlements. Dunedin's Andersons Bay, Sumner at Christchurch and Seatoun in Wellington, to mention just three tiny hamlets, first relied on small boats as the only means of escape to the outside world.

Harbours and waterways were first crossed with sails and oars, before paddle wheels and propeller-driven steamers provided seaside residents with regular transport. In more recent times, Wellington was blessed with quaint steamers which ploughed across the harbour to Days Bay in the teeth of even the worst southerlies, and in Auckland ferryboats are still synonymous with the harbour.

Ferries have plied the waters of the Waitemata Harbour in Auckland since 1854, when an open four-oared whaleboat subsidised by the Auckland Provincial Government began a service between Auckland and the North Shore. 'Michael row the boat ashore' would have been a hit tune on the shore had the song been composed when this 20-passenger whaler, manned by a crew of two, first bridged the north and south shores. The call was 'Yo-heave-ho' for male passengers when there was no wind to fill the sail. They were expected to turn to and lend a hand with the oars.

Quicker transit across the Waitemata Harbour soon became a lively topic of discussion. The newspaper *The Zealander* felt the time was ripe for a steam ferry. In 1860 the paper put forward a suggestion to bridge the waterway with a pontoon and telescopic bridge from Stanley Point, at a cost of £16,000. Another idea in *The Zealander* suggested that 'scientific men had declared that the North Shore could be brought into touch with the town further west, about Watchman Island, utilising a viaduct, chain bridge and drawbridge'—just about where the harbour was finally conquered by a bridge 99 years later. Was this clairvoyant thinking or great wisdom a century before its time?

After a few false starts, regular paddle steamer services soon became part and parcel of the daily way of life on the North Shore, and in an endeavour to foster settlement, a newly formed company, the Devonport and Lake Takapuna Tramway Company, proposed a venture in 1885 to give seafaring types a swift, modern land passage from the Devonport Wharf to their homes. Horse tramlines were to reach Takapuna, Narrow Neck, Cheltenham and Stanley Bay. The first section to Cheltenham was opened in September 1886.

On opening day the 12.30 pm ferry left Auckland for Devonport with shareholders and guests. The weather was fine and very favourable for the occasion, making the harbour crossing on the paddle steamer ferry *Takapuna* a pleasant interlude from the bustling city. From the open promenade deck (where the only weather protection was close by the funnel) the spectacle of the broad white wake from the churning paddle wheels which encased the vessel on each side gave the passengers a feeling of power and freedom. At the large helm stood the captain, exposed to all weather. Ferry captains were men of the old school who could handle these plucky paddlers against the treacherous currents of the inland waterways.

When the *Takapuna* reached Victoria Wharf, Devonport, two brand-new summer horse-trams awaited the guests and officials. At a brisk pace each car, drawn by two horses, covered the distance to Cheltenham Beach for refreshments and an inspection of the new stables. The stables and car shed were a short distance from the Cheltenham terminus on the corner of William and Lake Streets, a siding leading into the structure, which had been adapted for the comfort of the horses. The light and airy bodies of the trams, each capable of carrying 30 passengers, were built by Messrs Cousins and Atkin, of Auckland, and the wheels by Mr Masefield, making the cars an entirely local product.

At about this time the ferries plying to Devonport, including the *Victoria* and the *Alexandra*, were joined by a glamorous new paddle steamer named *Britannia*. The height of sophistication in harbour transit, *Britannia* was big and sturdy with all the trimmings. In her elegant ladies' cabin oil paintings hung on each wall panel, and brass plates covered the door steps to her cabins with the name of the harbour queen, *Britannia*, embossed on each. Such paddle steamer luxury had never been heard of before on the Waitemata, especially the separate cabins for women and an exclusive 'smokers' den' for businessmen. One could certainly move around on this sleek vessel and flex one's legs while experiencing the nautical life.

Although *Britannia* was scooping the 'townie' trade to the shore, the horse line failed to attract summer pleasure seekers. Even a drastic reduction in fares made no difference, whereupon the company went into liquidation and in March 1887 called tenders for the sale of all holdings, only five months after the grand opening. Messrs Duder Brothers took over the service, only to struggle through the winter of 1887 with empty cars. In desperation the owners gained permission from the Devonport Council to run the trams only during the summer months. The following year saw the end of horse tramways on the North Shore.

The horse-tram line in King Edward Parade that was laid by the Devonport and Lake Takapuna Tramway Company for their service between Devonport and Cheltenham, Auckland. Lack of patronage saw the line close within two years. *Author's Collection*

CHAPTER THREE

Magic Carpet Travel

After visiting San Francisco in 1889, Rudyard Kipling wrote: 'A cable car without any means of support slid stealthily up behind me and nearly struck me in the back . . . I gave up asking questions about their mechanism . . . If it pleases Providence to make a car run up and down a slit in the ground for many miles, and if for twopence ha'penny I can ride in that car, why should I seek reasons for that miracle?'

Taming the Hills of Dunedin

ROSLYN

To people who knew only the horse and the steam engine as forms of locomotion, a vehicle climbing a steep hill with no visible means of power must have been an awe-inspiring sight. In endless procession, like the stairs of a modern escalator, the tiny cable-powered cars were soon to conquer the hills that rose abruptly from the heart of Dunedin.

It was George Smith Duncan, a young New Zealand engineer, who first suggested a cable tramway for Dunedin in 1879. Duncan, of the engineering firm of Reid and Duncan, was the driving force behind the founding of the Roslyn Tramway Company, and in 1881, when only 29 years of age, he engineered the first cable tramway to operate outside the United States. George Duncan's proposals were in principle based on the design of Andrew Smith Hallidie, an Englishman who built the world's first street cable cars at San Francisco in 1873. Duncan, who had never seen a San Francisco cable car running, must have gained all his knowledge from technical papers.

This pioneer line south of the equator ran up Rattray Street from the corner of Rattray and Maclaggan Streets, taking a broad curve to the left by St Joseph's Cathedral, before continuing up the 1 in 7½ grade. Just beyond Arthur Street the line steepened to 1 in 6¼ and entered a large earth cutting on a private right-of-way through the Town Belt. On level ground high above this long incline the line came to an end outside the original powerhouse. Two crossing loops, one at Arthur Street and the other on Cathedral curve, were designed for downhill running. The gripman would drop the cable, coast through and around the loop, and pick up the cable again on re-entering the single track.

OPPOSITE PAGE: A night view of the last of the Dunedin cable cars. The Mornington line was replaced by buses in March 1957. A photograph of the city terminal in High Street shortly before the cable car's closure. *Graham Stewart*

Andrew Smith Hallidie

With a strap and a toehold, Dunedin workers ride the Rattray Street cable line to their hillside homes. *Author's Collection*

The original city terminus of the Roslyn Tramway Company's Rattray Street cable car by Maclaggan Street. *Otago Early Settlers' Museum*

Duncan solved many problems associated with cable tramway construction while building this 'goat track'. Much of his engineering had to be experimental to meet local conditions. A major problem was how to haul up cars round the curve outside St Joseph's Cathedral where the grade was 1 in $7\frac{1}{2}$ (Parnell Rise in Auckland is 1 in $8\frac{3}{4}$). Duncan designed the 'pull curve'—a number of small wheels, known as 'drum pulleys', which gently eased the wire rope around the curve and still allowed the car to grip while taking the curve on this hair-raising incline. A first for cable traction in the world, Duncan's invention was later to be adopted by major cable systems in other countries.

Propulsion for the toy-sized trams was provided by an endless cable running in a tunnel beneath the road, this being gripped by an arm hanging down under each car and passing through a slot in a centre rail. The strong crucible steel wire cable, with a circumference of approximately 9 centimetres, was hauled through a vault, about 60 centimetres in depth, by stationary steam engines situated in a powerhouse adjacent to the depot on each line. The cavern below the road could be seen through the centre rail slot. Cast-iron manholes of a chequered pattern were provided above each pulley for oiling and maintenance. Travelling at an official speed of 7.95 miles (13 kilometres) per hour, the wire rope could be heard humming mysteriously in a deserted street with not a cable car in sight, for the cable itself never stopped during the hours the service was running. It was the driver, known by all as the gripman, who controlled the passage of the small vehicle. Standing in the centre of the car, he was able, by means of large levers, to pick up the moving rope by a vice-like grip at the end of the arm projecting through the slot in the centre rail and thus enable the vehicle to be moved along the tracks by an invisible form of traction reminiscent of a magic carpet. With the same ease, the gripman could let the rope go at any time. Other levers were for braking.

In a city centre seemingly overshadowed by insurmountable hills, the cable car was to become a landmark for Dunedin, three private companies serving the suburbs of Roslyn, Mornington, Maryhill and Kaikorai by the Christmas of 1900.

1298 P. RATTRAY ST. DUNEDIN N. Z.   Muir & Moodie

The final city terminus of the Rattray Street cable line at the intersection of Princes Street. *Postcard, John M. Bettle Collection*

A thick mantle of snow made no difference to the Dunedin cable cars. Looking down Rattray Street from the Queen's Drive Bridge during winter in the 1920s. *Author's Collection*

A Roslyn cable tram passing through a cutting in the Dunedin town belt. An 'up car' can be seen in the distance. *Graham Stewart*

Four flimsy four-wheelers about 4 metres long with seats for 16 passengers started the Roslyn service. The cars were completely open except for a glassed-in platform at the northern end, a rather odd accessory as the prevailing weather came from the south. At first a large horizontal control wheel was used to operate the gripping gear, and the gripman and conductor often had to use their combined strength to stop with a full load. Two novel cars, a coal-tram and a water-tram, were built to keep the fiery boilers of the stationary steam engines alive. As there was no water supply on the hills, the water-tram was equipped with tanks to carry water from the city for the thirsty boilers and it ran when traffic was light.

For passengers there was a breathtaking element of danger while hanging from thin leather straps as a car pulled up Rattray Street. Some passengers would pause for a moment at the top of the hill and watch the huge steam engine's flashing rods, and listen to the exhaust beat, as the cable took the strain of a loaded gripcar on the grade. Snow white were the wooden boards on the floor of the engine house, and the engine itself was kept spick and span by engine drivers. Within four days of the opening on 24 February 1881, 14,000 passengers had experienced the thrill of gliding up a hill — a ride that was for many years fondly called 'the eighth wonder of the world' by visitors to Dunedin.

The original line to Roslyn was duplicated in 1884, and by 1906 the line had reached its final form, with an extension down into the Kaikorai Valley (an earlier attempt had not been feasible). The city terminus was now at Princes Street. Hidden under the street at this point was the terminal pit, below steel plates in a brick and cement excavation. In this pit a wheel almost 3 metres in diameter returned the rope toward the hill. Brighter enclosed cars for passenger comfort and lever-actuated grips on new dummies made for more efficiency.

The Roslyn cable line extension down into the Kaikorai Valley involved a steep descent down a private right-of-way on a gradient of 1 in 4.7. A Fell centre-rail braking system was used on this section. *Graham Stewart*

MORNINGTON, MARYHILL, ELGIN ROAD

David Proudfoot, who had been successful with the city horse lines, soon realised the potential in a cable line up the hill to the expanding district of Mornington. Reid and Duncan, the engineers who had built the Roslyn line, also applied to the city fathers for authority, but the council would not sanction the schemes proposed by the two syndicates. Proudfoot then lost interest and withdrew his application, and the council finally bowed to Reid and Duncan, who were granted rights to construct a line up High Street. The Mornington Tramway Company was then formed and work started from the Exchange to the Mornington township in 1882.

Dunedin's father of the cables, engineer George Duncan, journeyed to the United States in 1882, to study the latest techniques in San Francisco and while there ordered four trailer cars from the Jones Car Company of New York. When the Mornington line was completed, Duncan crossed the Tasman to build and engineer the extensive Melbourne cable tramways. With 74 kilometres of double track serving 17 radiating routes, Melbourne was reputed to have had the best laid-out cable tramway system in the world — truly a great tribute to the New Zealander.

The first of four open cable dummies, fitted with lever-type grippers, which became standard on cable cars, was hauled up the hill to the Mornington sheds by a team of four horses, and a locally built coal trailer completed the fleet. Thirty-two horses were required to haul the first cable — 3500 metres in length — up in the slot between the rails. The animals were supplied and controlled by James Duthie and Company.

On 16 March 1883 the line opened with a staff of five gripmen and four conductors, the chief conductor and trackman being qualified to drive when there was demand. For working a 57-hour week with no overtime, and being on duty every other Sunday, a gripman received a weekly wage of £3. The uniform was a blue-fox serge, each man being required to supply his own. Since it was a copy of

This photograph of the original Mornington cable trams and trailers in High Street, Dunedin was taken in 1883. With the ornate Victorian residence in the background, this could easily be mistaken for that most aristocratic of hill slopes in San Francisco, Nob Hill. *Author's Collection*

These Dunedin women do not appear flustered at being asked to pose for a photograph while sitting on the Maryhill cable tram, at the edge of a slope reputed to be the steepest tramway in the world.
Alexander Turnbull Library

American practice, the double-track Mornington line worked contrary to the New Zealand rule of the road, the cars running on the right-hand side of the street. The terminal crossovers at each end were gravity worked, and the practice of right-hand running was not rectified until the 1920s.

In March 1885 the company completed the extension line to Maryhill. To ride this branch line, which was only about 800 metres long, passengers had to alight from the High Street car at Mornington and walk through the depot to the Maryhill car, which would be waiting at the side of the building. This was the star attraction of the line and the nearest thing to a roller-coaster ever instituted for public conveyance. As it left the short terminal section the car suddenly tipped forward and plunged down a grade of 1 in 4 which smartly steepened to 1 in $3\frac{1}{2}$ (and even more precipitous) for a good 160 metres into the valley below. It was reputed to be the steepest cable tramway in the world and after having experienced a spine-chilling trip, few passengers would dispute the claim.

Cable car No. 10 obliges the photographer by stopping on the 1 in $3\frac{1}{2}$ gradient on the Maryhill cable line in Dunedin.
Muir & Moodie, Author's Collection

A watercolour painting by John Crawford of Dunedin in 1885 of the Mornington cable car ascending High Street, showing William and Alva Streets. The American practice of running on the right-hand side of the road continued until 1928. *Otago Early Settlers' Museum*

BELOW LEFT: The Maryhill tram, loaded with schoolboys homeward bound, descends into the valley one sunny afternoon in the 1950s. *Reginald McGovern*

BELOW: Heading back to the Mornington terminal along Glenpark Avenue in the 1950s is Maryhill cable tram No. 106, now preserved at the Otago Early Settlers' Museum in Dunedin. *Reginald McGovern*

A view of the Kaikorai Valley from the Dunedin and Kaikorai Tramway Company's cable line which ran into the city down Stuart Street, terminating at the Octagon. *Postcard, John M. Bettle Collection*

BELOW: Dunedin College students boarding a city-bound cable car and trailer at the Mornington terminus in the 1950s. *Reginald McGovern*

Cable Car. High

The company refused, on economic grounds, to extend the Mornington line to Elgin Road in 1902, and following public agitation the council was forced to take over the lines under the provisions of the Public Works Act. Unfortunately, while the Arbitration Court was in session to finalise the price in February 1903, an early morning fire destroyed the tram sheds and plant, together with three houses and a shop.

A strong south-west wind fanned the flames, which had a good hold when first discovered in the tramway office, and they quickly spread through the car shed and plant. Next door lived the tramway engineer, Joseph Lowden, in a home owned by the tramway company. Great tongues of flame soon engulfed his residence and spread to the next home in the street, occupied by G.W. Grigg. From there the fire leaped to the local police station where Constable Power lived. At 3.20 am the Dunedin City Fire Brigade was summoned, and under the command of Captain Mitchell a machine headed up the hill. In Maclaggan Street the captain and his men realised that the inferno was outside the city boundary and that it would be against regulations to proceed farther. Mitchell then returned to the station and dismissed his men. Engineer Lowden realised at about the same time that the whole street was in danger of destruction and telephoned Mitchell. The latter first called the Mayor,

The Mornington tram terminus at the junction of High and Princes Streets during the First World War. The City Corporation Tramways Department were now running the service. *Author's Collection* BELOW LEFT: The sole surviving piece of rolling stock following the 1902 destruction of the Mornington Tramway Company's tram sheds and plant was trailer No. 4. *Otago Witness* BELOW: Later renumbered No. 107 by the Dunedin City Corporation, this cable car trailer, seen arriving at the port of Auckland in 1958 for preservation, is now an exhibit at the Museum of Transport and Technology, Western Springs, Auckland. *Graham Stewart*

Dunedin schoolboys and shoppers returning home to Mornington on an afternoon cable tram. *Graham Stewart*

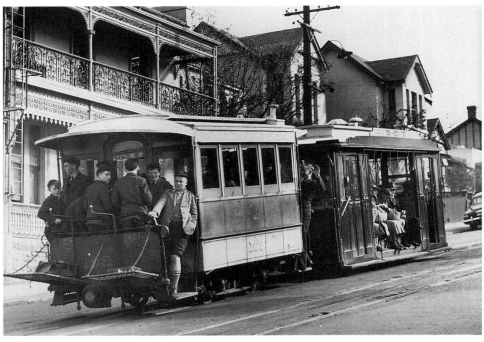

J.A. Park, but as there was no answer he took the responsibility on his own shoulders and, with half a dozen men and a house reel, returned at full gallop on a manual wagon.

Their arrival was greeted with hearty cheers from the hundreds of helpless spectators. By this time, close on 4 am, the fire had a good hold in the store occupied by John Weir. From a cellar full of water at the butchery and a large tank belonging to the tramway company, the brigade soon confined the flames to Weir's store and saved other homes down the street from destruction. For the burnt-out plant and the sole survivor of the rolling-stock, a lone trailer that had been pushed to safety, the borough council were committed to paying the handsome sum of £20,000 for the takeover. This sole surviving piece of original stock is preserved at the Museum of Transport and Technology in Auckland.

April 1903 saw the line open again with two roofless, patched-up dummies working the service as a temporary measure until the new cars were ready. Surplus horse-trams from the city were pressed into use as trailers.

With the Mornington Borough Council now in control, Lowden, as engineer, was instructed to build the Elgin Road extension, which opened in the October of 1906. Though the first rope, in spite of having a totally new line to wear off the rough spots, lasted the life of a normal cable in use on the main line, subsequent ropes lasted only half that time. Rope troubles saw the line closed for three months in 1907 and for another four months in the following year. This excessive wear caused the line to be abandoned, after a short and a spasmodic life, in January 1910. Although the extension was only 1.3 kilometres long, the sharp curves had proved too severe for cable traction.

BELOW: The short-lived Elgin Road cable line. *Postcard, John M. Bettle Collection* BELOW RIGHT: Mornington cable cars and trailers passing late one afternoon in High Street, Dunedin, in the 1950s. *Graham Stewart*

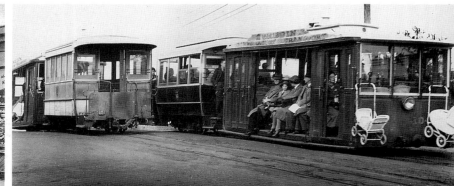

Kaikorai and Dunedin
Tramway Company cable cars
at the Nairn Street terminus in
the Kaikorai Valley shortly
after the line opened. *Otago
Early Settlers' Museum*

KAIKORAI

The third private venture to scale the hills of Dunedin with cable cars was first mooted in the December of 1894, the originator being an engineer, E. Roberts. From the Octagon, a double line was to run up Stuart and Albert Streets at varying grades through the Town Belt and down into the Kaikorai Valley, a distance of 1.8 kilometres. At the first meeting of shareholders of the newly formed Dunedin and Kaikorai Tramway Company, Roberts was appointed engineer for the project.

Five years were to pass before construction was completed. Then, on 9 October 1900, 40 civic leaders rode in dignity on a special car from the Octagon as guests of the chairman, H.V. Haddock, to a formal opening held at the powerhouse. Alas, the public service was further delayed until the 22nd, as the company awaited the delivery of another gripper car to run the service. Patience was rewarded when over 250,000 passengers were carried in the first 23 weeks.

These picturesque but springless little boxes were now a common sight, with their passengers clinging precariously to whatever hold was available. But in December 1900 alarm was expressed about safety by the Public Works Department's District Engineer, E.R. Ussher, in a letter to the Under-Secretary of Public Works in Wellington. 'The car thus loaded,' he said, 'resembles a swarm of bees — if this is continued no doubt a frightful calamity will occur some day.'

Many on the sidewalk privately held the same view, as there had already been two fatal accidents in Dunedin due to failure of equipment. Only two months after the Roslyn line opened in 1881, a car rolled backwards from Cathedral curve and capsized at the foot of the grade. One man, Thomas Garrett, died of injuries a fortnight later. In October 1900 another Roslyn car raced out of control from the Town Belt, and a Chinese man, Kim Hay, either jumped or was thrown off near the Girls' High School and killed. Improved equipment replaced the horizontal emergency screw-down brake wheel and gave Dunedin and its cable cars a remarkable safety record. There were the inevitable accidents, but they were few when related to the thousands of passengers who rode the mechanical mules each year.

Passengers about to board a
Kaikorai cable car at Highgate
for the city in 1938. Until 1936
the Maori Hill electric tram
crossed the cable line at this
junction. *Author's Collection*

'THERE'S ALWAYS ROOM FOR ANOTHER!'

Travel by cable car was different; no queues waited to enter the quaint Victorian cars as they reached the terminus, the waiting crowd surging around them in a circular movement. By habit, women and youngsters made for the tiny glassed-in saloons fore and aft, while men took the open-air seats on the outside and latecomers selected whatever footholds they could find. A strap and a toehold on the footboard were enough for any energetic male. As the car bobbed off and took the grade, a passenger hanging by a thin leather strap, which soon cut into his fingers, experienced an element of danger which gave him the feeling that the world was still for the brave.

The conductor, an agile acrobat, would swing monkey-like along the side of the crowded car, with punch and tickets in his hands. To collect fares he worked from strap to strap, climbing through cabins and around toeholds on the luggage racks. The gripman, an expert at his specialised task, was treated with reverent respect by the regulars. In the centre of it all he heaved on his big levers to stop and start the car, a constant source of fascination.

There was a friendly intimacy about the ride — one couldn't be snobbish when sharing a toehold with a dozen others. Tunes were played on the cable car bells by the gripmen, who had a code all of their own. Two distinct 'dongs' chimed after an up car passed a down car, the chimes telling the other crew that an inspector was close by. A symphony in steel was played as the pulleys slapped and rattled and the hum and skip of the rope buried deep below the slot fluctuated in crescendo. To those who live near a cable line this was music to their ears — part of the familiar sounds of their locality.

When the car entered a cutting, a passenger hanging from a stanchion would often have one foot dangling in the tall wet grass beside the track. When it rained there were advantages in standing one or two deep, for those on the outside provided welcome shelter. Climbing steeply above the city the happy but crushed assortment of passengers had a panoramic view of the city and harbour. The squat little car bursting out all over with humanity would reach the top of the long pull with ease and efficiency. After unloading some of its burden, it would then plunge with a sickening lurch over what seemed like a vertical cliff, giving that sudden sinking sensation that sent a chill up the spine as the car descended into the Kaikorai Valley. Diehard strap-hangers who loved the open-air freedom of these family lines would nod a greeting of thanks to the crew as they headed for home.

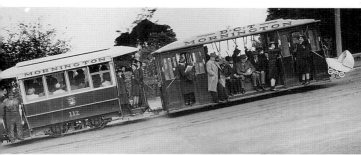

Passengers, prams and agile conductors photographed on the Roslyn and Mornington cable cars of Dunedin in September 1951. *Graham Stewart*

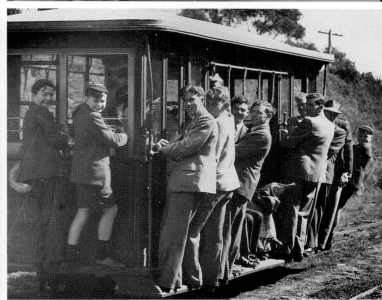

The birth of a new Wellington suburb. Initial formation and cuttings along Upland Road, Kelburn, showing the power house in the foreground for the Kelburne and Karori Tramway Company. No. 1 cable tram is being used to test the new lines. *Author's Collection*

The Kelburne & Karori Tramway Company, Limited

HOLIDAY TIME-TABLE

Cars will NOT run on CHRISTMAS DAY

Otherwise, throughout the holidays, the usual running hours will be observed, cars leaving at intervals of ten minutes—increased to five minutes when traffic warrants.

J. K. DARLING, Manager.

The Kelburne & Karori Tramway Company, Limited

EASTER HOLIDAYS TIME-TABLE

GOOD FRIDAY, CARS WILL NOT RUN.
SATURDAY—
       7 a.m. to 11.20 p.m.-10 minutes' service.
       5 minutes' service when necessary.
SUNDAY—Ordinary Sunday Time-table
       1.40 p.m. to 10-10 p.m.
MONDAY and Tuesday—
       7 a.m. to 11.20 p.m., 10 minutes' service.
       5 minutes' service when necessary.
WEDNESDAY, Ordinary Time-Table.

J. DARLING, Manager.

One of three Palace-type Wellington horse-trams which were purchased from the Wellington City Council and used as trailers on the Kelburn cable tramway until withdrawn in July 1954. *Gordon Burt Collection, Alexander Turnbull Library*

Kelburn—The Only Remaining Link

Valuable suburban land waiting to be exploited was the primary motive in the building of a cable tramway from the heart of Wellington to Kelburn at the turn of the century. The conquering slopes which rose over 150 metres above the embryo city's Lambton Quay were slowly tamed by men wielding picks and shovels and removing spoil in wheelbarrows. Tunnelling through ridges and spanning gullies with bridges was gruelling work for engineers and labourers alike on this mountain face. Even teams of prisoners from the old Terrace Gaol were put to work, slogging to build the incline. The Kelburne (as it was then spelt) and Karori Tramway Company was formed, with shareholding held by the Upland Estate Company, to develop the open farmlands and scrub areas of the Pharazyn and Copland estates. Cutting through back gardens and bush, the double track right-of-way was 785 metres in length, with a ruling and steady grade of more than 1 in 5.

On a Saturday morning, 22 February 1902, the slap of cable over well-oiled pulleys was heard for the first time. From the skyline terminus at the top, horse-coaches owned by the company and a Mr Spiers met the cable cars to convey settlers to the then remote village of Karori. The cableway was a brilliant success, new homes spreading like an infectious rash as real-estate sharks flourished. So great was the demand that three 'Palace' horse-trams were bought from the Wellington

City Council for use as trailers to cope with the traffic. These cars were dragged by a team of horses up Glenmore Street and through Kelburn to Upland Road, where they were shortened and converted for their hill-climbing role.

Although designed as a true cable tramway, the two cars were joined together by a second wire rope known as the tail-wire. This cable was independent of the main drive cable and ran round a drum at the top so that one car balanced the other. Only the descending car gripped the driving cable and, as it was pulled down the track, it hauled the ascending car by the tail-wire. Therefore the term 'cable car' was really a misnomer, as the tramway was technically a funicular worked on the counterbalance principle. But the trams retained and used the true cable-tram grippers and brakes.

A familiar landmark until the engine-house was electrified in 1933 was the smokestack towering above the steam-driven winding machinery at the top of the incline. The drift of smoke from this chimney became a convenient weather vane for the town. To cater for the upsurge in commuting from the hilltop suburbs, the

Nearing the top of the climb shortly after the line was built in 1902. Passengers on the Kelburn cable car leave the last tunnel to find paddocks and farmlands, a welcome change from the horse-congested streets of Wellington city below. *Author's Collection*

As this 1903 photograph shows, the outside side seats of the Kelburn cable cars were originally not 'stepped' as in later years to avoid a passenger sliding, with embarrassment, down the car on to other passengers. *A.P. Godber, Author's Collection*

ABOVE: Kelburn cable car No. 3, one of the first generation of cable cars which gave 76 years of service, was the only gripcar with open-ends. *Graham Stewart* ABOVE RIGHT: Talavera Station in the days of the original cable line. *Graham Stewart*

company later formed a subsidiary, the Kelburn-Karori Motor Bus Company, which used a fleet of motor-buses for feeder services. To the delight of shareholders, traffic grew from 425,000 passengers in 1902 to 2,000,000 in 1926. In December 1946 the Wellington City Council exercised its right of purchase and the cable line became an integral part of the city's transport system. With the scrapping of the street cable lines in Dunedin after the Second World War — in spite of a large section of the community strongly voicing claims for their retention — the Kelburn cable cars became the last remaining link with the tramway age. Wellington had grown fond and proud of these novel wooden trams with their garden-type seats, coupled to diminutive little trailers harking back to the days before the horseless carriage. Through dark tunnels and out into daylight the cars were carrying over $1\frac{1}{2}$ million passengers each year.

In July 1974, Wellingtonians' sentimental attachment for their cable cars came to the fore. Following an accident, the then Ministry of Works suddenly ordered the removal of the brakeless trailer cars, halving the cable cars' capacity, as they did not conform with modern safety standards.

A battle between the council, citizens and the ministry followed, with a report by a panel of engineers recommending that, even if the present system were given a stay of execution for two years while the system was upgraded, the lifespan would be only another eight years. Since 1902 the cable cars had carried 100 million people and there had only one fatality. Seventy-two years of almost accident-free running had suddenly become a safety hazard.

The Mayor of Wellington at the time, Michael (later Sir Michael) Fowler, fought hard for the original system to be retained. When the council finally conceded to a new Swiss system, Michael Fowler expressed dismay when discussing the replacement of the old cable cars with 'modern Swiss tin cans'. The new cable cars would, he said, spell the end for one of his favourite pastimes — kicking the tunnel walls, while sitting on the outside seats. He and his family had been doing it for years, as had many other people. The contract for the new cable car system went to Habegger AG of Switzerland. The line would be a single-track of metre gauge, with a crossing loop at the mid-point, Talavera station.

On Friday 22 September 1978 the original cable cars made their last trips. 'Thousands thronged Cable Car Lane and the Kelburn terminal to farewell Wellington's most-photographed asset,' reported the *Dominion*. Throughout the afternoon every trip was packed with people taking their last ride on the 76-year-old tramway. Just after 11 pm, cable car No. 2, loaded with invited guests, made the last historic journey from Lambton Quay. At Talavera, about 20 young people sang 'Auld Lang Syne'; then, as the tram passed Salamanca station, students from Weir House marked the last trip by throwing eggs and water bombs at the tram. Hundreds of people surrounded the cable car as it reached the upper terminal where a pipe band played a last tribute.

Just over a year later, on 20 October 1979, the Swiss system, with new chalet-style stations, opened. Thanks to Michael Fowler, a noted architect, who insisted the new trams have incorporated in their design some 'old world' atmosphere, the

The second generation Kelburn cable cars introduced in 1979 continue to serve Wellington residents and visitors. *Graham Stewart*

interiors were furnished in varnished hardwood and synthetic woodgrain panelling — a decision that must have helped the new Kelburn tram to retain the former system's rating as a front-line New Zealand tourist attraction. Workers, residents and university students still mingle with visitors from around the world, who make a trip on the tramway to experience a unique mode of travel in this part of the world and to view the panorama of Wellington.

Tourist itineraries make a ride on a San Franciso cable car a 'must'; perhaps these hill-climbers and a similar topography give Wellington some claim to the title of the San Francisco of the Southern Hemisphere. San Francisco has its Market and Powell Streets, Hong Kong has 'The Hill' and Wellington has Kelburn.

The final 1970s days of the original 1902 cable tramway system which gave passengers the enjoyable freedom of riding on the open sides of the trams.
Graham Stewart

An intricate pattern of steel.
The laying of the tramlines and
points at the busy Queen
Street-Customs Street
intersection in Auckland in
1902. The old Waitemata Hotel
is in the background. *Author's
Collection*

Laying the electric tracks at the
Cuba Street-Manners Street
intersection, Wellington, in
1904. *Alexander Turnbull
Library*

CHAPTER FOUR

The Jazzy Electrics

Farewell Dobbin

The 19th century drew to a close with the emergence of internal combustion engines for carriages and electric steel-tyred giants to carry the masses, but two-horse landaus and traps continued to prance on regardless, zigzagging their way up to hilltop suburbs, or proceeding sedately along the city boulevards. Close on 1000 horses were being employed to haul tram-cars in six different centres. Horseless carriages running wild in the streets of cities overseas were the talk of the town. P.R. Skeates of Auckland imported a belt-driven Star motor car in 1900, and two years earlier William McLean, of Wellington, had imported New Zealand's first motor cars, two Benz machines, which had forced the passing of the McLean Motor Car Act 1898 that dispensed with the need for a man to walk in front with a red flag. Even with a running jump start from the opposite incline, and a 20-kilometre-an-hour dash across Queen Street, cars of Skeates' type generally needed a gentle push to make the top of Wellesley Street East.

But despite the novelty of the new-fangled motor car, the marvels of electrification now dominated future planning for tramways, with many schemes and propositions being put forward by English and American traction companies. People were becoming impatient with delays associated with the lumbering, easy-going horse-cars. On a long haul, fresh horses would be required to meet the car halfway. The unyoking of the tired horses and the coupling of an already-harnessed new team took a good five minutes. Horses, their sides heaving with exhaustion, were always given a spell at the top of a steep hill.

Tramways had first been laid to overcome the poor road surfaces of broken shingle or mud, but the excreta from hundreds of horses made the streets far from pleasant. A shovel brigade with two-wheeled carts did a stout job keeping the main thoroughfares reasonably free from this nuisance.

Apart from the water-bound macadam which extended for only 45 centimetres each side of the track, citizens of the Victorian era had to combat the slush which prevailed in winter between the sidewalk and the footboards of a tram-car. Tarmac, wooden blocks and concrete had not yet been developed as permanent road surfaces. Trackmen swept clogged rail grooves and junction points in a battle to keep the tracks from being swallowed by the roads. Tramway lines generally traversed the most populous suburbs, with horse-buses supplementing the horse-trams and serving the outer suburbs. Disorderly movements of drays and wagons clogged the traffic streams, with pedestrians, cyclists and hand trolleys adding to the bustling atmosphere. Gradually the faithful 'hay-burners' hauling their now dingy saloons with flapping canvas blinds were becoming outmoded.

However, the use of horses as a form of traction was far from finished, and tramway companies found them an invaluable asset. Special teams were used to haul heavy powerhouse machinery from the docksides, and to transport the bodies of the new electric tram-cars from the coach builders. Farmers readily bought the tramway horses and found that they worked to the call of a whistle. Some of the these horses survived until the late 1920s. One deed of transfer when electric motive power took over contained the names of over 100 horses then in service.

Soon the familiar sound of faithful old Dobbin's hoofs pounding on the metal road, or the hollow boom of a horse-car trotting across a bridge at an exhilarating speed of 10 kilometres an hour, were to disappear as the horse became redundant.

One of the first electrics, car No. 2, on the Maori Hill line shortly after this pioneer electric tramway opened along the hilltops of Dunedin in 1900. *Author's Collection*

The First Notch

At the startling speed of over 30 kilometres an hour the first electric-powered line in New Zealand, between Roslyn and Maori Hill at Dunedin, created something of a sensation when it opened in October 1900. The first electric trams represented the height of both enterprise and luxury, as such a swift form of travel had been unknown to city dwellers. They were described at the time as noiseless and graceful, with the comfort of a drawing room. People flocked to ride on these speedy wonders that glided with such ease along the hilltop.

The line was built for the Dunedin and Roslyn Tramway Company by the contracting company of Noyes Brothers, of Sydney, to replace a short feeder horse-tram service which connected at the Town Belt with the Rattray Street cable tram from the city. Folk rode the Rattray Street cable cars in droves, eager to boast an electric tram ride, which the private company had introduced while city fathers pondered over the new forms of propulsion now offering for suburban transit. After a trip to Maori Hill, the return to the main thoroughfares of the city and to the slow old horse-cars was an anti-climax. Everyone now regarded horse-cars as chariots of the past.

To erect the overhead wires, workers had manned a large wooden sledge carrying a tower platform, this contrivance being pulled by a docile horse borrowed from Halfway Bush. The 2.3-kilometre length of track, which had a crossing loop between Selkirk and Fifield Streets, was laid to the same gauge as the old horse line, 3 feet 6 inches. Hard times had forced the company to use second-hand railway track and when the three electric trams arrived from the United States in wooden crates on the *Westralia*, one car had to be placed in pawn until more solvent days arrived. Although short of funds, the management boldly announced that it was not their intention to disfigure the cars with enquiries about the state of one's liver, or to command patrons to take Dr Snodgrass's green spectacles for sore eyes. Advertisements would not be allowed. An enamel of deep lake colour graced the exterior panels of the trams, which were built by the J.G. Brill Company of

Philadelphia for the princely sum of £660 each.

The *Evening Star* of 29 September 1900 gave this enthusiastic description of the 20-passenger accommodation:

> Inside we have all the comfort without the inconvenience in the way of bric-a-brac that a drawing room affords. The gangway leaves ample room for the conductor to walk up and down without apologising at every step or calling forth unuttered exclamations from his fares; the seats and backs are upholstered in figured velvet pile; the roof is lined with ornamented satin wood. There are two bevelled plateglass windows at either end, and the inside of the doors is panelled in Georgia pine.

Canopies were built over the dashboards so that those on the platforms below escaped the dripping of rain water, and at each end headlights produced an unbelievable brightness from lamps of 32 candlepower. At night pedestrians were dazzled by the brilliance of light blazing forth from the trams, in vivid contrast to the pale glimmer of the gas lamps that for so long had been the only form of illumination.

On 23 October the mayor and councillors of Roslyn were guests of the company for an inaugural run, which was followed by a luncheon in the Maori Hill tram shed to celebrate this historical milestone. On opening day the two cars carried 1100 people without a hitch, and negotiated the tricky loop section where the overhead was only a single wire straight through. Northbound cars had to take a flying jump at the loop, dramatically speaking, and coast around the loop line while the conductor pulled the trolley pole from the wire as the tram diverged from the mainline power supply. An electric tram without its overhead source of power was like a yacht without sails.

Personalities at the controls often gave first riders on the electric cars thoughts of 'back to the horse-cars please!' When the car was full of rubberneck tourists, motorman Jack Paterson, known locally as 'Hellfire Jack', made a habit of notching the tram up to full power and then placing both his feet up on the front apron, coolly leaning back and taking a swig of cold tea which he subtly kept in a beer bottle. Passengers bred to the pace of horses were already apprehensive about this fast mode of transport, without the added antics of a daredevil driver.

W.G.T. Goodman, of Noyes Brothers, who had come from Australia to supervise track construction and the equipping of cars and powerhouse, later became engineer for the building of the Dunedin city electric system when his company was appointed engineers to the City Corporation. When construction work had been completed, Goodman accepted the position of City Electrical Engineer, an office he held until returning to Australia in 1907 to become manager of the Adelaide Tramways. An ironic twist of fate for the man responsible for establishing these early electric lines was his return 40 years later as Sir William Goodman, to report on the future of the Dunedin electric and cable tramways. Sir William's report to the council pronounced the death sentence on the very services he had so ably helped to introduce.

One of the original Maori Hill electric trams trundling along Highgate, Roslyn.
Author's Collection

Electric and cable trams of the Roslyn Tramway Company of Dunedin at the 'Junction' in Ross Street on the town belt where passengers from the city on the Rattray Street cable line could transfer to the Maori Hill pioneer electric tramway. *G.C. Ditchfield Collection*

Two early postcards of Maori Hill tram No. 1, New Zealand's first electric tram, in Highgate and City Road. The fronts of the tram were glassed in to give motormen protection from the weather. *John M. Bettle*

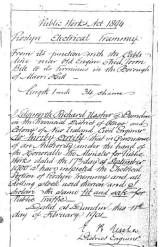

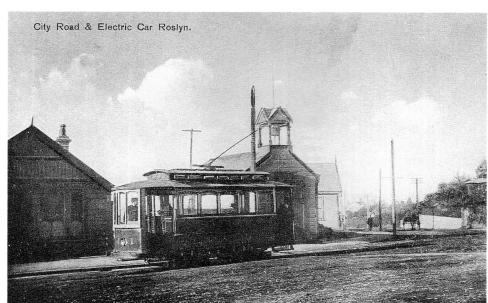

City Road & Electric Car Roslyn.

The ticket issued to Sir John Logan Campbell to ride on electric tram No. 1 on opening day. *Author's Collection*

In the days when a woman's place was in the home! There are scarcely any women to be seen in the huge crowd which greeted the first Auckland electric tram when it trundled across the Queen and Customs Street intersection with Sir John Logan Campbell at the controls. Why are they all looking skywards? The trolley-pole has come off the overhead wire—the first, but not the last, time that such an incident would halt a busy tram. *Author's Collection*

Private Enterprise to the Fore—Auckland

Triumphant celebrations acclaimed the opening of electric tramways in Auckland on 17 November 1902, when thousands of citizens packed Queen Street to see the Phenomenon, a tram-car which ran without horses. A marvel of the 20th century had come to town, to give workers a new deal, enabling families to settle in the outer suburbs of Mount Eden and Kingsland, with speedy 'electrics' to whisk father to and from his daily toil. Proceedings opened with the switching on of the electric current at the Hobson Street power station by the Mayor of Auckland, Alfred Kidd, Hunter's Garrison Band adding tone to the occasion. In his speech the mayor made a brief reference to the first electric line: 'There was a small tramline in Dunedin—a fine piece of work of its character.' Then with parochial pride he went on to say that 'every Aucklander would feel proud of the fact that Auckland was the first city in New Zealand to go in for a complete electric tramway system'. This remark was followed by a thunder of applause. An open carriage then took the official party to lower Queen Street, where six trams were standing in readiness.

With much pomp and ceremony, the white-bearded Sir John Logan Campbell, the 'Father of Auckland', was asked to set the first car in motion. The band played 'For He's a Jolly Good Fellow', flags waved in salute, and bearded men wearing boaters applauded as Sir John took his place at the controls. Taking hold of the driving handle, he said, 'Success to the Tramways Company. May its cars never cease to run in the city of Auckland.' Then amidst renewed cheering the first electric car, gaily decked with bunting and flags, surged forward up Queen Street.

The six official electric trams about to leave lower Queen Street at the conclusion of the inauguration of electric traction by the Auckland Electric Tramways Company in November 1902. *Author's Collection*

A five o'clock scene in lower Queen Street as depicted by an *Auckland Weekly News* artist. *Auckland Weekly News*

The steamer *Elingamite*. *Author's Collection*

Following were the other five cars laden with invited guests bound for the Choral Hall, where 300 citizens sat down for an official luncheon. Excited townsfolk lined the footpaths to watch the cars pass through the streets. Several people were observed placing coins, pins and other articles upon the rails in front of approaching cars. On being picked up afterwards, these flattened objects appeared to give their owners much satisfaction.

That evening a ball at Rocklands, Epsom, the residence of P.M. Hansen, local director of the Auckland Electric Tramways Company, brought a momentous day to a fitting close. An electric wire had been strung along the streets from Manukau Road to supply electric light for the social occasion. At Rocklands 260 guests danced in the spacious rooms illuminated by electric light bulbs. On the lawn outside, a brass band played a selected musical programme. Auckland could now lift its head high and take its place alongside major cities of 'that great Empire upon which the sun never sets'.

It had been intended to start the public service to Ponsonby on the following day. Unfortunately, 11 motormen on their way from Sydney to take up employment in Auckland were shipwrecked when the steamer *Elingamite* struck one of the Three Kings Islands, three of their number being drowned. To enable the survivors to recover and to become acquainted with the routes, the company delayed starting the service until 24 November. The public therefore had to wait a week after the gala opening to experience what one privileged guest described as 'the exhilaration of being whirled through the air at the rate of knots'.

So great was the rush when the regular service began that bona fide travellers were jostled out of seats by crowds eager to ride on an electric tram. Ten cars, eight small four-wheelers and two bogie-type 'combinations' carried 15,000 passengers and it was estimated that 10,000 others missed the memorable event. All day long, and far into the evening, a large gathering waited at the foot of Queen Street. As each tram arrived there was a scramble to get aboard and then a fight for seats. In a flick of the fingers, the car was packed tight, the rear platform crowded, with men and women still struggling to climb upon the steps, some hanging on to the last. Five company officials aided by two policemen were required to clear the crowded saloon before the tram could glide away and disappear up Queen Street. Many local residents who required transport to reach their places of business in the morning, or their homes in the evening, had to walk the distance. Some Aucklanders spent hours enjoying what today's five o'clock commuters will be surprised to learn were called 'pleasure jaunts', riding back and forth between Queen Street and Ponsonby. One man bought 3 shillings' worth of tickets (a trip cost only twopence) and, taking his seat, remained until the tickets were exhausted. Several women spent the

Auckland tram No. 1 city bound on Parnell Rise in 1904 after the trams had been painted a light orange colour, relieved by narrow blue and red lines, to combat the dust problem. *Postcard, John M. Bettle Collection*

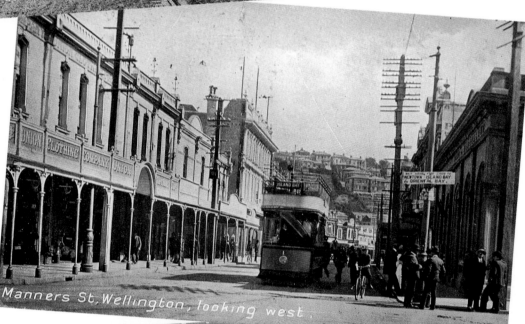

Wellington tram No. 1 in Manners Street, about to cross the Cuba Street intersection en route to Island Bay. *Postcard, John M. Bettle Collection*

Courtenay Place, Wellington, in the 1900s was a busy tramway junction. The tram on the right is heading for Oriental Bay. *Postcard, John M. Bettle Collection*

Greeting cards featuring the new electric trams were popular in the early years of the 20th century. *Postcard, John M. Bettle Collection*

Many happy Returns of the day.

Though we are so far apart,
Though we for a while must sever.
Let this say, with all my heart
Old friends are old friends for ever.

Trams dominated all traffic in Princes Street outside the old Exchange building in Dunedin for over 50 years. *Postcard, John M. Bettle Collection*

Princes St., Dunedin.

The business Centre

A Kitson steam-tram hauling two double-decker trailers along Cashel Street heading for Cathedral Square in Christchurch. *Postcard, John M. Bettle Collection*

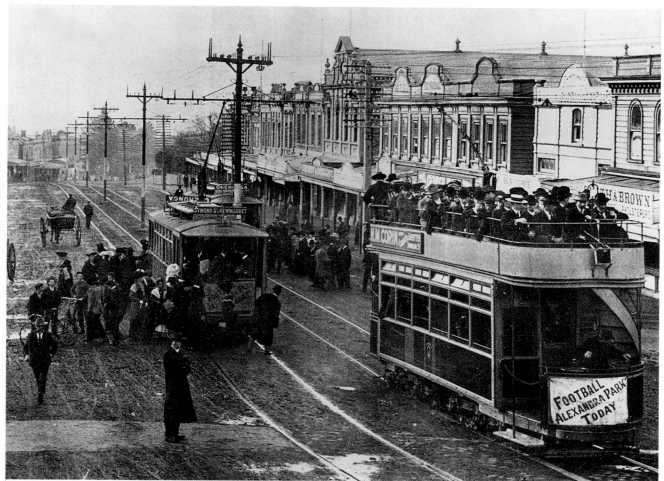

Hardy Auckland rugby
enthusiasts find the open-
top deck a bracing form of
travel in 1905. Symonds Street
from the top of Khyber Pass
Road. *Author's Collection*

afternoon in similar fashion. Some, who were removed because of overcrowding
and told to catch the next car, argued that there were no horses to suffer because of
the extra load.

The *New Zealand Herald* was full of praise for the gaily painted cars: 'Once the
travelling public, pedestrians, and the horses have become used to the system it will
rank as one of the finest services of rapid transit in Australasia.' Commenting on
the cars, the *Herald* wrote: 'Smooth and comfortable, not to say luxurious, transit
which so recently would have been impossible even for the richest is now being
brought into the everyday use of all.'

Horses, as usual, objected to the then novel electric vehicles. At about quarter
past five in the evening, Dr Goldie was being driven down Queen Street by his
groom in a light trap when the horse slipped and fell across the rails in front of the
Herald office. A large double-decker tram coming down the street at a fair speed
could not be stopped in time and struck the horse, to the accompaniment of frantic
screams from several women passengers. Unnerved spectators were relieved to see
that the wheel-guard prevented the wheels from running over the animal's head, as
it became wedged under the front platform. As soon as the car stopped, it was
reversed, and the horse, after a little coaxing, regained its feet and was led away,
badly bruised. Earlier in the afternoon a horse ridden by a young man was
frightened by a car at the top of Pitt Street and jumped onto the footpath, falling on
the rider and breaking his leg. Elsewhere, wagon teams shied off the roadway and
one trap capsized into the gutter.

Notwithstanding such incidents, by the end of the first week more than 70,000
people had enjoyed the technologically advanced mode of conveyance represented
by the electric tram-car. The Auckland Electric Tramways Company was a subsidiary
of the British Electric Traction Company, which owned and operated a large
number of tramway systems throughout Britain, and also at Bombay (India),
Nelson (British Columbia) and Caracas (Venezuela). In all, the parent company
controlled 526 route kilometres of tramways by December 1903. Englishmen arriving
in the colony were quick to spot the familiar 'magnet and wheel' insignia of the
BET tramway empire displayed on the side panels of the cars.

It was a social occasion when the first electric tram arrived at the Auckland suburb of Grey Lynn in May 1910. *Author's Collection*

Electric trams and horse-buses dominate a busy scene in lower Queen Street in 1905, when the Auckland Railway Station was on the site of the old post office. A lone motor car is parked behind a photographer standing on top of a stepladder at right. *Author's Collection*

Private enterprise meant that the ratepayers need have no fears of transport levies, the company having been given a 30-year concession by the council; only the shareholders would suffer if the services ran at a loss. Threepence had been the fare on horse-cars irrespective of the distance travelled; now, as promised, it was one penny a section on the new-fangled electric contraptions, and Aucklanders became a community to tram-riders. They had outgrown the days when they were dignified, unhurried pedestrians.

Electrics Become the Fashion—Dunedin

Public oratory reigned supreme at the official luncheon when the opening of the Dunedin city electric service was celebrated in December 1903. Following the feast, privileged guests rode over the line to Normanby in a convoy of decorated trams. Shopkeepers closed their premises to allow their employees to witness the grand procession, but unfortunately the eating, toasting and speech-making lasted for three solid hours, and thus it was mid-afternoon before the public, who had been waiting patiently, were rewarded by a glimpse of the new city toys. A second outing for the decorated convoy in the evening conveyed the guests in comfort to the Botanical Gardens, where an open-air concert by combined bands marked the coming of electric traction to Dunedin. For the next week motormen were given the freedom of the new steel road for training and instruction purposes.

On Christmas Eve, when the service finally started, the clanging of warning gongs could be heard far and wide. Motormen were determined to make the day accident-free. On the previous evenings an illuminated car had taken the Premier, the Rt Hon. Richard John Seddon, for a trip over the rails. With typical political diplomacy he was quoted as saying that the Dunedin tramway system was 'the smoothest running and most comfortable electric installation south of the line'. It was not reported at the time whether his remarks referred to south of the equator or south of Wellington! The first tram for public patronage was driven by A. Lenz, and the conductor, W.H. Mackenzie, later rose through the ranks to become manager in 1920. As expected, joy-riders were out in force, many refusing to leave the trams.

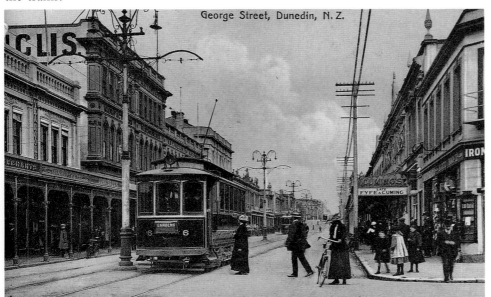

George Street, Dunedin, N.Z.

One of the smart new electric trams in George Street, Dunedin. Women still rode bicycles into town. *Postcard, John M. Bettle Collection*

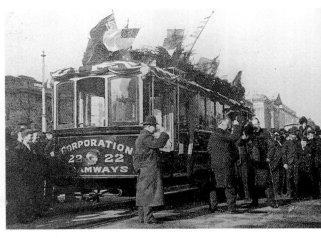

ABOVE: Dunedin Californian combination tram No. 22, loading for the Botanical Gardens in Princes Street, in the early years of electric trams in Dunedin. *Auckland Weekly News* ABOVE RIGHT: No. 22 decorated for use as a vice-regal tram for the carriage of the Governor, Lord Plunket, in 1904. *Otago Witness* This tram has been restored to running order by the Tramway Historical Society of Christchurch.

Electric cars were now a possession any city worthy of the title could boast about — something to be shown to guests with a display of pride — and Dunedin, after all, was the first city corporation in New Zealand to go it alone in this new field. When the Governor, Lord Plunket, made his first visit to Dunedin in 1904, a ride in an electric tram was arranged. At the appointed time, combination car No. 22, decorated with flags and foliage, pulled up outside the Grand Hotel, the crew wearing freshly pressed uniforms with buttons gleaming. His Excellency and the vice-regal party took their seats, with the mayor, T.R. Christie, and the City Electrical Engineer, W.G.T. Goodman, in attendance. Then, without stopping on the way, the electric car journeyed in style through the city streets to the North East Valley School. Drawn up at attention to meet the vice-regal tram was the school cadet battalion. Lord Plunket alighted from the tram with dignity and stood by the step, while young buglers sounded the Royal salute. The Governor inspected the cadets and spoke to the assembled school children, mentioning that he himself had been a bugler in a cadet corps. Then he returned to his electric steed. To a ring of the foot-gong, the vice-regal party waved a polite farewell and the tram sped the King's representative back to his hotel.

Dunedin city fathers inspecting one of the new imported American electric trams. Third from left is W.G.T. (later Sir William) Goodman, who was engineer for the building of the Dunedin system. *Evening Star*

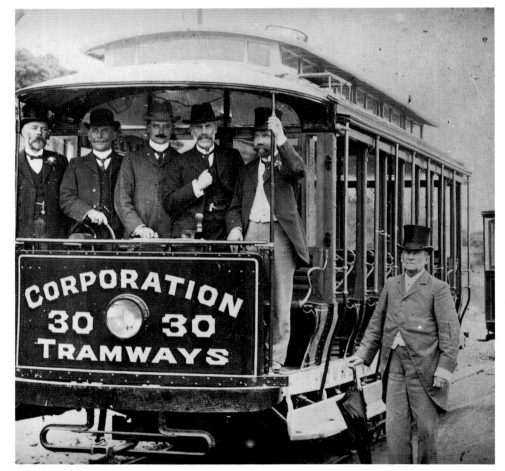

Trams Illuminate the Streets — Wellington

For several years Wellington had been associated with other centres in studying the latest overseas developments in urban transport with a view to electrification of the capital city's tramways. Generally speaking, it had only been the protracted business of finalising contracts and finance which put one city ahead of another in inaugurating an electric service. It was an English company, Macartney McElroy and Co. Ltd, of London, which was given the task by Wellington's city council. On 8 June 1904 engineers carried out the first trial run just a few minutes before midnight. Those present for the occasion were impressed by the display of lights in the dead of night. As one newspaper reporter wrote:

> Slowly and steadily the car came down the track from the Newtown shed, brilliantly lighted inside with eight 16-candlepower lights, having a 32-candle power headlight, and the destination lights (showing the words Wellington and Newtown at each end) were of 16-candlepower. Besides this lighting, frequent flashes of electricity were thrown off from the works beneath the car and the point of contact of the connecting arm with the trolley wire overhead showed a vivid blue light. The whole spectacle as the car proceeded along the track was unique and brilliant.

On the last day of June 1904 the first section from the Newtown sheds to the gates of St Patrick's College in Kent Terrace was opened for passenger traffic. At

Wellington electric tram No. 1 turning into Lambton Quay from Willis Street in 1906. Those were the days when Wellington had two railway terminals, the government station at Lambton and the Manawatu Railway Company station at Thorndon. *Author's Collection*

nine o'clock that morning the mayor, J.G.W. Aitken, accompanied by councillors and Public Works personnel, boarded a double-decker car opposite the Basin Reserve and were carried through Newtown and into the car shed. After inspecting the facilities and posing for the inevitable photographer, the party returned in a single-deck car to the Kent Terrace terminus. Rounds of hearty cheers were given for the mayor, who had acted successfully as motorman, and for R.W. Wright, the electrical engineer who had designed the system. It was agreed by those who had experienced electric services in other parts of the world that 'Wellington's was as good as any, and much less noisy than Auckland's'. There was no public opening ceremony as the total length of electrified line represented only a penny section, a horse-tram providing a connecting service to the commercial centre of the city.

The newspapers had this to say:

At present the Wellington motorman is, like the Premier, going slow. If he keeps to the present pace, there need be little fear of accident, but should he venture to get up to the Auckland pace, there will be considerable danger. The gauge is narrow, but when the double line is down there is little left for anything but the tramcar. At one of the principal business corners of Wellington, where Manners Street joins Cuba Street, there is a marvellous network of rails, which would make the most daring of pedestrians stick resolutely to the path, and even then he might be in considerable danger of having his knuckles dusted by a passing car.

Tracks extending into the main business area were not brought into use until the end of the year. When all sections of the system, as originally planned, were finally working in January 1905, the mayor and city councillors seated themselves in an illuminated double-decker for an official night trip. With much civic pride, the car traversed all routes adorned with flowers and greenery, and outlined in electric lamps of red, white and blue, with a line of lamps being carried up the trolley-pole to complete the decorations.

An unbelievable token of goodwill by comparison with commercial relationships today (according to several old tramwaymen who told the author the story) was the gift of a small convertible tram of American design from the contractors who installed the system. Furnished with padded seats and curtains, the car—which carried the road number 33—was given for the exclusive use of the mayor and city councillors! This believe-it-or-not story did not finish there; the gift tram was too

wide for Wellington streets and had to be sliced down the centre from end to end and a section removed before it could be used in the narrow thoroughfares of the capital.

In February 1905 a red-faced motorman received a dressing-down from a very angry Premier. Instead of stopping his tram in the narrow thoroughfare outside the Premier's residence in Molesworth Street when he saw a carriage ahead only centimetres from the track, he proceeded in the belief that there was clearance for the tram to pass. The tram struck the carriage and carried it along 3 or 4 metres, until the horses were dragged off their feet. It seemed likely that the car would run over the legs of the horses, but the speedily assembling crowd cried out in time. J. Lane, a well-known cab proprietor, who was waiting by the carriage to drive Premier Richard Seddon to the Manawatu Railway Station, had signalled the motorman to stop because he considered that his horses were too restive to bear a tram passing so close to their heads. While arguments were in full cry as to the right of the road, and the harness was being cut to relieve the horses trapped between the two vehicles, the Premier arrived on the scene and soundly rebuked the motorman before setting off for the station in another cab.

Even baby was brought to
town when the first electric
tram rumbled through
Cathedral Square,
Christchurch, on the inaugural
run to Papanui in June 1905.
*Press Collection, Alexander
Turnbull Library*

Fashionable women now used
the electric cars—the corner of
High and Cashel Streets,
Christchurch in September
1905. *Muir & Moodie,
Dominion Museum*

Steel-Shod Armada Decorated with Toetoe Grass — Christchurch

Organisers always fear that a carefully planned ceremony will be marred by mishap. Such a dreaded possibility became reality when Christchurch dignitaries went riding in eight spanking new electrics to open the first line to Papanui in June 1905. Like many modern motorists the motormen appear to have been driving their trams too closely in formation, and the fifth tram in line astern heavily bumped the car in front. The sixth car was unable to stop in time and ploughed into the fifth with considerable force, demolishing the back platform. A grinding, screeching thud, accompanied by metal twisting, woodwork splintering and glass breaking, shocked the top-hatted guests with flowing moustaches, who were experiencing a jaunt with their wives, dressed to the nines.

Much to the credit of all concerned there was not a single scream or any panic in the saloons. Four people on the platform of the fifth car were injured, including the Inspector of Police, R.J. Gillies, whose right thigh was crushed by the crumpled wreckage. With the convoy reduced to six vehicles, the procession continued undaunted through Cathedral Square, where the sidewalks were lined with sightseers. Mrs W. Reece, wife of the Tramway Board's chairman, had driven a double-decker through a ribbon stretched across the tracks to start the steel-shod armada, all cars being decorated with patriotic ribbons and toetoe grass. It was prominently recorded that a 'kinematograph photograph' had been taken of the inaugural run.

Next day the first revenue car left the Clock Tower in High Street at about 6.45 am. F.H. Chamberlain, the Tramway Engineer, was at the controls as motorman, and Mr Wood, the Traffic Manager, stood beside him on the platform. The *Lyttelton Times* report stated:

> There seemed to be some competition among the passengers for the distinction of paying the first fare. One cornered the privilege by securing himself in the conductor's first port of call. The reporter, however, bagged the honour of throwing the first punched ticket on to the floor. The citizens of Christchurch played with their new tramway system all day yesterday, and late last night, until they were tired. The patronage was unprecedented and entirely unexpected. The cars as they ran through Cathedral Square held large numbers of bystanders in a kind of fascination. They were the cynosure of every eye ...

There were five cars, including two double-deckers, running on the section from 6.37 am to 11.7 pm.

Some of the Christchurch tram bodies had been built locally by Boon and Company in Ferry Road, and these featured interior panels of mottled kauri, which contrasted favourably with the maple panels of the imported cars. To protect the swarms of bicycles which clogged the roads, large steel fenders with a net of steel mesh projected a metre in front of each tram-car. If a cyclist was likely to be struck by a tram-car, the motorman only had to push a trigger with his foot and both bike and rider would be scooped to safety. Electric heaters under each seat made winter travellers reluctant to leave the cars but, unlike those in Wellington, the seats did not have cushions. Management was of the opinion that cushioned seats were not hygienic!

A ticket issued on the last day of electric trams in Christchurch, 11 September 1954. *Author's Collection*

Christchurch residents discussing the new horseless wonders in Cathedral Square on the opening day of the electric tram service. *Press Collection, Alexander Turnbull Library*

TOP: Race day in Auckland. A double-decker tram in Queen Street, loaded with punters, passes a 2-cylinder 1907 Oldsmobile. This horseless carriage was the fourth motor car on the North Island motor registry. *Price, Author's Collection*
ABOVE: The same scene during the last week of trams in December 1956. *Graham Stewart*

CHAPTER FIVE

Penny Section Days

Across the Auckland isthmus, like a foreshortened transcontinental railway, the electric tramways came in stages from the Pacific waters of the Waitemata Harbour to meet the Tasman Sea at Onehunga. The first section to Newmarket was opened on Christmas Eve 1902, and as the car crossed the city boundary into Newmarket Borough, all the dignitaries on board stood while the mayor called for three hearty cheers for the tramways company. Adjournment to a public house seemed the order of the day as the steel rails probed forward. Officials on the inaugural run to Newmarket alighted as soon as the car whined to a halt and celebrated the occasion in the Newmarket Hotel. Only a week before, Parnell Borough had 'wet the head' of their new electric baby. On the way back from that jaunt, a short stop had been made at the Exchange Hotel in Parnell Road. Male passengers assembled in the bars where they drank toasts accompanied by musical honours, while the women were left to discover the discomfort of wooden tram seats.

Gradually the coast-to-coast line snaked its way through Epsom, Royal Oak and down Queen Street, Onehunga, to Church Street, where members of the management and councillors on a 'show-the-flag' first trip, patted each other on the back over ale at Graham's Hotel. To the ringing cheers of about 100 school children who had gathered to witness the great event, the party re-entered the tram and returned to Auckland. The arrival of the tramway was not without a tinge of parochialism, for at an Onehunga Borough Council meeting that evening, concern was voiced over the crowding of Onehunga tram-cars by inconsiderate Auckland residents. In September 1903, with much clinking of glasses, the narrowest part of New Zealand was finally transversed by a tramway 11 kilometres long.

Aucklanders about to board a city-bound tram at the Onehunga terminus after a journey into the 'country' and afternoon tea at the Sans Souci tea kiosk. *Price, Author's Collection*

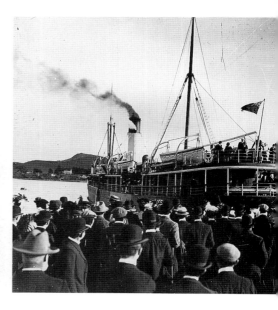

Paul Hansen

Author's Collection

The contentious subject of running trams on Sunday came to a head in this month with a poll being taken to decide whether the restful quiet of the Sabbath should be shattered. Letters to the editor of the *New Zealand Herald* voiced strong resistance. A typical protest:

Sir—I am afraid it will be a bad day for Auckland if the tramcars are allowed to run on Sundays. I have seen letters re Continental Sundays. May God save us from having them here! We are going quite fast enough as it is. It is only the thin edge of the wedge to open the shops. We are getting too fond of pleasure in Auckland. I am, etc, N.Z.

And yet another:

Sir—I have endeavoured to view the subject impartially. I feel it my duty to declare my conviction that to run the trams on the Lord's Day would tend to degrade and debase the people. I never make man or beast work for me on Sunday. I am, etc, Alfred Jowitt.

On polling day advocates for Sunday trams wore dark blue ribbons; their opponents wore white ribbons with the word 'Peace' printed on them. The ballot paper was worded: 'Proposal to run the electric tramcars on the Lord's Day.' Citizens gave their sanction to Sunday trams by a narrow majority of 22 votes, which was reduced to 19 on a recount. The company, for its part, had pledged that trams would not run during church hours. During those hours, from 11 am to 12.30 pm, and from 7 pm to 8.30 pm, trams stood motionless on the Choral Hall branch in lower Symonds Street, and in Hobson Street. For some unknown reason, motormen were paid for these enforced stoppages, but not conductors.

In the New Year the Mayor of Onehunga, D.A. Sutherland, formally hoisted a Union Jack to open the Sans Souci tea kiosk which had been built at the Onehunga terminus by the Auckland Electric Tramways Company. Visitors to Onehunga could admire a view of the Manukau Harbour while relaxing in the ornate interior, and sip afternoon tea from a silver service with sandwiches and fancy cakes. So popular was this innovation that the company extended the building on an elaborate scale to accommodate 150 patrons. The decor was grandiose—walls painted cream, red and gold, with a frieze of Japanese leather, dados and a cream ceiling adorned with electric lights of various colours. All this was crowned by a centrepiece consisting of 50 lamps set in mirrors and surrounded by glass pendants. A visit to the Sans Souci soon became a social highlight.

Concerts were now the vogue on alternate Wednesday evenings during the summer months. Paul Hansen, the local director of the company, returned from England with a Monarch gramophone which became a principal attraction at these functions. The music box was duly unveiled under the glare of 100 electric lamps in the plush Edwardian surroundings, the audience wearing evening attire for the occasion. Madame Melba singing Tosti's 'Good-bye' opened the selections, and other scratchy recordings which held the guests spellbound included songs by Signor Enrico Caruso, Signor Francisco, Mr Edward Lloyd and Mr Ben Davies.

On the coast-to-coast tramway, both motorman and conductor adopt a pose befitting their responsibilities. The Onehunga terminus in 1906. *Author's Collection*

BELOW: Looking down Manukau Road from the Royal Oak junction with Mount Albert, Campbell and Mount Smart Roads in 1905. *Author's Collection* BOTTOM: A similar scene from the same intersection during a morning peak period towards the end of the tramway era in Auckland in 1956. *Graham Stewart*

Out of the tunnel and into the country—a Wellington tram emerging from the Seatoun tunnel shortly after it opened in December 1907. *Author's Collection*

The extension of the tramway into the country brought with it communication problems. How could a motorman report back to headquarters in town if he ran over a wild pig or into a flock of sheep? To overcome the difficulties of serving such far-flung outposts as Onehunga, telephone lines—with connections suitably spaced—were strung from the roadside poles supporting the electric trolley wire. Christchurch and Auckland both instituted similar systems, each car carrying a magneto telephone which, in case of accident or breakdown, could be plugged into a terminal box on the nearest pole.

Rural operation certainly had its moments. In the Auckland Magistrates' Court in 1905, Alfred Buckland and Sons sued the tramway company to recover £7 10s, the value of 10 sheep alleged to have been killed by a tram in Manukau Road, Newmarket. Drover William Jones said in evidence that he was driving about 1300 sheep along the road on a clear night when a fast-moving city-bound tram ploughed into the mob. Jones maintained that the motorman did not attempt to stop until halfway through the flock, by which time the wheels were clogged with bones and wool.

In this age of jet aircraft it may be hard to realise that Aucklanders wishing to travel south started their journey in the city by boarding a tram for Onehunga, where it would connect with the steamship service to New Plymouth and ports farther south. The Union Steam Ship Company had started the first regular passenger express service between Onehunga and Lyttelton, calling at New Plymouth and Wellington, back in November 1883. In the heart of the North Island, while men

A tram descending the steep gradient from the Dunedin suburb of Opoho in the 1920s. *Postcard, John M. Bettle Collection*

Opoho Car off to the City, Dunedin, N.Z.

The Wellington tramway terminal outside the original Lambton Station at the Featherston Street and Lambton Quay junction in 1912. *Postcard, John M. Bettle Collection*

The same busy tramway terminal outside the Wellington Railway Station in the 1950s. *Graham Stewart*

laboured with picks, shovels and primitive machinery to build the Main Trunk railway line, completed in 1909, the coast-to-coast trams thrived on the boat trade.

Southbound travellers would step out onto a rough roadway and lift their burdens up to a tram platform, find a wooden bench, pay their fares and be whirled off to Onehunga at speeds which sometimes reached as high as 50 kilometres an hour. One consolation of this section of the journey was that on arrival at the port the walk from tram to steamer was downhill. The overnight sea voyage took about 13 to 14 hours, depending on the weather, and travellers' endurance as sailors was usually taxed to the utmost. At the port of New Plymouth there was the upheaval of transferring to a train drawn by a smart-looking steam locomotive adorned with flashy brasswork, snorting impatiently to whisk passengers the short distance into the township. While waiting for the mail train to Wellington on the bleak station platform, the jaded travellers had time to regain their land legs. Then, for the umpteenth time, there came the struggle with luggage, this time onto the rack overhead, before selecting an upright seat upholstered with leather cushions firmly padded with horsehair. Settling down for the final, wearisome 400 kilometres, travellers soon found themselves inhaling the acrid smell of coal smoke sifting through the window frames and ventilators of their carriages as the train laboured up the many stiff inclines. Arriving in the capital city some 14 hours later, travellers had the choice of a horse-drawn cab or a tram-car, both standing in attendance at the Manawatu Railway Company's station. On the tram a fee was charged for luggage, because it was classified as freight. Relieved at having arrived safely after a night and a day of continuous travelling, weary travellers usually paid up without a murmur. A journey from Auckland to Wellington, which began and ended with a tram-car ride, was not an expedition to be undertaken lightly.

Colombo Street Christchurch. N.Z.F.G.R 5651.

Pedestrians and trams—looking down Colombo Street from Cathedral Square, Christchurch during the First World War. *Radcliffe Collection, Alexander Turnbull Library*

'Move down the car, please' ... the ring of the conductor's bell ... the whine of electric motors under the floor ... the struggle for a foothold, the rear platform jammed tight with homeward-bound workers ... the car gathering speed along the shining rails embedded in the roadway ... the saloon lights fading slowly to a glimmer as the power was sapped from the overhead wire ... the metallic rattle amid a shower of sparks as a trolley-pole came off ... these were part and parcel of daily life in the cities of New Zealand during the bustling Edwardian era, as also were the dignified women with big hats and stately parasols, and top-hatted males with flowing moustaches, high collars and floral buttonholes as big as cauliflowers. The sidesteps and narrow entrances of trams amused pavement observers of the time. Women wearing wide-brimmed Merry Widow hats had to tilt their heads to one side to pass through the doorway. Their hobble skirts were tight and long, and the steps were high, so that when a woman put her foot on the step her skirt would slide up and show her ankles.

Travelling at speed was fun. This extract from a letter written at the time by a Wellingtonian on holiday in Auckland to a friend back home captures the enthusiasm that prevailed:

Wellingtonians boarding a double-decker electric tram at the Island Bay terminus after a day at the seaside in the early 1900s. *Alexander Turnbull Library*

Riding about in the new electric cars is a great game here. It is nothing unusual for a family party to get into a car and ride back and forward the full length of the route several times. The service is a huge success and very popular. For a penny you can go a distance equal, say, to the section from Thorndon terminus to the Opera House in Manners Street. At night each car makes a great illumination as it threads the streets.

The enchantment did not apply to all; on leaving the tram-car first-trippers sometimes experienced a feeling of nausea akin to seasickness, and some less fortunate people even had to get off in a hurry. This could have been due to excitement, or the unaccustomed motion. Static electricity in the air was one theory held by those opposed to such advancement.

David Low, the great political cartoonist, said in his autobiography that when he was a young man he found Cathedral Square to be an excellent observation ground, the Piccadilly Circus of Christchurch, so to speak. He would stand sketching and making rough notes on the back of an envelope to catch some nob waiting for his tram a couple of metres away. Some nob? What little class distinction existed in those years—compared with that which existed in other countries—came in for a wigging when the Wellington City Council instructed conductors that they must not allow shabbily attired persons on the tram-cars. Any passenger whose dress or clothing might, in the opinion of the conductor, soil or damage the lining or cushions, or the dress or clothing of any other passenger, was to be refused transit. It was alleged that the by-law savoured of class distinction, and that to give conductors such authority would result in working men, whose calling led to their being generally begrimed and dishevelled in appearance, from riding in the cars. The council countered this with plans to run special cars for the convenience of working men. Workers' 'specials' and workers' concession tickets were instituted in Auckland.

Hatpins became the bane of the tram conductor's life. The sharp point of a woman's hatpin was a dangerous thing and some conductors had scars as evidence that ladies should be compelled to use guards on their pins. One conductor, interviewed on the issue, said that he never knew the minute when the fate of one of his eyes would be sealed by a sharp point as a woman leaned over to pay her fare

FIVE O'CLOCK TRAM.

We're Labourites, and Tories,
The Opposition too,
But we don't apply the closure
On anybody's view
As we stand on the back platform,
The usual privileged few,
On the tram that takes us home
At 5 o'clock.

There's a plumber and a printer,
A natty office toff,
A porter and a policeman—
Who pops in on and off—
And a little pale bookkeeper
With a nasty kinda cough,
On the tram that takes us home
At 5 o'clock.

There are always cheery greetings,
And many a hearty laugh,
There are serious discussions,
And much good-natured chaff,
And we sometimes gather stories
Fit to tell our "better half,"
On the tram that takes us home
At 5 o'clock.

A diversity of comments
Upon the state of trade,
Gives way to talk of football
And how Otago played.
We learn tips on bulbs, and gardens,
And what Grand Jury paid
On the tram that takes us home
At 5 o'clock.

We have no standing orders,
Or any other guide,
For all debates are friendly—
No heat on either side;
We forget our work-time worries,
And feel better for the ride
On the tram that takes us home
At 5 o'clock.

D.W.S.
Evening Post.

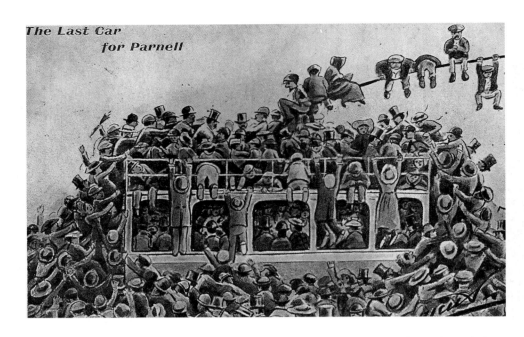

The Last Car for Parnell

or rushed up to get out: 'The conductor has enough to put up with, without being bayoneted in the discharge of his duty. Why can't women wear elastic under the chin as they did in the old days?' It was said that hatpins were generally the last thing snatched up when a woman prepared to go out shopping, and to affix a guard to them might mean an afternoon tea, a tram or a bargain missed.

Corporations and companies found it prudent to publish pamphlets setting out the correct way to alight from a car in motion, because of a large number of accidents—minor and serious—which had occurred through people getting off the wrong way. A large poster illustration made it clear that passengers should not alight from a moving car while facing the rear of the vehicle. The printed warning added, without comment, that if they did so the concussion between the back of the head and the wooden paving blocks would convince them of the error of their ways!

A new phenomenon—the five o'clock rush—was born with the coming of the trams. Some considered the rush to board a car as good training for potential All Blacks. And there were 'ladies' in the scramble and crush who could wield a deadly elbow while complaining loudly about the rude tactics of brutal males. These

'Of course, when you've been on the job a bit longer, you'll know better than to go inspecting tickets on a five o'clock tram.'

'Well! If that wasn't the tightest squeeze of any ride I've ever had!'

Island Bay, Wellington was a popular seaside picnic destination when groups and organisations would hire special electric trams for a day at the beach. This photograph shows the tram terminus as crowds prepare to return home in the early 1920s. *S.C. Smith, Alexander Turnbull Library*

struggles over seats usually took place at a terminus while the conductor was swinging the single trolley-pole on these early models to the other end of the car in readiness for the next trip. An amusing letter in the *Lyttelton Times* in 1905 complained bitterly about this dangerous necessity for swinging trolley-poles:

> At the terminus, with a double-decked carload the conductor alights smartly and plunges everything in darkness while he angles with the 'fishing rod' in the reversing operation. A few nights ago several young ladies had to wait on the top of a car during this performance, not daring to stand upright on account of the wanderings of the pole and unable to see their way downstairs.

Dunedin, incidentally, gave up double-decked trams when it pensioned off the horses, but the other main centres each had electrics with open top decks.

If one was accustomed to heights, loved the rush of fresh air and could stand the swaying, a ride on the top of a double-decker was a great thrill. Apart from the threatening swirl of the pole and the feeling that one was about to be decapitated every time an overhead bridge loomed on the horizon, the view of the passing countryside was magnificent. Young folk loved the upstairs deck, where they could relax without having the beady eyes of some puritanical conformist glaring disapprovingly at their antics.

Len Robinson, who rose through the ranks of the Wellington Tramways to the position of transport superintendent, once related this story about conducting on a double-decker:

> One evening a young couple got on and proceeded to the top deck. I went up to collect the fares in the semi-dark, and was given a shilling for two penny fares. On descending to the back platform, I was running my fingers through the cash when I saw a gold sovereign in with the single shillings in my bag. I realised at once that the top-deck passenger had made a mistake, so climbed the stairs to tell him. The young man took his arm from around the girl's waist, and said to me, "Don't be silly, I never make mistakes like that." So I returned to the platform again. On further thought, I assured myself that the only shillings I had taken were in daylight and that the sovereign must belong to the young man. Upstairs I went again to be met with, "For goodness sake, keep downstairs, and if you are nineteen shillings over, well keep it." Sure enough, when I cashed in that night I was nineteen shillings over, so I just took the young man at his word, and pocketed the change.

Penny courtships on top of deckers were all the rage. Courting couples couldn't ask Dad for the family car in those days.

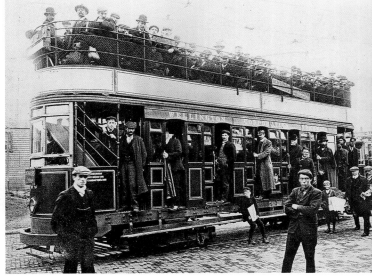

While all this snuggling was going on above, motormen, fully exposed to the elements, kept a sharp weather eye on the road ahead. Plenty of brawn and muscle, and a cast-iron constitution, were the main qualifications for a successful 'trammie'. Minimum weight for motormen was 70 kilograms; some strength was necessary to handle the heavy handbrake which preceded the popular Westinghouse airbrake. It was certainly no job for weaklings. Oilskins and gumboots were worn in wet weather, and during the summer months, crews sported straw hats with wide brims. If they were not being pelted by rain, their faces and uniforms would be covered with dust. But a motorman was eyed with envy by men, both young and old, despite the many drawbacks to the job. On all lines it was common to see someone waiting at a tramstop with a billy of tea or cocoa and a batch of freshly made scones. Against all regulations a conductor would sip his tea, on the front platform because the rear end was invariably in a cloud of dust. Citizens took a great interest in the tramwaymen. A young man controlling unknown and reputedly dangerous forces became the more fascinating to impressionable young women. He was an exotic figure in his uniform with its shiny silver buttons and peaked cap. Horse-bus drivers had not worn anything resembling a uniform.

Regulations required tramwaymen to be neat in appearance and polite to all. They were not to 'constantly frequent' drinking places when off duty, or to indulge in any form of gambling, 'including the laying of bets'. They were not to enter into unnecessary conversations with passengers, smoke, chew tobacco or read books or newspapers while on duty. The rules stipulated that a motorman should 'stand erect, one hand on the controller handle, and one on the brake'. This position was to be maintained throughout the journey. Sitting down or leaning against the door while in transit was not allowed.

Speed was relative. The rules laid down a method of computing it by counting the number of poles passed per minute, and stated that motormen should use the system frequently. Road courtesy was set out in some detail. Motormen were to 'avoid ringing the gong if possible in the face of an approaching horse', and to 'stop quickly if the horse objected to passing the car'. Wide spaces were to be given to winged wagons and heavily loaded teams, and motormen were enjoined always to be patient and give other drivers time to draw out of their way. Motor cars were few and limited to a speed of 13 kilometres an hour, so the fast electric trams were the kings of the road. They had the right-of-way over all other traffic.

The conductor's call of 'Fares, please' would echo from one end of the tram to the other. Conductors had to be careful when swinging their way along the footboards around a tram not to come into collision with the cast-iron centre-poles which supported the overhead wires, and which were located between the 'in' and

ABOVE LEFT: An Auckland motorman and conductor pose at the Grey Lynn terminus for a photographer in the days of open-fronted trams. The conductor with a cigarette in his hand was permitted to smoke only at the terminus. *Author's Collection*

ABOVE: Beware of a flying machine that cuts the corner from Customs Street West into Queen Street in Auckland, 1905. *Muir & Moodie, Author's Collection*

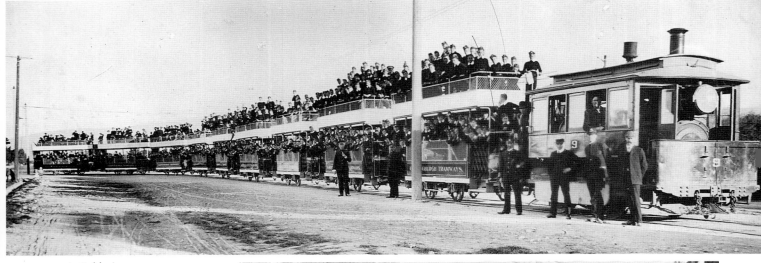

A Baldwin steam-tram locomotive was imported second-hand from Sydney to assist with the increased passenger loadings during the New Zealand International Exhibition at Hagley Park, Christchurch, in 1906. This photograph shows No. 9 hauling nine trailers loaded with public school cadets to a picnic in 1910. *Author's Collection*

A temporary loop line was constructed for the convenience of visitors to the New Zealand International Exhibition in Christchurch in 1906. It ran from Victoria Street along Peterborough Street, Park Terrace and Salisbury Street. People can be seen alighting from the electric tram in Park Terrace. A special service ran from the Square to the exhibition. *John M. Bettle Collection*

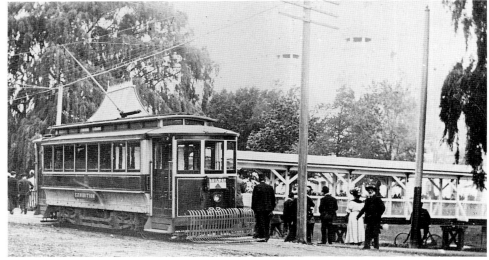

Christchurch Tramway Board.
Exhibition Special.

2D
EXHIBITION to SQUARE.
SQUARE to EXHIBITION.
15432
2D Exhibition Special.

This Ticket is good only for use on Car and Trip to which it is issued. It is not Transferable. Please destroy on leaving Car.

This Ticket must be shewn when demanded, or another Fare will be charged.

'out' tracks. The danger presented by these poles brought this letter to a newspaper: 'Seeing that our electric tram conductors are beginning so badly in knocking their heads against the poles along the route, might I make the suggestion that the poles be padded, so that the impact of head on pole will be less great and be met with less injury.' From this, perhaps, came the saying 'Pull your head in'.

The conductor's job called for iron self-control, plenty of tact, patience and a strong heart. There was for the passenger an element of sport about his chances of being asked to pay before his journey ended. Conductors were told never to go inside a car or to the front without first counting the number of passengers on the rear platform, and if more were there on his return, he was to call out, 'Fares, if you please', without addressing anyone in particular. Passengers had already complained about the objectionable habit some conductors had of licking their fingers when tearing off tickets. Small tin cases, containing a sponge for wetting the fingers, were issued to counter such complaints.

A conductor, in addition to being able to punch tickets with precision, had to be an encyclopaedia of local information: put Grandma off at 'Mrs Brown's place along Main Street—she's lived there a long while—you must know her'; know all timetables of trains, boats and service cars; accept the blame for not stopping ('I pressed the bell three times'); and take responsibility for the common phenomenon of a passenger's florin becoming a half-crown when the amount of change was queried. He had to act as a guide to tourists and point out beauty spots of the city. It was an advantage that, when the breaker switch on an overloaded tram groaning up a hill blew with a terrific bang, he remained calm. Other virtues were the ability to force a welcoming smile for pushchairs and inspectors; to memorise the instruction book and the list of lost passes, as well as Cup winners back to 1902; to explain pleasantly to young matrons that the ticket box was not provided as a distraction for their offspring. Furthermore, he had to be prepared to change a pound note for

The crowd outside old
Parliament Buildings when Sir
Joseph Ward declared New
Zealand an independent
Dominion of the British
Empire on 26 September 1907.
Zak, Author's Collection

a penny fare and keep an unlimited supply of threepences for Sunday mornings.
Finally, good eyesight was necessary for discerning coins left on the floor.

Discipline was strict in the service, and there were always about six men chasing
each job. Inspectors would suddenly appear from nowhere to check discrepancies
in tickets, crew behaviour and general neatness of cars. A sort of guerrilla warfare
developed between the staff and the ticket inspectors. Special signals between trams
warned of the approach of inspectors. Inspectors in turn were under close managerial
surveillance, their job being to maintain the essential link between management and
crews. My father once told me a delightful yarn about a former Auckland traffic
superintendent of tramways, H.H. ('Pop') Morgan, who ruled all traffic staff with
an iron hand. Morgan, a huge man with a bark like a bear, was feared by the men.
It was New Year's Eve at the bottom of Queen Street and Morgan invited my father
to come up into the despatcher's cabin to watch the crowd celebrate. At five
minutes to midnight a parked tram started to rock slowly from side to side.
Morgan, sighting this behaviour, barked at an inspector: 'Smithers, go and stop
those fools.' Smithers obeyed, donning his regulation cap and overcoat, and dis-
appearing into the jostling crowds that were packed around the tram. Breaking the
silence, my father dared to remark, 'By Jove, that was a pretty tough order.'
Morgan looked at him and said, 'If he's got any sense, he'll get lost in the crowd!'

Inspectors had their own frustrations. In his most official manner an inspector
once broadcast his entry on the scene by a sonorous request for 'All tickets, please!'
He came to a halt before an inoffensive old gentleman who tendered a number of
tickets hastily extracted from a waistcoat pocket. An impatient shuffling and careful
comparison of figures failed to disclose to official scrutiny the requisite evidence of
good faith, and intimation to this effect was tersely conveyed to the passenger. A
further search in another pocket revealed another bundle of tickets, but here again
the right ticket could not be found. After a further search the passenger handed up
what was instantly recognised as the correct one. 'That is the last ticket I have,' he
explained apologetically.

'This is the ticket I have been looking for for the past five minutes,' thundered
the exasperated inspector.

'Oh! I thought you said "All tickets, please!,"' said the old gentleman, 'so I
thought I would let you have the oldest ones first.'

Inspectors, motormen and conductors—all had their duties, and on the whole
did them well, earning the respect of those who used the services.

The first collision in Auckland between a tram and its rival new-fangled form of transport, the motor car. It happened in Hobson Street on Labour Day, 12 October 1904. The car, owned by a Captain Subritzky, was extensively damaged, but its occupants escaped without serious injury. *Auckland Weekly News*

The tramway company's decorations were the highlight of the visit to Auckland by the Governor, Lord Plunket, in July 1904. All cars were most tastefully festooned, according to the standards of the time, with red, white and blue bunting, flags and streamers. Red strips of bunting carrying the word 'Welcome!' were draped around the front apron of each tram, and streamers flew from the trolley-poles. In Queen Street the centre-poles supporting the overhead wires were ablaze with colour. The focal point of all this gaiety was a combination car fitted up as a travelling illuminated display, which created considerable attention after nightfall. The patterns of lights were adorned with coloured bunting and a profusion of New Zealand ferns. Around the roof the outline of the car was picked out in red, white and blue lights, and between each window frame more globes blazed. To add the finishing touch, the trolley-pole was outlined with globes of red, white and blue.

Dr Parkes, a well-known Auckland doctor, almost made history the following month, but escaped without a scratch, thanks to the alertness of motormen. Driving his first motor car to Epsom through Newmarket, he decided to switch from one side of the road to the other. He carried out this manoeuvre between two tram-cars which were approaching each other at a relatively high speed. As the gap closed, the motor car skidded and left him between the tracks like the meat in a sandwich. Instant braking by the respective motormen saved the day and the doctor's life. A Mack Sennett Keystone Cops movie once featured a similar sequence with disastrous results!

History was made in October 1904 when the first accident between a tram and a motor car in Auckland occurred while the Labour Day procession was passing up Hobson Street. The car, owned by a Captain Subritzky, was extensively damaged, but its occupants escaped without serious injury. Benzine buggies were costly to buy and only the adventurous were game enough to discard the horse. One needed muscle to start them and each hill meant a battle against gravity; some critics said of these early motor cars that they had to be pushed just about as far as they were required to run—a most undignified procedure.

Ellerslie racegoers waiting in Customs Street East, Auckland for trams to whisk them to the course. *Author's Collection*

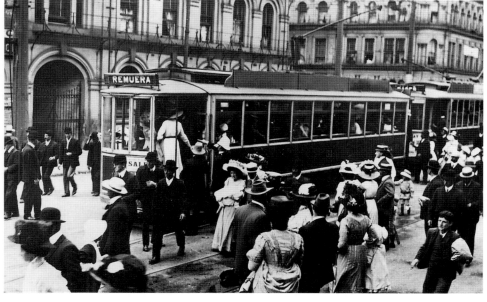

In the same month the Railways Department, which had enjoyed a virtual monopoly in the carriage of passengers to the Auckland Racing Club's course at Ellerslie, had to contend with strong opposition from the electric car service. Rather than face the discomforts of travelling in the tarpaulin-covered open goods wagons pressed into service by the railway authorities, visitors to the races preferred the run out and home in the relative luxury of the tram-cars, even if it meant walking to and from the terminus at Victoria Avenue.

The first electric tram reached Lyall Parade, Wellington, in December 1911. Photographers with large plate cameras on sturdy tripods can be seen recording the historic occasion, while the Wellington Corporation Tramways horse-drawn tower wagon stands at the ready in case of an emergency. *Author's Collection*

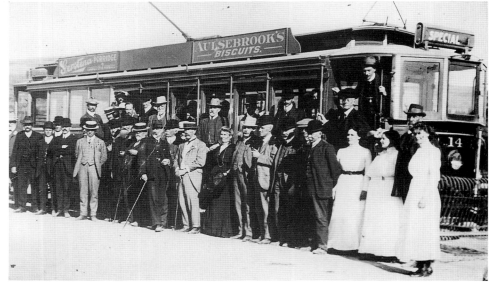

Christchurch officials and local residents were keen to be photographed in front of the first electric tram to the foot of Hackthorne Road, Cashmere, in December 1911.

Journeys to the seaside—to Christchurch's Sumner or New Brighton, Dunedin's St Kilda or St Clair, Wellington's Lyall Bay, Island Bay or Seatoun, or Auckland's Onehunga—were popular in the summer months when the cars were packed with 'beach belles' and their beaux, together with the inevitable picnic hampers. However the tramway authorities did not extend provision for beach picnics to family pet dogs. The cruel practice of making dogs run after cars all the way to the beach was soon noticed by conductors. Attempting to keep up with trams, the poor animals would be coaxed on by their owners at every stopping place, although obviously distressed. Correspondence reached a climax in newspapers when it was reported that, in one case, a big, long-haired pet collie, obviously out of condition, kept in the wake of its master's tram, arriving five minutes after the car, only to collapse and die.

The pioneer of mechanically propelled passenger vehicles in New Zealand. A painting by W.W. Stewart depicting the Hawke's Bay Motor Company's Straker steam-bus, working on the Napier-Taradale service in August 1903. *Author's Collection*

A photograph of the Straker steam-bus showing the alarming high-altitude seating on the top deck. *Alan C. Bellamy Collection*

Another story involving a dog took place at a depot, where a fox terrier was kept as a pet by the depot staff. Sometimes, mainly under damp conditions, a passenger could receive a minor electric shock from the metal support on a seat, due to a slight leakage of electricity. To find which seats were affected, depot staff would carefully place a small piece of meat against the cast-iron leg of each seat, put up the trolley-pole and watch their so-called 'pet' nibble his way through the saloon. The little bloke would eat his evening ration in this fashion, leaping back smartly from the odd seat leg, without even a whimper.

When the first omnibuses appeared as potential competitors, they were rather cumbersome-looking objects mounted on solid rubber tyres, with locally built bodies on imported chassis. Generally they resembled trams in appearance. One of the earliest mechanically propelled buses to run in New Zealand started in a service between Napier and Taradale in August 1903. Strange as it may seem, the source of power was steam, not petrol. Operators of this noble-looking contraption were the Hawke's Bay Motor Company Limited, who had Rouse and Hurrell of Wellington build a double-deck body on a Straker steam lorry chassis. Top-deck travel was not to be recommended, as the funnel of the steam engine expelled an embarrassing volume of smoke and smuts. A taller chimney, which could be retracted to pass under low-slung wires, was fitted, but even this did not abate the soot nuisance. Belching its way to Taradale, the steamer, with its bright red paintwork, certainly attracted a lot of local attention, but it was far from successful. Horses bolted at its approach and passengers were blackened by the snorting monster that was regularly stricken with breakdowns. Ultimately the company reverted to horses and sold the boiler and chassis to the Amners Lime Company for use at their quarry in Milton Road, Napier. The directors decided to wait until more reliable mechanical traction had been developed.

The first motor-bus propelled by an internal combustion engine outside the Christchurch Railway Station in May 1904. The driver of the hansom cab on the left seems to have trouble controlling his steed as the horseless contraption sounds a trumpet to gather its passengers. *Winkelmann, Auckland Institute and Museum*

On 7 April 1904 the *Lyttelton Times* reported the arrival of the first motor omnibus at Christchurch:

The men attached to a stables in Christchurch, were surprised last evening, when an immense motor, with drag-like dimensions, drew up at the door with the object of stopping the night. The vehicle is a motor bus. It is the first of the kind that has come to this city and is the herald of the change in traffic that has already set in many parts of the United Kingdom, Europe and America.

The owner, A.C. Thompson of Timaru, who had brought a party all the way from his home town that day, had purchased the horse-less machine while visiting Scotland the previous year. The journey had taken 14 hours from Timaru, which included a two-hour stop-over at Ashburton. Exhibition runs through the principal streets of Christchurch were arranged by Thompson, now the local representative for the manufacturers, the Stirling Company of Edinburgh.

Leaving Ballantyne's department store in July 1905 for the then distant Christchurch suburb of Riccarton. The open-sided body could cater for more passengers. *John M. Bettle Collection*

96

The debut of an internal combustion-engined omnibus attracted a great deal of attention in Christchurch. The *Press* in their 'News of the Day' column said: 'The big car was well handled by Mr Smith, the expert whom Mr Thompson brought out with him from the Stirling works in Edinburgh, though the Christchurch crowds present little trouble to the motor jehu, who has learned his business in the big cities of Britain.' Some people were treated to rides by the owner, there being seating accommodation for 16 people, on facing seats along each side of the saloon. The bus weighed 2 tonnes and travelled from 20 to 22 kilometres an hour, at a cost estimated by Thompson to be a fraction over a penny per 1.6 kilometres. Among the mechanical features of the bus were the lubricators (all parts being oiled from the holders, placed close to the driver) and the system of water cooling. The water being arranged to circulate by gravitation, from a series of tubes in front of the driver's seat and returning cold around the engine. The 12 horsepower Stirling motor was fitted with two independent systems of electric firing.

The outcome of these exhibition runs was the formation of the Christchurch Motor Omnibus Company towards the end of April 1904, to run a daily motor service between Cathedral Square and the Railway Station, via High Street and Manchester Street. After 15 months of service, the Stirling motor-bus had travelled 24,000 kilometres and carried 80,000 people. But the primitive contraption was no match for the trams when they started running over the same route in June 1905. So the omnibus was transferred to the Riccarton district, away from the steel-railed opposition.

In Auckland, the firm of W.A. Ryan and Company had been formed to import to New Zealand two motor-buses and a motor lorry. The company brought the two motor-bus chassis out from England. They were made in Germany for the Milnes-Daimler Company of London, and the tram-like bodies were built locally at the works of Cousins and Atkin, Elliott Street. R.B. Spinks, a prominent shareholder in the company, was the first man to drive the strange new vehicle and he taught Bert Barwell, one of the first professional drivers employed on a suburban motor bus in New Zealand. The two buses were transferred to the Howick Motor Bus Company for service between Queen Street and the distant township of Howick. The maiden run of the first bus, despatched by Sir Maurice O'Rourke in June 1904, was watched by hundreds of admiring onlookers, with flags hoisted and crowds lining the route. At Pakuranga school children, waving flags and shouting, stood in rows at the side of the road. When the bus arrived at Howick the township was en fete and a luncheon was held in the old public hall. Spinks had driven the guests to Howick in under an hour. Such speed, people thought, was miraculous, as the horse-buses used to take two and a half hours for the same journey.

Named *Pioneer*, this first bus was painted primrose and olive green and bore the Royal cypher 'E.R.', the company having secured the mail contract. The bus cost £1,366 to build and carried 18 passengers. Its top speed was only 32 kilometres an hour, and its hard seats and tyres of solid rubber must have made the journey a test of endurance for the passengers. The second bus, named *Advance*, arrived

BELOW LEFT: True to its name, the first motor-bus in Auckland pioneered a service to Howick in 1904. Jack Craig was at the wheel when his photograph was taken in Eden Terrace. BELOW: The second Auckland motor-bus with the city's 'Advance' painted on the engine bonnet after being transferred to the Mount Roskill service. *Author's Collection*

The steam passenger buses which were introduced to the North Shore of Auckland in December 1904. *Auckland Weekly News*

in October. This vehicle had an improved body with seats for 25. The saloon compartment was smaller, but more accommodation was provided for those who enjoyed fresh air. No benzine being available, the company imported stove naphtha from Melbourne for 2/10 per 4 litres. When a bus became stuck on a road, or a tyre came off—both of which mishaps were not infrequent—a small Oldsmobile, steered with a tiller, would dash off to effect repairs. In the end the bad roads proved too much for the buses and the company concentrated on a service from Mount Roskill along Dominion Road until the steel web was extended for the electric trams.

Four dignified steam passenger cars were about to cut a dash on a Devonport to Takapuna marathon on Auckland's North Shore. With locally built coachwork, the first three steamers were running for the Takapuna Motor Bus Company by December 1904. The first two vehicles were Clarkson steam cars and the third, a Gardner Serpolette. The steamer had certain advantages such as smooth operation (no gears) and quick acceleration. Disadvantages included waiting several minutes to get steamed up and having to have water tanks available at strategic points to replenish the boiler.

Buses were at that time regarded as flimsy and unreliable contraptions. Who could trust a smelly gasoline engine which vibrated and created such a din that passengers literally got the shakes? There could be no doubt in the mind of any reasonable person—trams were here to stay. Gracefully riding the boulevards of towns, the streetcar was reliable, quiet and gave a frequent service.

As if to prove the point, the Christchurch *Press* reported in detail the breakdown of a motor-bus in June 1904:

A motor vehicle engaged by sixteen people the other evening to take them to a card party at Sumner, broke down, for some reason, near the Woolston School. The driver informed the party that the vehicle could only proceed providing they got out. They did so, and as the tram for Sumner had passed them a few minutes before, the sixteen walked ruefully home again, preceded by the vehicle at a good pace.

A now rather suspect joke of the period summed up the regard and faith people had for and in the electric tram: 'Never run after a tram, my boy. You want to remember what they say in America. "Never run after a tram or a women, there'll always be another one along in a minute!"'

The Auckland rapid transit car, a solid-tyred Daimler charabanc which ran a service to the domain during the Auckland Exhibition of 1913. After climbing three rather large steps, passengers had a grandstand view of the passing scenery and a roll canvas blind was provided for wet weather. *Author's Collection*

Women's lib in 1916. Probably the first woman conductor in New Zealand, Miss W. Mitchell, on Searle's motor-bus at Oamaru in 1916. *Clarke, Author's Collection*

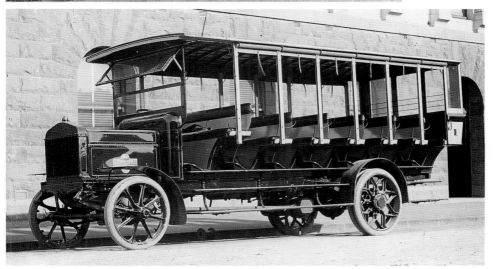

A bone-shaker of 1913. One of the Straker Squire buses purchased by the Auckland Electric Tramway Company in 1913 to carry crowds to the Auckland Exhibition. *Price, Author's Collection*

Cuba Street before the mall was built, from the junction of Manners Street. *Sorrell Snr, Author's Collection* TOP: When the horse was supreme. CENTRE: The open-front electrics of the early 1900s. *Author's Collection* BELOW: The third- and second-to-last trams making their final journey into Wellington on 2 May 1964. A trolley bus crosses in the foreground. *Graham Stewart*

CHAPTER SIX

The Final Spread of the Steel Web

Throughout the country public interest in the new improved forms of transportation reached fever pitch. Dreams and schemes included electric tramways for Whangarei, Pahiatua, Thames, Timaru, Stratford, Te Awamutu, Petone, Lower Hutt, Devonport, Nelson and Palmerston North. Hastings envisaged a tramway system on which would run cars powered by internal combustion engines. At Te Awamutu the talk was for a 2-foot 6-inch gauge rural line. The adjoining boroughs of Petone and Lower Hutt actually went as far as having a tramway board constituted in 1904 to investigate electric tramways. Originally a line along Jackson Street, as a feeder to and from the Petone railway station, was planned, but interest from the neighbouring borough called for an amalgamated system. In 1905 the Hutt Valley Tramway Board received a proposal from Tommy Taylor, the Member of Parliament, to install tramways and the Wellington Meat Company put forward a proposition to supply electricity. A poll of ratepayers, however, threw out the scheme.

At Devonport, on Auckland's North Shore, the borough council in 1898 considered a request from P. Hansen of British Electric Traction (represented by W.J. Napier) that his company be given a concession to run electric trams and to supply electric light to the council for streets and to private citizens for household use. Cars were to run at 14 kilometres an hour for penny fares. The idea was to popularise Lake Pupuke and the fine beaches nearby. The lines were to run from Victoria Wharf (the present ferry terminal), to Cheltenham Beach, around Mount Victoria, to Brick Bay (Stanley Bay), along Lake Road and around Lake Pupuke. A double line was to be built to the racecourse, via Victoria Road. In February 1899 the promoters cabled from London to the effect that a syndicate had taken up options on the North Shore and in Auckland city. Negotiations continued for some time, but in November 1900 the council refused to extend the option and the scheme lapsed. Interest was revived in 1906 when E.R. Russell secured a concession which was later transferred to the Devonport Transport Company Limited. In December 1908 a poll of Devonport ratepayers voted solidly against a tramway.

The question of an electric tram between Rotorua town and the thermal wonders at Whakarewarewa was debated in 1906. Quite apart from visitors to the region, it was the popular Sunday walk for Rotorua residents, said the planners. Rotorua folk continued to have their constitutional at weekends, as the idea never got off the drawing board.

A novel twist was a private scheme in 1909 to run self-contained petrol trams in Hastings. The council favoured the conventional overhead electric system, to run over a distance of almost 6 kilometres, in conjunction with the electric lighting installation. Since then little has been heard about trams in Hastings.

Timaru went a long way toward running trams, at least on paper, with two unsuccessful proposals. Two routes were envisaged for the initial installation: first from a point near Hobbs Street, on the Main North Road, to the corner of Otipua Road, on the Main South Road; via Stafford and King Streets, with a branch on George Street to the Railway Station; and second North Street, Otipua and Wai-iti Roads, Le Cren and Church Streets, junctioning at each end with the first route, giving a total route length of 11 kilometres. Detailed specifications included designs for a fleet of seven trams, four combination and three single-saloon cars.

At Palmerston North a loan of £60,000 for a tramway scheme, involving a subway under the railway in the Square, was sanctioned by ratepayers in 1912. A large section of the citizens were determined to keep abreast of the times and

Closing the gap between suburb and town centre. A Sydney steam-tram locomotive working on the formation of the electric line to Gonville and Castlecliff, Wanganui, in 1912. This Baldwin locomotive is now an exhibit at the Museum of Transport and Technology, Auckland. *Tesla Collection, Alexander Turnbull Library*

wanted Palmerston North to be as much like a city as possible—with tram-cars on the streets. But opposition mounted and several months later another poll reversed the decision. Controversy continued in the years up to the First World War and the council at one stage rescinded a unilateral decision it had taken to install an Edison Battery tramway system. A Citizens' League deputation in 1920 cast the die for motor-buses, asking the council for a municipal bus service.

There were other plans, such as the cable tram proposed for Durie Hill in Wanganui before the present elevator became a reality. Many more schemes were pounded out across county and borough council tables. Invariably the only outcome was the retention of the faithful horse until jalopies with a can of benzine strapped to the running board became available to convey the foot-weary citizens.

Wanganui—First Provincial Electric Tramway

The first provincial centre to establish a streetcar system was Wanganui. But what a civic fight preceded the memorable day in December 1908 when the first electrics trundled out to Aramoho, the town's railway junction. Wanganui then had a population of 10,000, and businessmen returning from trips abroad spoke of the desirability and feasibility of a modern public transport system. Before Wanganui could develop and expand, it was claimed, the town must have an efficient transport system. The entire future of Wanganui as a commercial, industrial and residential centre depended upon cheap and regular transport being available.

At this stage, the government-owned branch railway from Aramoho into the town station on Taupo Quay, and the private Castlecliff Railway from Taupo Quay to Castlecliff wharves and beach, were the only means of travelling from one part of the town to another, apart from horse-drawn cabs and coaches. A few people owned horses and rode to town. Saddle horses and gigs could be hired, and livery stables were as numerous as petrol stations are today. Bill Gibson ran a two-horse Palace bus with side entrances, in which passengers sat facing each other for the journey between Aramoho and the post office. Gibson's Palace cars were a feature of Aramoho's life and if a play was being staged in town, Bill Gibson could be relied on to meet the convenience of his patrons. Gibson was killed in a level-crossing accident and his coaches and teams were taken over by Bert Finlay, who instituted drags with a rear door and long side-seats facing the aisle. These vehicles remained until the arrival of the trams.

A new electric tram body being loaded in the Christchurch railway yards for transport by train to the port of Lyttelton, for shipment north. Built by the Christchurch coach builders, Boon and Company, for the Wanganui Corporation Tramways. *Press Collection, Alexander Turnbull Library*

Alexander Hatrick, Wanganui's mayor from 1897, first suggested in 1903 that a committee report on improved means of communication. Hatrick relinquished the mayoralty during the following year to holiday in Europe, but returned in 1905 with information on streetcar services, as they were called overseas. He considered that the Paris steam motor system on rails, known to be planned for London, was the answer. What was good enough for Paris and for London, declared Hatrick, was quite good enough for Wanganui. Public interest quickened with another report from Councillor T.H. Battle, then in London, that three steam cars and trailers running over 8 kilometres of track would begin to pay for themselves within two or three years. A poll of ratepayers confirmed the 'steamers', but they were never to see the light of day.

Before the council could spring into action, the General Electric Company's Auckland engineers offered to install an electric tram system for the same capital outlay. A newly elected mayor, C.E. Mackay, now held the banner for the electrics, while the majority of councillors were against him. Wordy warfare raged, with the former mayor, Alexander Hatrick, campaigning vigorously for the steamers he had initially recommended. In fact, said Hatrick, if the council bought steam trams and they failed to pay, he would meet the annual loss up to £500.

After weeks of the electric-versus-steam controversy, a vote was taken at a council meeting. The division was even and a motion to investigate ways and means of adhering to the electric tram plan was carried on Mackay's casting vote. Two days later Mackay was requested by a petition to authorise the importation of a French-made Purrey steam motor car for trial on Wanganui streets. The petitioners undertook to meet the cost of operating the steam car if it was found unsuitable. Hatrick made one final plea for steam trams, but this fell on deaf ears. A second ratepayers' poll was then held to sanction the higher capital costs of electric trams, and this was carried with increased public support.

The scattered settlement of the town made it difficult to reduce the amount of track and the first route to the Aramoho railway station had to be duplicated by a circular route through Glasgow and Dublin Streets. By coincidence, this was in keeping with the Maori legend of the district, the correct form of Aramoho being Aramuhu, meaning a path forced through dense bush. Many decades before European settlement, a Maori named Hau-e-rangi had lost his way and died. When his body was discovered, it was seen that he had beaten a circular path through the forest in

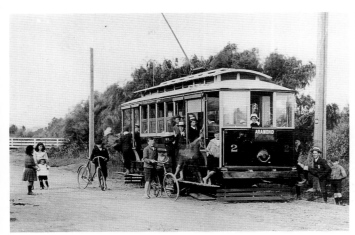

ABOVE: The first Wanganui electric to reach Aramoho in December 1908. *Ron Alexander Collection* ABOVE RIGHT: The shopping centre of Aramoho by the Wanganui River in the 1920s. *Author's Collection*

his struggles to find his way out. Wanganui East folk used the riverbank line to Aramoho and walked to their homes over a footbridge at Dublin Street, while to the south a track was laid down Guyton Street to the racecourse at Spriggens Park. The first engineer-manager in charge of the Wanganui system was Francis P. Talboys, who remained with the service until 1925.

Metal for ballasting the tracks was hauled in a slow procession by one-horse drays carrying only about one cubic metre at a time. To speed up the job a Straker steam-powered wagon was introduced. This steam engine with its steel wheels and large body was capable of hauling 3 to 4 metres of metal in one load. As a result of all this traffic, the roads became so badly cut up that cyclists were given permission to ride on the footpaths. Incidentally, a great deal of physical courage and endurance was needed to ride these bikes with their solid rubber tyres. The penny-farthing cycle — with a large front wheel and a tiny rear wheel — was also on the market, but it was not so popular.

On the opening day of the tramways women were well to the fore. Miss Norma McBeth, a niece of Councillor T.H. Battle, now the Tramway Committee chairman, switched on the current and the first car was despatched on its inaugural run to Aramoho by the Mayoress, Mrs C.E. Mackay. Glimpses of the picturesque Wanganui River made the tram ride to Aramoho different from most suburban journeys. Women's hatpins were in the news again when the corporation publicly warned offenders that regulations prohibited the wearing of unprotected hatpins which projected from hats, and that this rule would be rigidly enforced. Already the lost-luggage problem was present. The Town Clerk, George Murch, announced that lost articles could be recovered at the powerhouse on payment of a twopenny fee.

It was 1 o'clock on the old post office clock when this photograph recorded the first provincial electric tram cars in New Zealand, in Victoria Avenue, Wanganui. Tram No. 1 was still roadworthy when the system closed in 1950. *Price, Author's Collection*

Each conductor was given a pound in silver and pennies for use as change when he joined the service. He retained that amount in his own possession, with the requirement that he should produce it if called on to do so. A sudden decision was made one day to ask each man to produce the pound when he cashed in at the end of his day's run. The first man was caught out, but he tipped off the other conductors. Each reported in turn to pay in, and one pound note was used. The first man came out of the office and handed the note to the next man who, when he cashed in, was given the amount back again to hold until the next check. By this resourceful if unorthodox method one note went far enough to get a number of men over a spot of bother.

Extension of the line out through the sandhills to Castlecliff beach was the result of direct co-operation between the borough council and a separate tramway board established to serve Gonville and Castlecliff. Unplanned housing development, with resultant scattering of homes, made for worse problems than in the case of the eastern routes, and the tramway had to be duplicated through two separate areas where the aggregate population was barely sufficient to support one line.

The Gonville-Castlecliff Tramway Board found ample gravel in the district for track formation and a locomotive and ballast trucks were ordered from Australia for the laying of the permanent way from the beach to Hospital Corner. A former Sydney tramway locomotive, built in 1891 by the Baldwin Locomotive Works of Philadelphia, was imported for this work and became affectionately known as 'Puffing Billy'. Rails, sleepers and other equipment were discharged by vessels at Castlecliff. One sailing vessel with a cargo of Australian hardwood sleepers was wrecked on the beach. This was the barquentine *Pelotas*, inward bound from Eden, New South Wales, on 12 June 1911.

From the city the borough council extended its Guyton Street line to join up with the Castlecliff line by a detour and trestle bridge over the railway line. To help boost traffic, the tramway board gave the Castlecliff surf club monetary grants to be used to provide holiday attractions and amusement equipment for children at the beach. On the credit side, over a hectare of land was donated to the board as a beach reserve, upon which the board built a tea kiosk. Then came a difference with the Auditor General, who refused to authorise the sum of £59 donated by the board for beach amusements and the surf club grant 'even though by such expenditure the revenue of the trams may increase'. Eventually the local Member of Parliament, H.C. Veitch, had the expenditure validated by the inclusion of a clause in Parliament's washing-up bill.

With trams running to Gonville and Castlecliff, the Castlecliff Railway Company's passenger traffic to the beach began to fall away. Until now this traffic had been encouraged by the issue of combined tram and train tickets between Aramoho and Castlecliff. As the rot set in the railway company considered electrifying its line. Then the purchase of an Edison battery-electric car was debated, but rejected by the directors. Free carriage of perambulators, bicycles and hampers was offered, but competition from the trams became much too intensive for the trains which chugged along the riverbank and in 1922 the Castlecliff Railway Company discontinued its passenger facilities.

The tramway board paid a car mileage from the Post Office to the terminus and collected all fares until the amalgamation of the suburbs with the city in 1924, when assets and liabilities were transferred to the newly proclaimed City of Wanganui.

ABOVE LEFT: The trestle bridge over which Castlecliff and Gonville trams crossed the railway line in Guyton Street, Wanganui. *Author's Collection*
ABOVE: The Castlecliff tram in Wanganui would deliver beach belles and their beaux right on to the sand at the end of Rangiora Street. *Alan Jackson Collection*

Wanganui-Gonville-Castlecliff Electric Tramways.

Between 8th & 9th Sections.

4D

Not Transferable.

20396

Good only for car and trip issued.
This ticket must be shown when demanded or another fare will be charged. Please destroy on leaving.

ABOVE RIGHT: The Dublin Street bridge which gave the suburb of Wanganui East a direct road link in November 1914. *Author's Collection*
ABOVE: After the cutting of the ribbon, the first vehicle across the bridge was an electric tram. *Auckland Weekly News*

A tram was the first vehicle to trundle across the new Dublin Street bridge after speeches and ribbon cutting in 1914, giving Wanganui East a much-needed link. The all-purpose structure carried tramway, road and pedestrian traffic, and the line ultimately reached the Wanganui East railway station. Among the first to ride on the new Wanganui East tram route on that red-letter day were children from the Wanganui East School.

Wanganui was virtually surrounded by railway lines. Beyond the tram terminus at Aramoho the main line to New Plymouth crossed the river and Somme Parade, and how the tramway was to proceed further without recourse to a level crossing was a vexed question. A proposal to build a line to St John's Hill and up to Virginia Lake slowly fizzled out while new steel rails and hardwood sleepers deteriorated in the undergrowth on the hillside above Victoria Avenue. An overbridge spanning the railway branch line from Aramoho to Wanganui, at the foot of the hill, had been one of the stumbling blocks. Without this bridge the tramway would have had to cross the railway on the level. Fortunately, a similar problem at Aramoho was solved by the provision of a subway below the western abutment of the railway bridge, and the new track on the verge of the river bank was in use to Quick Avenue by April 1915. School concessions were first sanctioned in this year, allowing for penny rides 'provided always that the children are accompanied by a teacher'.

BELOW: Wanganui single-saloon No. 4 and an open breezer trailer at the Quick Avenue terminus, Aramoho. *Ron Alexander Collection*
BELOW RIGHT: The tramway subway under the railway bridge by Somme Parade, Wanganui, used by trams to Quick Avenue and the Aramoho Cemetery which opened in April 1915. *W.W. Stewart*

The launching of the ferry steamer *Pupuke* from George Nicol's yard at Auckland on 15 December 1909. *Price, Author's Collection*

Takapuna — Final Curtain Call for Steam in the Streets

Visions of a fast rural electric service opening up new housing estates led to a deputation of Takapuna businessmen calling on the Auckland Electric Tramways Company in 1907. Their proposition was for electric trams to be installed on the North Shore of Auckland. Such services, they hoped, would bring in their wake the rapid development of settlement that had eventuated in Auckland after the introduction of electric trams. Unfortunately, after a full investigation, the company decided to throw in the sponge, because of the sparse population. Not to be daunted, the group announced that an independent local organisation was needed to 'put the cart before the horse' and service the area with transport in the expectation that development would follow.

Thus the Takapuna Tramways and Ferry Company Limited was born. The turning of the first sod at Hall's Corner was celebrated to the accompaniment of popping champagne corks in the Takapuna Hotel. There was a property boom equal to that which followed the opening of the Auckland Harbour Bridge, large blocks of land being sold even before the tramway service was inaugurated. Electricity was to have powered the tramway, but because insufficient capital was subscribed to allow for the cost of a generating station, plus the fact that 'The Shore' was destined to be hooked up to the national grid, the directors asked the shareholders for approval to use an interim form of traction. Steam was chosen to cope with the expected rush of settlers, the final curtain call for this form of locomotion on a public tramway in New Zealand.

Track layouts originally designed for electric cars had to be modified to avoid the necessity for starting locomotives on uphill grades and the locomotives themselves were ordered from England. A fast ferry express steamer was ordered to carry over 700 passengers at a speed of 11 knots across the Waitemata Harbour, and at O'Neills Point (Bayswater) a deep-water channel was dredged to the wharf site.

BELOW LEFT: Takapuna Tramways and Ferry Company's No. 1 locomotive working on the ballasting of the new line from Bayswater on the North Shore of Auckland in 1910. *Price, Author's Collection* BELOW: The body of a new trailer car being lowered on to a scow for transportation across the Waitemata Harbour to Bayswater. The recently launched ferry *Pupuke* can be seen behind the scow. *Price, Author's Collection*

ABOVE: The locomotive and tram depot at Bayswater Point, Auckland. ABOVE RIGHT: The workshops and tram depot in Lake Road at Hall's Corner, Takapuna. *Author's Collection*

Powerful explosives, horse scoops, drays, picks, shovels and wheelbarrows were used in a battle to carve away the cliff face for the formation that was to carry the line down to the new jetty.

From Bayswater the line ran to Milford via Lake Road, Hurstmere Road and Kitchener Road, with a circular route around Lake Pupuke (via Shakespeare Road and Taharoto Road to Hall's Corner). A small locomotive and car depot was erected under the cliffs at Bayswater and a second at Hall's Corner on the site of the present car park. Six trailer cars were constructed in Auckland from drawings supplied by the Auckland Electric Tramways Company, with British Brush Company running equipment, which the Auckland tramways offered to service and supply with spares when necessary. These units were commissioned with a quick eye to electric conversion. They were literally electric trams, minus trolley-poles, controllers and motors.

The first sturdy little locomotives, named *Waitemata* and *Bayswater* respectively, were assembled and put to work for the contractors carting local black gravel for the ballasting of the tracks. Boat builder George Nicol built the ferry on a vacant section at the foot of Nelson Street. It was christened *Pupuke*.

Without fanfare a crowded *Pupuke* made its maiden voyage across the harbour in December 1910, to be met by a cheering throng on the wharf, where the steam trams were waiting to take the public out around the lake. The steepest haul on the tramline was the climb up from the ferry landing, but once over the summit of King Edward Avenue, it was a straight run to Belmont. Seated on stained wooden seats, passengers relaxed and enjoyed the thrill of riding what was virtually a train right down a suburban street. Unlike a train, however, it was not possible to move from one carriage to another, as there were no connecting walkways. Through pleasant rural country, with green meadows and tall hedges on each side, the tram hiked at 'the rate of knots', clanging and swaying and leaving behind the odour of

The steam ferry *Pupuke* at Bayswater. Passengers walk from the ferry jetty to the tramway carriages as No. 4, a Baldwin steam-tram locomotive, shunts in the foreground. *Jim Housego, Author's Collection*

coal smoke and a fine spray of cinders. From Belmont the downhill stretch was taken at a smart clip with open throttle, as the incline where the Takapuna Grammar School and the Wilson Home now stand was often a problem with a heavy load. An adventurous motorist with a speedometer fitted to his car once checked a locomotive and carriage doing 85 kilometres an hour from Belmont School to Clifton Road. To the accompaniment of clanking coupling rods, the driver of a Takapuna steam-tram would sound his whistle if there was no one waiting to be picked up at a stopping place, and in reply the conductor would lean from the carriages and give a hand signal to indicate whether any passenger wished to alight.

Weaving at a good pace toward Takapuna, the steaming juggernaut would lurch sharply to the right at the junction of the tram lines at Hall's Corner and enter Hurstmere Road, coming to a stop outside the Mon Desir Hotel. Passengers for

A two-trailer steam-tram travelling at a good pace along Lake Road toward Takapuna and Milford. The Hauraki Road corner is in the foreground. The date is about 1912. *Takapuna Public Library*

Now the heart of Takapuna City. Looking along Hurstmere Road with the junction of Lake Road in the distance. *Author's Collection*

Passengers boarding a steam-tram for Bayswater at Hall's Corner, Takapuna, about 1912. This view, looking north-west from the corner of Lake Road and the Strand, with Hurstmere Road (right foreground), shows the premises of W.H. Hall, baker and storekeeper, after whom the corner was named. *Takapuna Public Library*

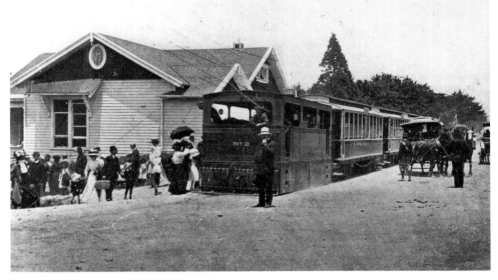

Takapuna steam-tram locomotive No. 2, which was named 'Bayswater', just after arriving at the Mon Desir Hotel in Hurstmere Road, Takapuna, with a load of Aucklanders bound for the beach. *Author's Collection*

Takapuna Beach swarmed off the cars with hampers and rugs to explore this fast expanding marine suburb of Auckland. Then on to Milford, with a view of Lake Pupuke through the tram windows to the left, to drop the remaining visitors and day trippers. Here bathing costumes and towels could be hired for a sojourn on the beaches. From Milford the tram circled the lake and returned to Hall's Corner for the homeward journey to Bayswater.

Camouflage was still the vogue for tramway locomotives, but whether by now the horses were more sensitive than their robust predecessors of the 19th century was open to question. On seeing and hearing a tram approaching, horses frequently bolted with their carts. Many were killed, particularly after dark when a stray horse would be a little too slow in moving off the tracks. Ray Parker, well-known skipper on the Devonport ferries for years, was a fireman on the engines and told me about the day the tram rounded the curve into Belmont with Bill Henderson, later a mayor of Takapuna, at the controls, and collided with a horse and cart. The local policeman, an Irishman, inspected the damage, took measurements, and then asked: 'How far were you from the cart when you hit?'

For night running acetylene gas generators were placed on each of the trailers, the gas flame being protected by glass globes. When these failed, the passengers sat in the dark while the locomotive crew hastily produced a kerosene hurricane lamp to hang on the front of the engine.

Carriage of freight, from passengers' luggage to groceries and general supplies for the shopkeepers, became good business. So much so that all the seats were taken

Takapuna Tramways and Ferry Company Baldwin locomotive No. 5 on arrival at Milford. *Jim Housego, Author's Collection*

out of the non-smoking compartment of one trailer for the conveyance of these profitable packages. Regularly attached to the tram which met the 5.20 pm boat from town, this trailer would be packed tight with businessmen and freight for the homeward run.

More powerful locomotives ordered in 1911 solved the problem of having to take 'a running jump' at the Clifton Road grade and helped later to carry the burden of traffic during the First World War, when maintenance suffered as a result of various wartime restrictions. Electricity, of course, was still in the air, but the company was in no position to go it alone. Paul Hansen, General Manager of the Auckland Electric Tramways Company, who was a director of the Takapuna Tramways and Ferry Company, had almost secured consent for electrification from his principals in London (British Electric Traction) when wartime conditions defeated him and the plan had to be abandoned.

Whatever critics the trams may have had, they could not deny that an era of prosperity on the North Shore had arrived with the whistle of the steam engines. Particularly successful were the real estate speculators who had opened up sub-divisions in readiness for the upsurge in population, and to them the Takapuna steam trams must have been a boon.

Invercargill city dignitaries and their wives were dressed in their best finery for the official opening of the southernmost electric tramway system in the world in March 1912. *Southland Museum*

On the official opening day of the Invercargill Corporation Tramways, motormen and conductors proudly posed for the photographer at the Leven Street car shed before the opening runs. *Southland Museum*

Invercargill — The Most Southern Tram-cars in the World

Southlanders were well up with the play when agitation arose for something better to succeed the horse-trams that had ground to a stop. Should they invest in those battery trams a Mr Edison was perfecting? What were the merits of the 'trackless tram' that was attracting a good deal of attention in England? However, it was the orthodox tram drawing its power through a trolley-pole from an overhead wire which won the day.

In January 1911, the first sod was turned by the then Governor-General, Lord Islington, before the laying of the tracks. The ceremony took place in Dee Street opposite the post office, with the Prime Minister, Sir Joseph Ward, in attendance. Sir Joseph, it may be recalled, had been senior partner in the old horse-tram company of the 1890s. Four routes, to North and South Invercargill, Waikiwi and Georgetown, were constructed, and 10 trams built in Christchurch. Despite wet weather, the opening day to Waikiwi and Georgetown in March 1912 was a gala day for Invercargill. Mayor W.A. Ott moved the first tram out of the depot through a ribbon held by the mayoress, after which three trams took guests on a tour of the two routes. At a banquet which followed, the mayor received a miniature gold controller as a memento of the day.

Crowds waiting to board the new electrics on opening day in Dee Street, Invercargill. A rainy day did not dampen the enthusiasm of the populace. *Southland Museum*

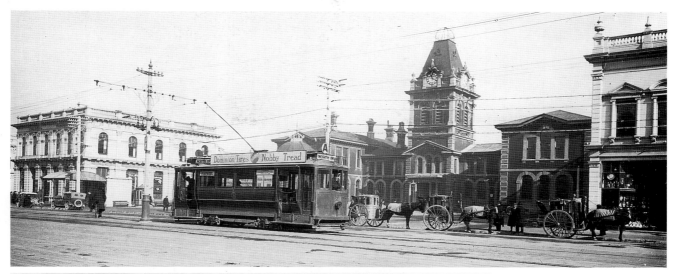

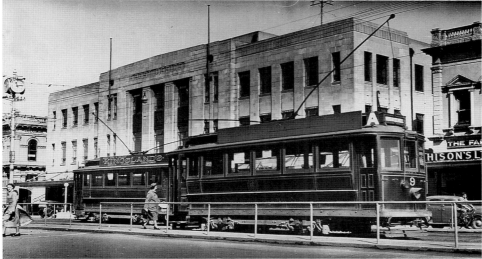

Hansom cabs and a tram waiting for fares outside the old post office in Dee Street, Invercargill. *Author's Collection*

Dee Street, Invercargill, 40 years later, with the same tram (No. 9) in the foreground. Gone are the hansom cabs and the old post office has been replaced by a new building. *Graham Stewart*

A report on the day headed 'The joy-riders' gives an insight into the excitement that prevailed in a town when the general public gained the rapid mobility which the electric tram provided:

After the important people, who got their rides for nothing, had done with the cars they became the proper plaything of their rightful owners, the people in general. And, it seemed, that nine tenths of the people in general consisted of women and children, mostly children. There was no doubt about them: they rode cars because they liked riding cars. They all wanted to do the same thing at the same time, and consequently there was a good deal of scramble. It all sounded something like this: — Mildred, if you dare leave go my hand, I won't wait till I get you home. They said they would be startin' the cars at three o'clock. It's a minute past now, and none in sight. It is — Mildred, come 'ere. There's Mrs Johnnie Smith there laughing at you. She'll tell all the street that I've got no perennial control over you. Maudie, I wonder who that 'andsome man is in uniform: yes, that one — Oh! dear, here's a car: at last! Mildred! M-I-L-D-R-E-D! What do you mean by lettin' go my hand. I wish I could be alone with you. Just for a minute m'lady. Come here, I wonder where it will stop. Thank you! You are very good to spoil me shoes by trampling on 'em, young man. What a crush! Mildred, come here! Up you go Maudie. Where's it going to? No, that's right, as long as it's going somewhere! I hope Mrs McBeamish will be at 'er gate to see us in the tram Maudie. Come on Mildred. What a squeeze! Can't you get up, Maudie? Only one step? How dare you push me sir! I've as much right — What? Too many on board? Well you needn't have pushed me like that, young man ... He may be a 'andsome man, Maudie, but he's no gentleman. We'll wait for the next car. Mildred, don't you go away, or I'll warm you!

Drivers of other vehicles on the streets were asked to exercise more caution and were exhorted not to wander from side to side at will. It was well known that the rule of the road had not been strictly enforced until now. Regulations were a bone of contention, with criticism being levelled once again at the provision regulating the length of hatpins protruding from women's hats. A unique feature of the Invercargill trams was the carriage of babies' prams, with infants riding in state in the comfort of the saloon, but passengers were forbidden to carry firearms. At last the businessman saw himself getting to the office in dry comfort on a wet day, and the speculator saw himself making a few hundred out of suburban sections bought unobtrusively at the most prudent moment. The canny ratepayer, meanwhile, began to live in dread of an increased rate bill to cover a possible loss on the trams. The tram carried the winsome suburban flapper, home from the theatre after seeing her hero rescue a wronged heroine from savage attempts on her innocent life. And it moved one correspondent to the papers to poetry:

> Many years have we suffered without the blooming cars
> Without the hurly-burly and without the jolting jars
> We have suffered long and sorely, but have reached the goal at last
> So fill your blooming glasses and we'll toast the smouldering past
> Here's health to Invercargill, here's a health to Ott as well
> Here's health to Joseph Hanan & health to my best girl.
>
> E.J.B.

It was appropriate that the southernmost electric trams in the world should be provided with a large heater for the passengers and a similar one in the motorman's enclosure. Invercargill can be bitterly cold when a southerly wind blows through the streets, seemingly straight from Antarctica.

A bold venture in Invercargill between the time the city horse-cars were incinerated and the electrics made alive, was the steam tramway to Otatara, crossing the Waihopai Channel on a long timber trestle bridge to Dunn's Road. This venture was floated by the Otatara Land Company to promote the sale of land and so to establish a new suburb. By this direct route, the 2.5-kilometre journey from the Invercargill railway station to Otatara took only seven to eight minutes. More than 220 freehold sections were offered by auction in December 1907, with a bonus of a free ticket on the tramway for two years as an inducement to any purchaser who erected a dwelling within 12 months of the sale. The idea did not flourish and the line passed into the hands of the borough council for use on the reclamation of the estuary.

The Otatara steam-tram and trailers on the trestle bridge over the Waihopai Channel at Invercargill. *Auckland Weekly News*

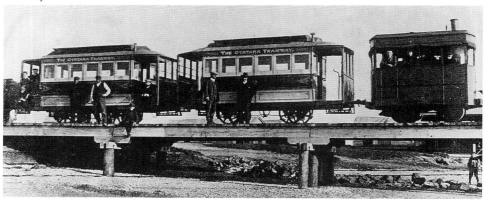

Invercargill No. 10 as originally built by the Christchurch coach builders, Boon and Company, at the southernmost tram terminus in the world. *Gary Lang*

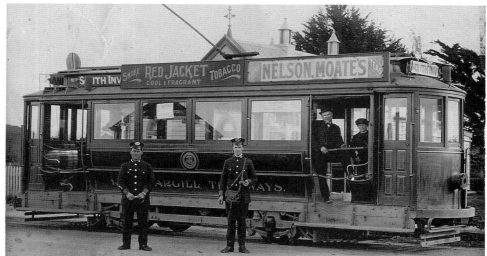

Gisborne — Battery-propelled at 16 Kilometres an Hour

There was no noise, no smell, no trolley-pole or overhead trolley wires to clutter the thoroughfares and only light track was necessary to accommodate the latest advancement in the tramway world. The cars in question were run on the accumulated energy of a specially designed electric storage battery invented by Thomas A. Edison and the body was designed by R.H. Beach. Installed under the seats of light tram-cars, the batteries could be charged with electric energy overnight at the car shed. They were already running in the United States, in Washington DC, in Jersey City and at Concord, and were said to be perfect for centres with a flat terrain. They sounded just right for Gisborne, where the council had been debating a municipal tramway for years, but where finance had always been the stumbling block.

When W. Douglas Lysnar took office as mayor, he became the champion of battery trams, although he faced many a bitter and stormy verbal battle with

The first trip of the battery trams in Gladstone Road, Gisborne, 1913. Car No. 1 was suitably decorated with Union Jacks, bunting and ferns for its maiden run. Author's Collection

Gisborne battery tram No. 1 in Gladstone Road, working the post office-Lytton Road service. S.C. Smith Collection, Alexander Turnbull Library

councillors opposed to his crusade. He was labelled high-handed in his actions, but he finally won the day and sailed for London to procure a loan. Passing through the United States on his way home, he met the famous inventor Thomas Edison, and arrived back 'fully charged' for the task ahead. Two Edison-Beach cars were duly ordered in 1912 from the Federal Storage Battery Car Company of New Jersey and track-laying began from the post office, along Gladstone Road to Roebuck Road, and to the car barn in Carnarvon Street.

In the same year, in order to convince the sceptical public, the American manufacturers shipped an Edison-Beach storage-battery car to Australia for demonstration on the Sydney tramway system. New Zealand engineers and municipal representatives were offered expenses-paid passages to view the trials. It was suggested as a suitable vehicle for such towns as Palmerston North, Wanganui and New Plymouth.

A week before the Gisborne service was inaugurated in April 1913, a trial run was made with the Mayor, William Pettie (who had succeeded Lysnar), at the controls. Because the Public Works Department was not happy with the brakes, speed was restricted to 16 kilometres an hour, although the cars were designed for a top speed of 32. On the opening day a staff of three motormen and three conductors coped with the rush when free rides were offered. From the outset the receipts did not cover the running expenses and after the first year, in an endeavour to put the undertaking on a more self-supporting basis, a 'pay as you leave system' was introduced, thus enabling conductors to be dispensed with.

The mayor's first report sounded quite optimistic. 'It is,' he said, 'quite one of the wonders of the age that a tramway car heavily laden with people should be propelled up and down our streets all day long by invisible powers stored up in a few metallic cells hidden under the seats of the vehicles, and the ease with which the power is liberated and controlled and its effectiveness at varying loads and rates of speeds as demonstrated by our cars gives hopes that the experiment Gisborne has so boldly ventured on will be eminently successful.' The mayor's enthusiasm was not shared by the citizens as the tiny cars meandered up and down Gladstone Road at irregular intervals, and with no financial improvement in sight, plans to find an alternative method of propulsion came before the council.

Mr Mansfield, the Borough Engineer, suggested that the trams be converted to petrol cars, while the Gisborne Engineering Company sought to put forward a plan by which the double trolley system should be used, the rails not acting as an electric conductor in any form whatever. The double trolley system was in use in Cincinnati in the United States, and in Havana, Cuba, the second trolley wire being used for the current return, on the same principle as a trolley bus.

Unfortunately, these bouncing chocolate-and-cream babies had been born heavyweights and were destined to continue as a burden on the ratepayer for a long time to come. From a tourist viewpoint, Gisborne did have something unique—it was the first town in the Southern Hemisphere with Edison-Beach battery trams.

No. 2 Gisborne storage battery tram at Te Hapara in 1930.
A.P. Godber

Napier launched its electric service in September 1913. Residents board the first three trams in Hastings Street, at the foot of Shakespeare Road, after the conclusion of the official speeches. *Stevenson, Author's Collection*

Napier — Another Link in the Municipal Chain

Trams had been talked about in Napier since a private company, the City of Napier and Suburban Tramways Company, had been formed in 1886. This ambitious project had envisaged a horse-car tramway between Napier and Taradale on a steel-railed line laid to a gauge of 2 feet 6 inches. The enterprising promoters issued a prospectus inviting the public to become shareholders and appointed provisional directors with H.S. Tiffen as chairman. After months of bargaining with the county council over roading and track alignment, the problems and differences remained unsolved and the plan was abandoned.

'Another link in the municipal chain of Napier' was how the Mayor of Napier, J. Vigor Brown, described the projected electric tramway from a decorated dais in Thackeray Street before he turned the first sod in March 1913. In his speech he said he hoped to see the trams running past the sports grounds, out to the golf links, through Taradale out to Clive and back to Napier. Then, with a few vigorous strokes of the pick, he turned up a portion of the roadway amidst applause. Preceding this milestone had been council debates, for and against, and a poll of ratepayers. The line as built was to run from the depot in Faraday Street, up Thackeray Street into Dickens Street, turning at the present post office corner into Hastings Street, then along Hastings Street and over the hill via Shakespeare Road to the inner harbour at Port Ahuriri, terminating at Hyderabad Road. There was also a short branch to the Napier railway station.

NAPIER
MUNICIPAL TRAMWAYS

BETWEEN DEPOT & AND PORT BRIDGE
Please destroy on alighting.

3 D.

NO. 142

NOT TRANSFERABLE.
Available for trip of issue only.
Must be shown on demand or
another fare paid. Issued subject to the Tramways By-laws
and Regulations.
TURNBULL, HICKSON & GOODER, PRINTERS.

Tram No. 2 of the Napier fleet passes contemporary cars in Hastings Street. In the centre a chauffeur-driven car is trying to overtake another car and a cyclist, who seems to prefer to ride between the tram tracks. *Author's Collection*

A view of Hastings Street, Napier, at the intersection of Emerson Street just after the First World War. Tram No. 5 is inward bound from the port. *Aldersley, John M. Bettle Collection*

Frederick Black, of Wellington, the council's consulting engineer, designed the first five trams, which were built in England and shipped out on the SS *Indrapura*. Tests followed the assembling of the royal blue and cream cars. Sleepy householders, startled by the rumbling noise which accompanies the passing of a tram-car, dashed to their front gates early one morning to witness something that was to become a feature of the town. Car No. 4 was loaded with $2\frac{1}{2}$ tonnes of pig iron as a simulated load for one test by Black. Before opening day, J.W. Callaghan, who had been appointed tramways manager, wrote to all the schools asking headmasters to address the children and warn them of the dangers and risks they would incur if they did not discipline themselves on the roads.

From the platform of the leading tram, the mayor was once again asked to address the crowd, estimated at 1500, who had gathered to see the lines opened to the public in September. Vigor Brown's address was brief and to the point. On behalf of the city and corporation he declared the lines open for traffic, adding 'and I hope that at the end of the year you will not have to put your hands in your pockets for extra rates … Three times running you declared at the polls that you wanted trams,' he said, 'for you, we have procured the most up-to-date conductors and motormen it was possible to have in New Zealand.' The mayor then invited passengers to board the cars, at the same time informing them that there would be no free 'joy riders'. All three cars filled quickly and were soon lost to sight. Later that afternoon, in Hastings Street, a gig driven by a Mrs W. Ward of Awatoto backed into a tram, 'with the result that the axle of the gig was badly bent'. Overall, everything was up to expectations, the five cars carrying 7899 passengers on 77 round trips on the first Saturday.

The accident involving Mrs Ward's gig may have been the first on the Napier Tramways, but it was not the last. On the first Sunday a tram proceeding across the intersection of Tennyson and Hastings Streets crashed into Sherwood's express, bringing both horses to the ground. There were no injuries, damage being confined to the glass shield in front of the tram and the pole and harness of the express. Other running-in troubles included cars meeting on the single line, because of a fault in the automatic signalling system, and the collapse of 150 metres of overhead in Shakespeare Road brought down when a trolley-pole came off and became entangled in the wires one Saturday afternoon when cars were carrying big loads to the football. This caused embarrassment as the council had still to get around to ordering an overhead tower wagon, which in those years was drawn by two horses.

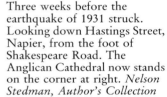

People continued to mob the service to such an extent that within a month recommendations were before the council for the purchase of two large double-bogie cars to handle the Christmas traffic. In the next report, council was asked to consider extending the line to Napier south, along Hastings Street and, if funds would permit, down Vigor Brown Street to Kennedy Road. March 1915 saw the first additions to the fleet — two four-wheelers carrying bodies built in Christchurch, and of a similar design and seating capacity to the original cars.

In the mornings a tram took folk to the railway station to join the express train to Wellington and on the return run, a load of high school girls from the Hastings school train would be dropped at the top of Shakespeare Road. As in other towns which had experienced the tramway craze, the residents of Napier liked the freedom of mobility provided by the trams. They appreciated having a chauffeur-driven 28-seater to take them home at regular times.

In Dickens Street it was a common sight in the evenings to see four trams in line astern, blazing forth light, with an inspector holding back any early starters until all cars were ready to be packed by homeward-bound theatre patrons. Within minutes of the curtain falling the first car, loaded to the steps, would grind away disappear along Hastings Street, the other three waiting patiently for the stragglers. A common sight was a convoy of three trams, each loaded with 60 to 70 people, whining slowly up the Shakespeare Road hill.

Three weeks before the earthquake of 1931 struck. Looking down Hastings Street, Napier, from the foot of Shakespeare Road. The Anglican Cathedral now stands on the corner at right. *Nelson Stedman, Author's Collection*

Another view of Hastings Street, Napier, from the Emerson Street intersection. In the foreground is No. 6, one of two trams built in Christchurch by Boon and Company, when the council expanded the fleet in 1915. *Frank Duncan, John M. Bettle Collection*

119

Devon Street, New Plymouth, shortly after the electric service started between Fitzroy and the port, and to Westown. *Frank Duncan, John M. Bettle Collection*

New Plymouth—An Air of Briskness to the Town

'The effect of trams on the town has been little short of wonderful,' wrote Town Clerk F.T. Bellringer in his report for 1916—17. 'The running of the cars has given an air of briskness to the town, due principally to the great number of people who now come in frequently from the suburbs, and who prior to the installation, owing to the difficulty of transit, only came in at long intervals.'

New Plymouth boasted it had become the smallest municipality in the world to run an overhead trolley system. Five trams started the service between Fitzroy and the Terminus Hotel (now the Tasman) in March 1916, the full service to the port being delayed a month because ships carrying essential parts were held up at wartime British ports. In May the Morley Street extension was opened and the usual official opening for such an enterprise, with flags, speeches, ribbon-cutting

The pride and joy of the borough, No. 3 electric tram in Devon Street, New Plymouth in 1916. *Author's Collection*

and good food, was laid on. Three of the four flags flying from the trolley-pole rope of the official car were displayed upside down—the signal of distress!

Until this time, wagonettes and horse-buses had coped within their limits, a Mr Page being the first in the field with a one-horse wagonette from Fitzroy. M. Jones had become the first proprietor of a horse-bus which he purchased in Auckland in 1893, and which had been driven to New Plymouth by the man who was to become the first regular driver, W. McIndoe. McIndoe would announce the departure of the iron-shod bus by blowing a bugle, and 'Mac's Bugle', as it became known, was a familiar sound to residents. Courtesy was the keynote of the early horse-bus service. Women would call out to the driver that they were coming, then put on their hats and coats, while the bus waited. But the same Mr Jones had an eye for business. Just before the trams swept all opposition off the main streets, he advertised a motor-bus service. He must have still regarded the horse as the only reliable means of locomotion as his advertisements warned customers that 'no responsibility will be taken for delays through blow-outs or other motor troubles'.

The shiny new trams became the pride and joy of the town, two cleaners working through each night, polishing windows and brasswork and disinfecting the interiors. With no triangle or balloon loop to turn the cars around, it was soon found that the city's playthings suffered corrosion along one side on the port run, because they always had the same side facing the wind and sea spray. As a result it was recommended that at regular overhauls the car bodies be turned completely. An improvement in traffic conditions was called for as motor vehicles, horse vehicles and bicycles were often seen on the wrong side of the road. Drivers had the habit of turning corners without consideration for following traffic and vehicles on the footpaths drove pedestrians on to the road. Life in a provincial centre such as New Plymouth proceeded at a leisurely pace in those days. People left vehicles unattended to obstruct a street, while the drivers discussed the war or some item of local gossip.

Tram travellers were asked to remember that they should board cars on the left side in the direction in which the cars were proceeding, and women were reminded again about those unprotected and potentially lethal hatpins. Picnic trams became popular, schools and church groups hiring special cars for excursions to the port. The life of the town became geared to the trams. The smallest of New Zealand's cities to possess a fully equipped tramway system, New Plymouth was also the last city in the country to install electric tramways.

NEW PLYMOUTH TRAMWAYS.
Must be shown on demand or another fare paid.
Issued subject to Tramways By-laws and Regulations

4d

OUT					IN		
1	2	3	4	5	6	7	

Available for trip of issue only and for section punched
Not transferable. PLEASE DESTROY ON ALIGHTING

L 49204

'Breakwater' was the original destination on New Plymouth trams running on the port service. *Author's Collection*

ABOVE: A Dunedin combination tram passing the University of Otago. *S.A. Rockliff* RIGHT: In 1930 the large advertisement on the roof of this Christchurch tram announced that a 'perfect set of teeth' could be yours for £2 12s 6d. Colombo Street at lunchtime. *Author's Collection* BELOW: A fresh air model. Wellington No. 38, one of the completely open summer trams known as 'Hong Kongs', after the early trams of that city, or 'toast racks', which they resembled. *Author's Collection* BELOW RIGHT: Combination trams with large open sections must have helped to breed a hardy generation of Wellingtonians. *Author's Collection*

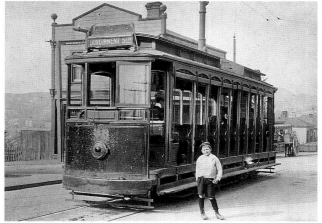

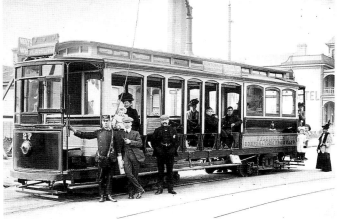

CHAPTER SEVEN

Always a Tram in Sight

Seldom do public utilities and essential services endear themselves to their users and assume a personality of their own. The electric tram-car, however, was different. It had an individuality that reflected the city it served. To a visitor from Auckland, a Christchurch tram looked strange and exciting. A Wellingtonian found the Auckland cars bulbous, even huge, after the narrow-gutted cars he was accustomed to see inching their way through traffic in the confines of Cuba Street. Trams were unsurpassed in their ability to move great masses of people speedily at cheap rates, and to stand the day-in, day-out strain of dragging around corners and vibrating along streets. Often grossly overladen, they had to be built to stand abuse with the minimum of maintenance.

They were built to last — and last they did. Many were to survive for 50 years, a credit to their designers, but detrimental to the image of tramways in an age of technological advancement. People would have refused to ride in a 1913 motor-bus even 15 years later, but because the tram-car was like an old soldier, and old soldiers never die, municipalities and companies kept the faithful old vehicles, seemingly gifted with perpetual life, plodding on. Standardisation of design often resulted in new rolling stock being built to the same layout as the original cars and powered with equipment that dated back to the Ark.

Designs varied from the box cars — also known as 'dinghies' because they behaved like small boats in a swell — with their enclosed saloons (which were to win through in the end because of New Zealand's changeable climate), to open cars for summer months, known as 'Hong Kongs' or 'toast racks', which they resembled in having a roof supported by a row of stanchions on each side. On these open cars smoking was allowed on the four rear seats, the motion of the vehicle carrying off the objectionable tobacco smoke.

Dunedin had a fleet of genuine American streetcars, built by the J.G. Brill Company of Philadelphia to a selection of styles. How passengers endured winter travel on these breezy electrics was a matter for wonder. The long overhang on these four-wheelers made them prance along the tracks when running at any speed, and nicknames such as 'jumping jacks', 'bobtailers' and 'galloping gerties' became local colloquialisms. Heavy loading saw a number of the little box cars coupled permanently together as twins, each vehicle pitching in the opposite direction to its twin like two ships under tow in a gale. In addition to the box and Hong Kong styles, a most popular design in the southern and provincial centres were the combination types originating in California, with a centre enclosed saloon, and an open section at each end with back-to-back lateral seats. The combination cars catered for those hardy souls who liked the open air, or for those who enjoyed the comfort of a club while travelling to the corner of their suburban street.

Fittings were of the finest quality. Tapestry curtains hung from brass rods supported by elaborate brass brackets and ceiling lamps carried art metal fittings with crystal shades. A more mundane touch was provided by the notice above each saloon door, 'Smoking and Spitting Strictly Forbidden'; other cars had notices reading 'Do Not Expectorate'. Some cars had seats covered with handsome Wilton carpet and spring-roller blinds were provided to shade tender complexions from the sun. Roller blinds of striped duck could be pulled down to floor level to protect the open sections in wet weather, and perforated metal tablets were placed on the stanchions for the striking of wax matches.

The interior of an Auckland combination tram showing the ornate ceiling light covers and the curtains for after-dark running. *Author's Collection*

The ornamental carved interiors of the imported cars were of polished oak, showing the natural grain, polished bird's-eye maple being mainly used for the ceilings. Window sashes made of quartered oak were set in felt runners to prevent rattles from vibration. To avoid the throat clearings and frowns that inevitably arose from differences of opinion on ventilation, cunningly concealed ventilating windows were built into the coachwork, thus leading the 'draught-maniac' to believe that the interior was safe from any rush of oxygen. Fresh air flowed in and out of cars at a rate of governed by speed. Exterior painting was a work of art, many coats being applied before the final lining-out, corner ornamentation and other fancy decorative patterns, and varnishing ensured that a car was ready for public display.

Auckland's first locally built passenger model was produced in 1905, a Californian combination, especially for the Remuera service. Its seats were sprung and for the sake of hygiene were covered with closely woven but somewhat slippery cane. In the centre saloon the seats ran longitudinally on each side, and going up Parnell Rise, passengers could not stop themselves from sliding toward the rear. By the time the car reached the summit, those passengers who had gravitated rearwards must have felt like sardines in a tin. Although the car had graceful lines with curved sides, it remained an orphan in Auckland.

British influence was obvious with the adoption in some cities of double-deckers of marked English descent. Both hands were needed to negotiate the narrow,

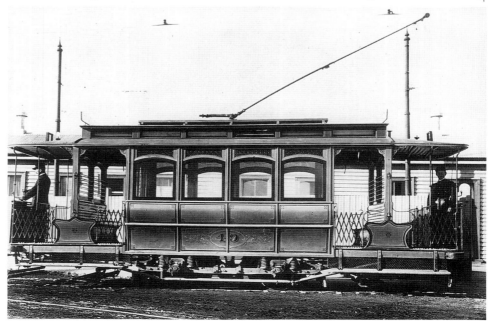

Once the society tram of Auckland. The regal-looking Californian combination car built especially for the Remuera service in 1905. *Author's Collection*

spiralling staircase and passengers on the unroofed upper deck sat on garden-type seats, any moisture running off beneath. From this vantage point the roof-top fares were monarch of all they surveyed, looking down disdainfully at the midgets dashing around in the street below. Above the passengers' heads rose the trolley-pole, terminating in a little wheel that whizzed along the wire, clattering through cut-outs and negotiating points in the overhead. What a majestic monster was the double-decker as it lumbered through the street like a regal elephant, scattering pedestrians in its wake. The large seating capacity and the simple segregation of smokers and non-smokers were two of the main advantages of the open-toppers. Managements and crews disliked them, however, mainly on account of their slow loading characteristics, and because they lurched badly at speed.

Nevile Lodge

"HE WANTS TO TRANSFER TO A SINGLE-DECKER—HEIGHTS MAKE HIM DIZZY."

Civilians and soldiers boarding Christchurch double-decker trailers for Sumner in the Square during the First World War. These old trailers started their life as horse- and steam-tram vehicles. *Author's Collection*

Criterion Coach .. Factory..

Victoria, Peterborough and Kilmore Sts.,
CHRISTCHURCH.

First Prizes for Circular Broughams   First Prizes for Buggies.

W. MOOR & CO., COACH and TRAMCAR BUILDERS.

Have your Tyres set by West's Patent Tyre Setter.

SPECIAL.—MOTOR CAR BODIES BUILT TO ORDER AND REPAIRED.
MOTOR CARS PAINTED & RE-UPHOLSTERED.   *Estimates Given.*

Christchurch No. 51, the daddy of all 'decker trailers', christened *Rotomahana*, was known to have carried 200 passengers home from race meetings. *Christchurch Tramways*

Christchurch must be given credit for building one of the first tramway vehicles in New Zealand, in November 1880. The tram, a double-decker horse-car, was built by Moor and Son for the Canterbury Tramway Company. The car was a facsimile of the imported carriages; with ash framing, panelling of American white-wood and roofs and window frames of oak and hickory. All the brass fittings were supplied by Scott Brothers of Christchurch, the only imported parts being the chilled cast-iron wheels. A contemporary report described the car as a most creditable specimen of local industry. The coachwork was equal to that of the American vehicles and a much-needed improvement had been made on the roof 'by the addition of a board running along the outside, for the special benefit of the female patronisers of the tramway'. Christchurch was renowed for its double-decker trailers, which snaked through Cathedral Square like a brood of ducklings following their mother. The daddy of all 'decker trailers' was launched during the early years of the electric tramways in Christchurch as an experiment, being two open-top trailers joined together. This jumbo seated 92 passengers and on race days it was not uncommon for it to carry 200 on both decks. Unofficially this trailer was known as *Rotomahana*, after the well-known express steamer of the day.

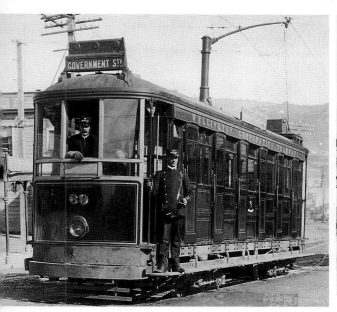

A type of vehicle exclusive to Wellington was the Palace electric tram. This design, copied from the Sydney tram-cars, was rather similar to the old English railway carriages. There was no centre aisle and the seats, which faced each other, extended across the width of the car, thus dividing it into compartments. A continuous running board along each side and sliding doors gave access to the compartments. In order to collect fares, conductors inched their way along the running boards and clung to the handrails as they swung from one compartment to the next. With the introduction of the first Palace cars built by the Wellington coach builders, Rouse and Hurrell, the council ordered six large double-bogie, double-deckers having five Palace compartments downstairs and an open upper deck. The 'Big Bens', as they were known, could really carry a crowd, swallowing an estimated 200 rugby fans from Athletic Park in one gulp.

Palace cars of the single-deck variety soon became commonplace on the streets of the capital, but casualties among the conductors as passing vehicles swept them off the running boards were increasing at an alarming rate. In 1913 the Tramways Amendment Bill was passed, requiring all trams to be equipped with a passageway through the centre. This bill, known as the Davy Act after the Member of Parliament who was instrumental in having the legislation made law, also governed the height of steps and led to the modification of tramway cars throughout the Dominion.

An interesting postscript to the saga of the Palace trams was the sudden nostalgia Wellingtonians felt when they found that the trams they had condemned for so long were no more. There was public outcry for the sole remaining car, No. 53, to be retained for future generations to view. The Dominion Museum was then housed in an old wooden building at the rear of Parliament Buildings and had to refuse the offer. Other sites were suggested, but slowly the public agitation waned and No. 53 was converted to the new style. This must surely have been the first attempt in New Zealand to preserve a tramway vehicle.

In Auckland the city council kept a close eye on the workings of the tramway company. The city's sole traffic inspector was detailed to check on regulations such as no standing, quiet running of cars, cleanliness, and failing to stop when requested. One day he sent 20 trams back to the depot for both noise and dirt, so the company had to employ a man to sweep out cars at the bottom of Queen Street. The council ruled with an iron hand, demanding the correct number of trams on the road in proportion to the rising population, as contracted in the deed of delegation. Being in the red with a shortage of rolling stock, the company must have been perturbed when the council issued an ultimatum, after repeated warnings, that if a new tram was not on the road by 1 August 1906, it would be liable to a fine of £8 a day. In the barn at the corner of Wallace Street and Jervois Road, Herne Bay, the coachwork of a new tram was being built by the company's tradesmen. With the swiftness and precision of a brilliantly executed military manoeuvre, the company stowed a serviceable tram at the back of the depot, removed all its electrical equipment and bogies, installing them in and under the

Auckland electric tram No. 57, built by the employees of the Auckland Electric Tramway Company at the Wallace Street Depot, Herne Bay, seen here hauling a redundant horse-tram as a trailer in the Labour Day parade of October 1907. *New Zealand Graphic*

new sparkling body, making the tram instantly roadworthy. Little did the council know of the skullduggery that had taken place as No. 57 graced the city on 1 August, not a day late.

In 1907 the company was once again embarrassed by a lack of trams and asked for help from its head office in London. In reply to the SOS, four complete trams from the London Metropolitan Electric Tramways Limited were shipped to Auckland and placed in service with London tram tickets still scattered on the floors. Not a day could be lost in getting the cars mobile, so off into Queen Street went the immigrants, still dressed in their London livery of bright red and cream. The colours worn by the Auckland fleet to combat dust tarnishing were now light orange, picked out with narrow blue and red lines, so the London cars were promptly dubbed 'The Lobsters' by Aucklanders.

In new condition, the London Metropolitan Electric Tramways single-decker type E tram as built in 1905. Four of these London trams, numbers 135, 136, 143, 144, were sold to the Auckland Electric Tramway Company in 1907. *Author's Collection*

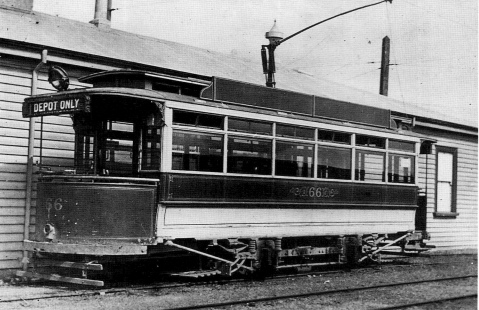

The first of the four London trams which were shipped, in running order, to Auckland in 1907, photographed at Epsom Depot. This tram, formerly No. 135 in London, was renumbered 66 on being commissioned for service in Auckland. At the time, both the London and Auckland operations were owned by the same parent company. *Author's Collection*

The Auckland freight and parcels electric delivery tram No. 44 (left), heading up Queen Street for Onehunga, loaded with parcels and produce. *Author's Collection*

There were some trams on which a fare was never collected or a ticket issued. 'Our motto — speedy delivery small profits and quick returns' was the heading of the advertisement published in the *New Zealand Herald* in October 1904 to announce a freight service which the Auckland Electric Tramways Company started in competition with the railways between the city and Onehunga. A special goods-van tram was built, its city terminal being at the foot of Queen Street for the convenience of merchants. This car provided a faster delivery service than the normal horse-drawn lorries and, unlike the trains, it went right through the heart of Onehunga borough. The advertisements read like a television commercial today:

> The freight car, the business man's friend. Rates very considerably reduced. Move with the times and send your parcels by the electric freight car. The cheapest, quickest, safest, and best way to have your parcels delivered to any part of the city and suburbs. Give it a trial, then tell your friends of the great convenience of Electric Delivery.

Freight rates were 4 shillings a tonne and the crew would unload right at the shop door. To cope with business the company opened a goods depot at the Onehunga Wharf, where parcels could be collected by horse and cart.

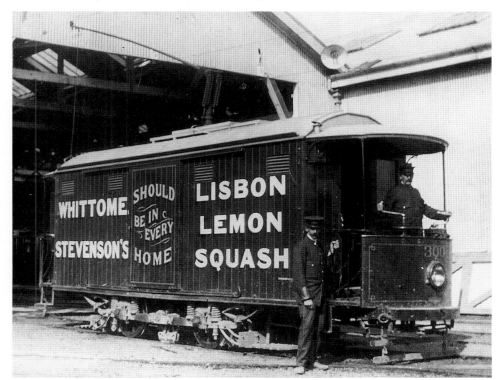

The Auckland freight tram leaving Epsom Depot after being recommissioned and renumbered 300 in 1908. This tram ended its days as a security tram carrying revenue boxes. *Author's Collection*

Wellington, N.Z.

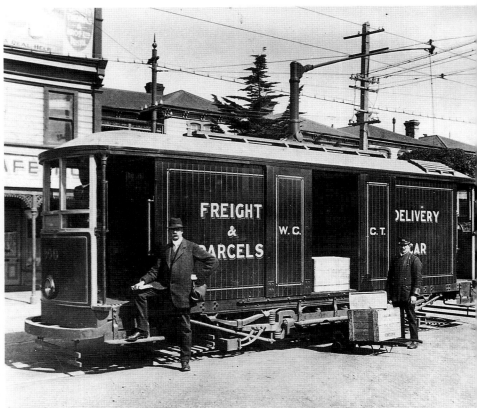

Wellington's freight trams ran a similar service to the suburbs. On a special tramway siding outside the old Wellington Post Office in Customhouse Quay (above), a freight tram is seen loading goods. *John M. Bettle Collection* ABOVE RIGHT: The Wellington City Corporation freight tram No. 200 which would deliver freight and parcels to your front door if you lived on a tram route. *Author's Collection*

Wellington built two similar windowless box cars for freight and small goods. Coal to Brooklyn, potatoes and flour to Cooper's store in Karori, beer to hotels — all commodities of freight were carried to and from goods depots at the tramway office (opposite the Lambton Railway Station), in Manners Street and Courtenay Place. While business was brisk, a receiving depot for goods was in use at the Post Office Square, Customhouse Quay. One 'freighter' would meet the Auckland Express daily at Thorndon Railway Station for passengers' luggage. After leaving their suitcases on the goods tram, passengers climbed aboard a passenger car for a fast passage to the city's hotels, and following in close attendance came the freight car. This service enabled travellers to retrieve their luggage right at the front door of a hotel. A de luxe model, with combined luggage and seating accommodation, ran from the Christchurch Railway Station to the Cathedral Square until motor vehicles defeated its purpose.

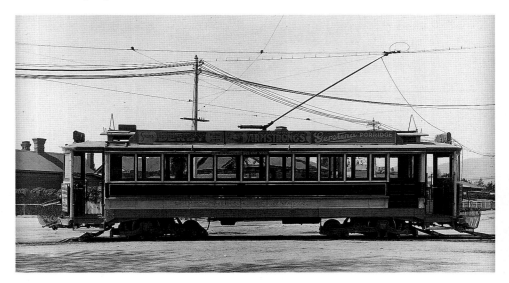

The Christchurch combined passenger and luggage tram No. 30 which was originally used for a service between the railway station and Cathedral Square. This tram ended its days as a 'bicycle tram'. *Christchurch Tramways*

Dealing with Dust

Speed stirred the dust on the macadamised roads and to help abate this nuisance the four principal cities ran electric water-sprinkler trams. In an era when women were still performing the time-honoured ritual of beating carpets slung over clotheslines, the Dunedin City Corporation put to work a unique vacuum cleaner-sprinkler car. The suction plant plucked dust and gravel from the rail grooves while a nozzle sprayed the road with water.

In Wellington a baby-sized model with a cylindrical tank — the motorman standing rigidly at his post, wearing goggles as protection against grit, one hand on the controller lever and the other on the swan-neck handle of the handbrake — would waltz along while people dodged down alleyways to escape the dust storm. Baffle plates inside the tanks prevented the water from surging and thus affecting the stability of the tram. A similar car in Christchurch, called 'Wet Willie', proved inadequate for the number of roads transversed by rails and was soon joined by two towering tankers, each having a capacity of 1500 litres, and equipped with a 9-kilogram air-pressure pump which sprayed water to 15 metres on both sides of the tram lines. Between them, these cars could distribute a total of 605,000 litres of water each day, helping to make bearable the unsealed roads that were rapidly becoming unacceptable in built-up areas. Dual-purpose cars these, for they had equipment to fight fires and clear snow.

A pollution problem of yester-year. One of the jumbo-sized sprinkler trams used to spray the unsealed suburban roads of Christchurch with water during the dry summer months. No. 2 sprinkler seen at a refilling point on a siding in Worcester Street off Oxford Terrace. *Press Collection, Alexander Turnbull Library*

BELOW LEFT: The Dunedin City Corporation vacuum cleaner-sprinkler tram. The suction plant plucked dust and gravel from the rail grooves while a nozzle sprayed the road with water. *Ian Stewart Collection*
BELOW: The Christchurch sprinkler-track cleaner tram No. 1, which was used into the 1950s for the cleaning of track junctions and drains. *Graham Stewart*

Laying the dust. An electric sprinkler tram working at the bottom of Khyber Pass Road, Auckland. The Carlton Club Hotel can be seen in the background. *Author's Collection*

No. 301, the first electric sprinkler tram in Auckland, being tested at the Herne Bay terminus in Jervois Road. The old Bayfield School can be seen in the distance. *Author's Collection*

The Canterbury Tramway Company made unsealed roads bearable in the 1880s by using a water sprinkler wagon of similar design which was coupled to regular service steam-trams.

The Auckland Tramway Company made a business venture of dust pollution, watering streets with three large electric road-sprinklers under contract to the city council, boroughs and road districts. Sufficient water would be ejected to sprinkle one side of the roadway at a time, the opposite side being covered on the return journey. Electric sprinklers had advantages over the heavy, horse-drawn watering carts, for there were no wagon wheels to cut up the roads. Watering trams had been used as early as 1880 in Christchurch, when Mr Peterkin, Traffic Manager of the Canterbury Tramway Company, ordered the construction of two wooden trucks bearing iron tanks designed to drop water across the width of the line. These water wagons were attached to passenger trailers drawn by a steam-tram on timetable runs.

Wanganui's 'breakdown tram' No. 7 (right), heading out of the Taupo Quay depot to an emergency. On the left a 'Takapuna' tram is seen arriving from Gonville. *W.W. Stewart*

Cars We Never Rode

Oddities that flashed past the corner tram stop from time to time, leaving onlookers bewildered and asking 'Do they call that a tram?', were generally veteran passenger cars, rather neglected, finishing their old age by grinding the corrugations out of the rails, or assigned to the nerve-racking task of training budding motormen.

The old song, 'The Merry-go-round Broke Down', fits the story about one of these semi-retired cars which was fitted up to rescue comrades in distress on Wanganui Corporation lines. Painted a drab chocolate from head to toe, No. 7 was designated the 'breakdown tram', and was furnished with lifting jacks, chains and other gear. It was always kept in readiness to dash off to the scene of trouble. Like their fire brigade counterparts, the tramway depot staff answered calls promptly, leaping aboard old No. 7 and setting off to retrieve a derailed or broken-down tram. One day while passing through Aramoho at breakneck speed, poor old No. 7 parted company with the tracks and ended up in disgrace a few metres short of a shop frontage. It was more than a little reminiscent of the pre-war Flanagan and Allen song: 'What Happens to the Breakdown Van when the Breakdown Van Breaks Down?'

From as early as 1903 public transport in Christchurch suffered from bicycle competition. On fine days the cycles came out, on wet days they were abandoned and the tram-car used, said a newspaper report. These spindly iron steeds, still a popular form of transport in Christchurch where flat country makes cycling a pleasure, whittled away the profits of the Tramway Board. Everyone, it seemed, rode a bike, whether to work or to play. The board showed consideration when it found that men signing on at the out-of-town tram shed in the early morning had to walk more than 3 kilometres in the midday heat from Cathedral Square to collect their bikes at the end of a shift. A tram was modified and in place of seats, bicycle racks were fitted. This tram travelled to a small depot in the Square each morning, and returned in the evening to the main car sheds in Moorhouse Avenue, laden with cycles required when crews and trams returned at the end of a day. Where else but Christchurch would one have found a 'bicycle tram'?

The second Christchurch 'bicycle tram', No. 203, and trailer No. 103, loaded with bikes in Colombo Street, bound for the Cathedral Square depot. *Graham Stewart*

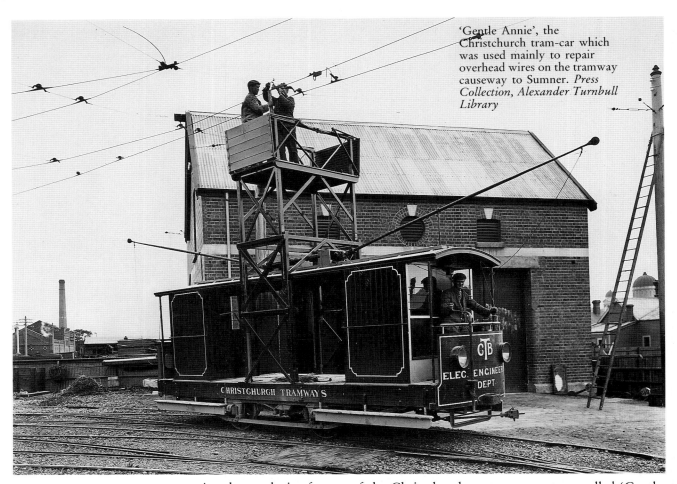

It's off to work we go — Auckland work trams leaving the tramway workshops in Epsom. No. 38 (left), a former double-decker passenger tram imported from England when the system opened in 1902, was used from 1936 to 1955 to grind corrugations off the rail surfaces. At right is the large freight tram No. 304, built in 1913 as a flat-top tram with a crane to carry rails around the suburbs. *Graham Stewart*

Another exclusive feature of the Christchurch system was a tram called 'Gentle Annie', which was used by the engineering department for the erection and maintenance of the overhead trolley wires. Gentle Annie, complete with an elevated platform, was built especially for the Sumner line on which causeway bridges prevented the use of road vehicles. Overhead emergency wagons drawn by horses were permitted to gallop to mishaps at fire-brigade speed, and to keep trams moving when there was a fire, portable ramp-rails were installed in a few minutes to bridge fire hoses across the tracks. Probably the most businesslike of all the work cars would have been the flat-top crane tram used to carry rails and heavy equipment about Auckland. During the peace celebration in 1919 a brass band, seated on the open deck, played patriotic music to the crowds as the tram rolled up and down Queen Street.

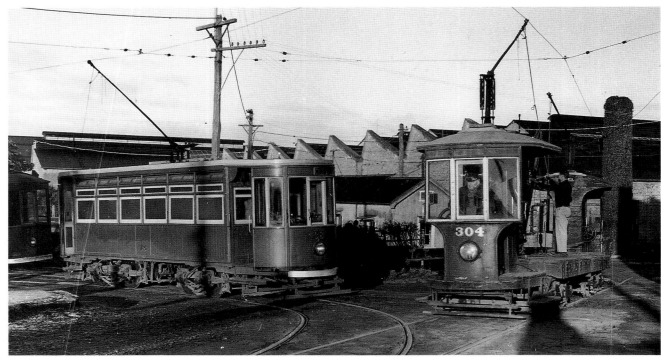

The Auckland flat-top freight tram No. 304 heading down Queen Street past the town hall in the 1950s. *Graham Stewart*

Old No. 2 in Christchurch, which ended its days as a track-grinding tram in the 1950s, seen waiting for a regular service Cranford Street tram to pass in Colombo Street. *Graham Stewart*

Replacing another battered safety zone. The Auckland flat-top crane tram lifting the remains of a motorist's nightmare, during the last month of tramway operation in Auckland, December 1956. *Graham Stewart*

'Gentle Annie', the Christchurch overhead tram, decorated for a First World War recruiting campaign in 1915. *Press Collection, Alexander Turnbull Library*

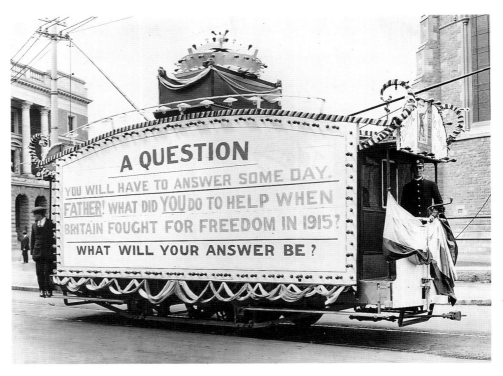

Before the days of Lotto — many New Zealanders will recall their delight in seeing what appeared to be a moving crystal palace: a tram covered with hundreds of small illuminated light bulbs ambling through the streets of an evening. One old Christchurch veteran would come out of hiding and brighten the streets in the final week before each Art Union closed. This old faithful, No. 4, is seen crossing the main south railway line in Antigua Street. *Graham Stewart*

A Christchurch centre-entrance tram built by the local coach builders, Boon and Company, in St Asaph Street, Christchurch. These trams became known affectionately as 'Boon' trams. *Press Collection, Alexander Turnbull Library*

Well Made New Zealand

Although English-type cars were ordered initially to fulfil contracts at Auckland and Wellington, as the fleets expanded New Zealand tended to favour American designs, modified variations of the California combination cars appearing in Wellington and Christchurch. Some had large open sections with a tiny saloon at one end for the protection of invalids, delicate persons and cowards! Others had a large saloon and a short open section. Some were grand for use as observation specials, to show off the local scenic highlights to visitors. A more practical adaptation of this format was the centre-entrance type, with closed saloons at each end and an open centre section.

Christchurch had many 'Boon' cars, so named after the builder, and Wellington adopted this design as standard. The open sections gave scant protection from Canterbury winter temperatures or a Wellington southerly, and in response to public clamour, the centre of each open section was provided with panels and windows. However, a doorway was left at each end of the now-enclosed centre section, thus providing four entrances spaced along each side, an excellent arrangement

A Wellington double-saloon tram No. 123, climbing the grade in Glenmore Street under the Kelburn Viaduct bound for Karori Park in the 1920s. The centre section had been closed for more passenger protection against the weather. *Wellington Tramways*

Known by the nickname of 'Big Lizzie', No. 1 of the Dunedin city fleet, originally a small single-bogie single-saloon tram, was rebuilt in 1919 to test the suitability of eight-wheeled cars for Dunedin. *Author's Collection*

for quick loading and unloading. Of similar layout were the twelve double-bogie cars built in Sydney in the 1920s to assist Dunedin's 50 'puddle-jumpers'. To gauge whether Dunedin was suitable for large eight-wheel cars, the corporation in 1919 tacked semi-open saloons onto each end of the original little box car No. 1 and, in what was described as a 'hybrid grafting job', produced the first double-bogie Dunedin tram, a rather odd-looking specimen which earned the nickname 'Big Lizzie'.

On the home market there were coach builders who specialised in tram-car construction. In Auckland, Cousins and Atkin (later D.S.C. and Cousins and Cousins), H.C. Williams, and Henderson and Pollard, built large numbers of trams. In Wellington the firm of Rouse and Hurrell, later Rouse and Black, supplied most of the early locally built cars. Local coach workers used several classes of timber for body construction. The pillars were generally of American ash, the window frames of cedar and the interiors lined with kauri, totara and other native timbers. All companies, boards and corporations eventually became geared to build their own rolling stock and tackled major modifications with competence.

Acknowledged as a leader in this field of industry was the Christchurch firm of Boon and Company, of Ferry Road, formerly Boon and Stevens, who had built

Four newly completed Boon centre-entrance trams for Christchurch outside Boons factory in St Asaph Street in April 1907. *Weekly Press, Bruce Maffey Collection*

When horsepower meant the number of horses. A team of nine draught horses pulling a new Auckland tram body built by D.S.C. and Cousins and Cousins, into Lower Symonds Street by St Andrew's Church, September 1910. *New Zealand Graphic*

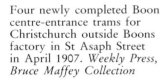

Coach builders were respected craftsmen. An Auckland electric tram nearing completion at D.S.C. and Cousins and Cousins factory in 1908. The American flags displayed on the far wall were in honour of the visiting American Naval Fleet. *Author's Collection*

horse-trams for the New Brighton Company, fulfilled orders for each of the provincial networks and built most of the additions to the Christchurch rolling stock. Boon's crowning achievement in streetcar manufacture was the construction of 23 48-seater saloon trams for the Christchurch Tramway Board between 1921 and 1926. Fitted with automatic acceleration and multiple-unit running equipment, these 12.5-metre cars with steel sheathed bodies, running coupled in pairs between Sumner and Riccarton and other suburbs, formed the backbone of the city's public transport fleet in the 1920s.

Three of the Christchurch semi-steel cars under construction in Boon's 'car shed' in St Asaph Street in the 1920s. *Steffano Webb Collection, Alexander Turnbull Library*

Front-liners of the 1920s — a multiple-unit pair of Christchurch trams running coupled, turning from Worcester Street into Oxford Terrace, heading for Riccarton. *W.W. Stewart*

Looking down Devon Street,
New Plymouth, from the
junction of the Liardet Street
tramline to Pukekura Park.
The trams are the American
one-man Birney safety cars
imported for the Westown line
in 1921. *Author's Collection*

A hardening of the economy, accompanied by the first pain from motor-bus competition, was felt shortly after the First World War. In the United States the J.G. Brill Company of Philadelphia was mass-producing a new, advanced lightweight streetcar to meet mounting competition from the motor omnibus. Design standardisation of trams had been unheard of until this car, the Birney Safety Car, was put on the world market. Its main feature was one-man operation, dispensing with conductors. Safety factors included air-operated doors to keep passengers safely locked in while the car was in motion, and the 'dead-man control', which automatically brought the car to a halt should the motorman collapse at the controls. Ultimately, more than 6000 Birney cars saw service throughout the world. Passenger loadings were still rising on street tramways, but so were operating costs, and the salvation of the tram-car lay in features that allowed for operating economies and the production of more net revenue.

One-man trams were to be the salvation of the tramways in provincial towns. In 1920 the Wellington agents for the Birney Safety Car, Richardson and McCabe, received orders from Invercargill for six and from New Plymouth for three. Napier wanted Birney Safety Cars, and asked for a reduction in the width of the aisle because of the narrow gauge. Brill could not, however, handle this request as their mass-assembly line was not geared for individual orders, so the order lapsed.

New Plymouth's little 'tin hares' were assembled and running by October 1921, becoming the first one-man cars in the Dominion. Shortly after the American trams came out, Gordon Coates, who was then the Minister of Transport, visited New Plymouth for a test run. N.F. Clarke, who was designated to drive the officials, was asked by the tramways manager, R.H. Bartley, to show the workings of the dead man's control. In full parallel, the tramway term for 'flat out', he lifted his hand off the controller, and the tram stopped dead, nose dived on its two front wheels, then slumped back with a shudder onto the track. As a demonstration it could not have been more effective, for Minister and all were pitched from their seats onto the floor of the tram.

The economies effected with one-man equipment meant that safety features

could be applied to many of the older cars. Veteran combinations were modernised and sprouted draught-proof doors. Later in the decade, Christchurch experimented with one-man operation by converting and electrifying three trailers. The low population density in Christchurch compared with the other main centres made the 'pay-as-you-enter' system workable, and helped to prop up the sagging revenue returns. During the Depression of the 1930s, the tramway board rebuilt the front row forwards of the fleet, the 25 saloons known as the 'Brills', to one-man cars. One unique departure from tradition was that the driving position was at one end only while in traffic, like a bus. Balloon loops and triangles therefore had to be laid to turn the 'Brills'. One advantage trams had over buses was their ability to reverse within their own length. The original arrangement of these cars was copied from the single saloons which remained standard right to the last in Auckland, a separate compartment being provided for the motorman.

Three of the famous Birney safety trams in Dee Street, Invercargill. *Author's Collection*

BELOW LEFT: One of three Christchurch tramway trailers that were converted to one-man-operated electric trams in 1927 to test the suitability of the 'pay as you enter' system. *Bruce Maffey Collection*

BELOW: The 25 Christchurch semi-steel trams known as the 'Brills' were converted to one-man operation in the 1930s. *Bruce Maffey Collection*

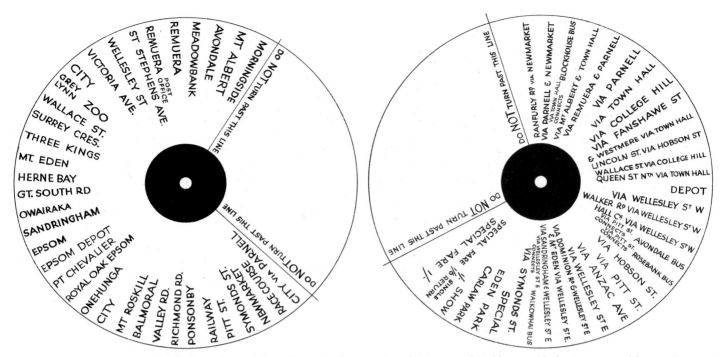

In the 1920s Auckland adopted large destination signs for their tram fleet. They were designed to be read from both sides of the street on an angle, the destination boxes being in a 'V' shape. They were known within the service as 'butterfly' destinations, with an upper and lower destination roll. The main destination appeared on the upper roll and a route variation out of the city could be shown just by altering the lower roll. The signs were altered by the crew by turning two wheels within the motorman's compartment. The wheel indicators are illustrated above, the upper destination roll on the left and the lower destination roll on the right. *Author's Collection*

OPPOSITE PAGE: The coloured destination light signals and the passing parade of trams turned Wellington streets into a fairyland in the evenings. You could always spot your tram from the bottom of Willis Street by its night signal lights. The combination on the Lyall Bay tram in the foreground was blue-white-blue. *Graham Stewart*

Sir Robert Anderson, Lord Mayor of Belfast, said during a world tour in 1912 that the Auckland trams were 'handsome looking'. Characteristics of the Auckland cars were the profusion of windows along each side and the destination-indicator boxes, known as butterfly signs, which were arranged in pairs to form a V. These signs were practical and easy to read, even if the ungainly units did not help to beautify the vehicle.

Reading the destination board on an approaching public conveyance can be infuriating and over the years attempts have been made to please the short-sighted and the elderly. Large numerical symbols to designate routes have always been popular for quick identification. An early version of this system was adopted in Christchurch where big circular tin discs carried numbers. Both Christchurch and Dunedin once used coloured symbols on destination blinds in various patterns and colours, featuring triangles, dots and squares. In Christchurch, Woolston was indicated by white with a large green dot, Lincoln Road by two squares of red and green; in Dunedin, St Kilda cars sported three red dots. Invercargill had a spot-the-tram system all of its own—alphabetical symbols. Route A ran between North and South Invercargill, and route B cars on the Waikiwi-Georgetown service. On some systems coloured route indication lights were used at night. Wellington will be long remembered for the combination pattern of lights as the passing parade of trams made Willis Street like a fairyland in the evenings; blue-white-blue for Lyall Bay, blue-red-blue for Newtown or red-green-red for Karori Park. Lights in Auckland lasted only for a short time; perhaps the 'Rangitoto Yanks' were colour blind. Ponsonby was indicated by red (which brought no protest from the moralists of the district), Remuera, by blue and red, Mount Eden, by red and white.

Colour was important on the tramways, and each system had its distinctive schemes. Steel poles, ornamental caps, finials and wrought iron cross-arms were part of the overall colour scheme. Auckland had all the hardware related to overhead painted olive green; Christchurch used a distinctive grey. Wellington and Dunedin cars were painted indian red, with the framework and dashers in yellow and gold, a livery similar to that used by the London County Council. Paris green and white were chosen by the Christchurch Board, whereas Auckland started with Midland red and cream, changing in 1904 to a light orange colour, relieved by narrow blue and red stripes. Three years later Auckland began repainting the fleet with the Christchurch colours of green and white. By 1912 some cars were green, others red and yellow, chocolate and yellow, and all red. The council muttered that the company had the fleet painted all the colours of the rainbow. So, red and cream became the standard livery.

An Auckland track maintenance gang relaying track in Ponsonby Road during the 1920s. *Author's Collection*

Lines of Steel

The tracks were the very foundation of the tramways, requiring a high degree of specialised engineering. Major road reconstruction, in the days of picks and shovels and horse-drawn drays and steam rollers, necessitated the digging up of existing roads for a solid metalled base on which to set the sleepers and rails. Then followed restoration of the roadway surface. This was labouring at its worst, even if the engineering needed to ensure a smooth line was an art. Some track laying was completed in a space of time that would make today's giant earth-moving machinery blush. The English firm of J.G. White and Company who, under contract, laid the original tracks in Auckland, had within 14 months completed no fewer than 43 kilometres of track. The Tramways Act, passed when only horse traffic plodded the ways, was a decided liability to undertakings as heavy motor traffic increased. The most onerous condition of this act was the stipulation that the road between the rails and 45 centimetres each side had to be maintained by the tramway authority to an approved standard as directed by the road authority. Even if only five trams transversed a road each day while convoys of heavy trucks or buses bombarded the same surface for eight hours daily, the damage done by those trucks and buses over the area carrying tram tracks was the responsibility of the tramways. Some local authorities even levied a sanitary rate on each tramway pole, as though the transport authority had any control over the instinctive habits of the canine population!

Motorists damned the trams as pot holes enlarged, never understanding that transport authorities were heavily subsidising a large proportion of the tarseal used by rubber tyres. Many suburban lines involved massive feats of engineering, including cuttings and tunnels carved through hillsides to give public transport access to a mushrooming district. Motor vehicles used the solid road surfaces made possible by this work, and their operators or owners took for granted the amenities provided. Wellington tunnelled through surrounding hills to enable the tram-car to penetrate new suburbs such as Karori, Hataitai, Seatoun and later Northland. The Wadestown line was built like a railway, with high cuttings and embankments, and it faced the same problems as railways with landslides blocking the line in the winter months.

ABOVE LEFT: Wellington
double-saloon No. 130 leaving
the Northland tunnel
in Northland Road.
W.W. Stewart ABOVE:
Wellington double-saloon No.
224 emerging from the Karori
tunnel. *W.W. Stewart*

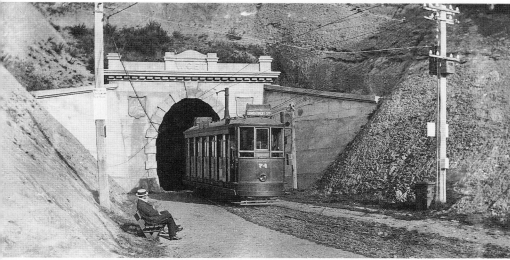

A Palace tram emerges from
the city portal of the Hataitai
tramway tunnel, Wellington.
Author's Collection

"STREWTH! IF WE STRIKE ANY MORE TUNNELS I HOPE THEY'RE NOT
AS TIGHT A SQUEEZE AS THAT ONE!"

BELOW LEFT: Morning peak-
hour traffic at the Hataitai
portal of the Hataitai tramway
tunnel in the 1950s. *Graham
Stewart* BELOW: The city
portal of the Hataitai tramway
tunnel when used by Miramar
trams in the 1950s. *Graham
Stewart*

Shades of a rural railway line. The original single tramway track which ran through a cutting to Wadestown in Wellington. *Author's Collection*

ABOVE RIGHT: Swinging and swaying on the back trailer to Sumner, Christchurch. A view out the back window of the 'Sumner Express', which usually consisted of a motor-tram with two trailers. *Graham Stewart*

Causeways across mudflats, together with wooden trestle bridges, carried the line to the Christchurch seaside suburb of Sumner.

Where railway and tramway tracks crossed on the level, semaphore-arm signals of railway pattern worked in conjunction with derailing points to control the passage of trams. If a tram went against a signal, the interlocked trap points would swerve the tram wheels to the left and onto the tarseal with a crunch. Safety precautions were not considered necessary for level crossings with seldom-used private railway sidings into industrial yards, such as were found at Dunedin, Wanganui and Napier. Napier did have two crossings with the private railway line owned by the Napier Harbour Board. In May 1920 a late theatre tram returning to town from Port Ahuriri collided with a Harbour Board locomotive near Milton Road, both vehicles suffering considerable damage. Fortunately the tram was empty and going very slowly, and the train did have the legal right of way. Another safety precaution designed to stop runaways where a terminus was situated on a grade, was the form of tram trap used in Auckland. Trenches at the end of each rail were covered with wooden supports, then tarsealed to stand the weight of all rubber-tyred traffic, but designed to collapse instantly when the dead weight of a steel wheel hit the trap, arresting any further movement.

A C class locomotive waits at the Colombo Street level crossing while a 'Hills' type tram with trailer crosses, inward bound to Cathedral Square, Christchurch, in the 1950s. *Graham Stewart*

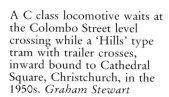

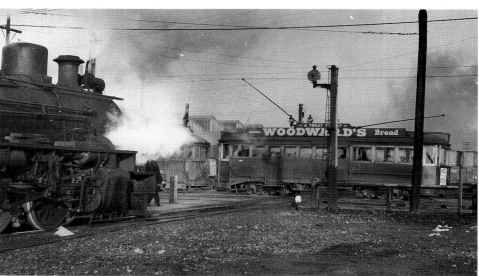

'I do like to be beside the seaside.' A double-decker tram with two double-decker trailers on the tramway causeway to Sumner. Rounding the curve in the background is Christchurch sprinkler tram No. 1. *Author's Collection*

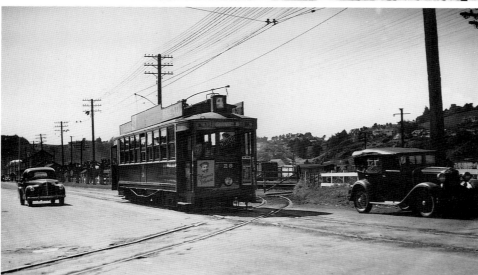

An industrial railway siding crossed the tram track in Taupo Quay, Wanganui. *W.W. Stewart*

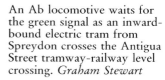

An Ab locomotive waits for the green signal as an inward-bound electric tram from Spreydon crosses the Antigua Street tramway-railway level crossing. *Graham Stewart*

TOP: Tram tracks being laid at the intersection of Pitt Street and Karangahape Road, Auckland, in 1902. *Author's Collection* RIGHT: The same intersection showing a Ponsonby-bound tram in 1908. *Muir & Moodie, John M. Bettle Collection* BELOW: The Pitt Street-Karangahape Road intersection shortly before the tram service to Point Chevalier was closed in 1953. *Graham Stewart*

The grandest of all tramway track junctions known as a 'grand union'. A bird's-eye view of the Queen and Customs Street intersection in Auckland from the top of the Dilworth Building. The upper tram is turning into Customs Street West. *Graham Stewart*

Safety measures for passengers as protection against the rising tide of motor cars in the 1920s included street safety zones, which were narrow platforms at kerb height, adjacent to the tram tracks. These were a boon for pedestrians, as intending passengers were in a safe position ready to board the car when it pulled up. Formerly, prospective passengers rushed out from under verandahs, dodging vehicular traffic and elbowing their way into the cars, much to the despair—and often to the discomfort—of old folk, women and children. Now everybody could be ready on the zone, enjoying sanctuary from the rush of vehicles screaming past. Motorists never really became accustomed to the zones, and rejoiced when they were finally removed with the trams.

In 1936 the then Minister of Transport, the Hon. Robert Semple, decreed that intending passengers must wait on the footpath until a tram stopped. Those who dashed madly out into the street did so not only at the risk of being knocked over by hurrying motorists, but also at the risk of being fined £2 for the infringement of a government regulation. A kerbside salute to the motorman was the technique expected, but people generally seemed unwilling to comply, probably because the average man or woman did not care much for making gestures in public.

Tram tracks had some advantages for motorists. By glueing one's eye to the outside track in heavy fog one could follow it to town with one's head peering out of the car window. Tram tracks had character, too, especially in their intricacy at junctions. The grandest of all tramway track junctions were in Auckland, where both the Wellesley Street and Customs Street junctions with Queen Street had an arrangement known in American tramway lore as a 'Grand Union'. This consisted of a right-angled intersection of two double tracks, with double-track connections in all four corners, permitting cars to make a 90-degree turn regardless of the direction from which they approached the intersection, or to proceed straight ahead. It involved four right-angle double-track crossings, with 16 pairs of tongue switches (points). Grand Unions were rare even in the world of tramways.

The relaying of the Queen and Customs Street 'grand union' in Auckland in the 1920s. The large flat-top freight tram No. 304 can be seen unloading sections of the complicated network of tracks. *Author's Collection*

A busy Christchurch Cathedral Square scene at the outbreak of the First World War in 1914, when most city people used trams to commute to and from their homes. *Press Collection, Alexander Turnbull Library*

"Well, you're always moaning about not being able to reduce the overhead."

Trouble overhead—repairmen fixing a break in the overhead wire at Invercargill. *Graham Stewart*

Auckland motor tower wagons
in the early 1920s. From left,
No. 2 of about 1912–14
vintage, No. 1 of about
1910–12 period and No. 3 of
about 1920–22. Windscreens
and cabs were fitted about
1928. *John Wolf*

Described at the time as a
'motor driven overhead
repairer, the first of its kind in
the Dominion. The latest
addition to the equipment of
the Wellington Municipal
Tramways.' *Weekly News*

The green tramway signal box at the Queen and Wellesley Street intersection during Auckland City Council tramway days. *Author's Collection*

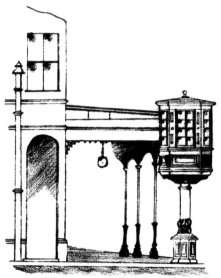

A drawing of the tramway switchman's tower on the corner of Queen Street and Wellesley Street West, Auckland. *Author's Collection*

At the Wellesley Street junction, mounted high upon a single pillar, was a green signal box from which all tramway traffic was directed by the flick of a lever. Semaphore signals at each corner indicated to motormen when, and when not, to proceed. The signalman had a responsible occupation, making sure that trams were sent on their right courses; he had to be careful not to switch an Avondale tram onto the Ponsonby route, or perhaps speed a carload of Mount Eden residents along the line to the zoo. Levers switched the various points on the street below, while plugs worked the semaphores. Traffic tallies in the 1940s showed 264 trams passing the box in the evening rush period from 4.15 pm to 5.15 pm; 153 passed on the 'up' track, an average of one every 32.4 seconds, and 111 came into town, an average of one every 32.4 seconds. From this remote perch a signalman would watch the city grow, see new fashions donned and discarded and a multitude of tiny incidents such as the day when an unfortunate predicament befell a certain motorman. It had been raining heavily and the tram rails had become swirling channels of water. The switching of a set of points caused a geyser of water to shoot upward, much to the discomfort of a woman upon whom it descended. For five minutes she held up the city's tramway system hurling abuse at a nearby motorman, who of course was absolutely blameless. The signalman was amused, and yet sorry, for he had not seen the woman when he pulled a lever at the switchboard.

The 2-metre octagonal cabin had all mod cons for signalmen who worked a straight eight and a half-hour shift—running water, a spirit heater for boiling up a brew and, under the sole seat, toilet amenities! Before the cabin was built, men controlled trams with flags by day and lamps by night.

The Wellesley/Queen Street signal box showing one of the semaphore arm signals on the pole in the foreground. *Jim Housego, Author's Collection*

Hazards of the Line

Hazards on the road for tramwaymen in the course of their duty have always been many and varied. During the long history of tramways in New Zealand countless millions were carried from their suburban homes to town centres and back in comparative safety. But no history of urban transport would be complete without reference to the 1903 Christmas Eve tragedy in Auckland which shocked the country. A heavily laden double-decker, No. 39, carrying carefree men, women and children on their way to a final shopping spree in Queen Street, was travelling from Kingsland just after dark with motorman Fred Humphrey at the controls. In Eden Terrace the car stopped, but the handbrake ratchet apparently failed and the car started to roll backwards downhill. Much to the consternation of the passengers the tram-car gained speed rapidly and the trolley-pole slipped off the overhead wire, plunging the interior into darkness. As the vehicle's speed increased, the trolley-pole swung back, hitting a cross wire and striking passengers seated on the open upper deck, instantly killing one unfortunate young woman.

Motorman Humphrey then ran to the other end of the tram and tried to brake

A drawing of the fatal 1903 Christmas Eve tram accident at Kingsland, Auckland, by an *Auckland Weekly News* artist, from accounts supplied by eyewitnesses. *Auckland Weekly News*

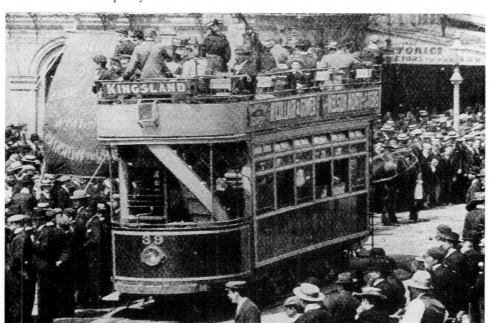

The rogue Auckland tram, double-decker No. 39, which ran away down Eden Terrace on Christmas Eve 1903, killing three people and injuring more than 50. *Author's Collection*

153

Another drawing by the *Auckland Weekly News* artist of the 1903 fatal Christmas Eve accident at Kingsland, Auckland, showing the wounded receiving attention. *Auckland Weekly News*

the heavy car, but his efforts were to no avail. By now the passengers were frantic, the women screaming and clutching their terrified children. After travelling for nearly 800 metres at a terrific speed, the uncontrollable vehicle, lurching from side to side, rounded the bend by the old Rocky Nook bowling green. Ahead the horrified passengers saw the headlight of another loaded city-bound car. Ernest Thompson, the motorman of this car, combination No. 32, just had time to slam his vehicle into reverse and shout a warning to his passengers but collision was inevitable. The concussion of the two trams colliding was heard over a large area of Auckland, the initial impact being followed by piercing shrieks and agonised groans. Several passengers were hurled from the top deck.

Lights were fetched from nearby homes to facilitate the rescue operations until another tram arrived to illuminate the scene of the wreck — a scene that resembled a battlefield. Women had fainted in the tangled wreckage, blocking doorways, forcing rescuers to lift people on stretchers through broken windows. Not a pane of glass remained intact in either car, and seats wrenched from their fastenings by the shock pinned passengers in a heap inside the combination car. G.C. Marris, who was a passenger, remarked later: 'Though I saw some pretty ugly things during the Boer War, I never saw such an indescribably sad and sickening sight as that at the Kingsland car accident.' Three people lost their lives and more than 50 were injured, some of them seriously. It was a miracle that the casualty list was not greater. The Premier, the Rt Hon. R.J. Seddon, sent a message on behalf of the government to the Mayor of Auckland, the Hon. E. Mitchelson, expressing sympathy with the many people who had suffered as a result of the accident. The inquest into the accident was held before H.W. Brabant, SM, and a jury. The jury found that the cause of the collision was 'the ratchet brake's failure to act, causing motorman Humphrey to lose his head, and through his want of knowledge he did not use the other brake'. The jury also considered that the tramways company's mode of teaching motormen and conductors was inadequate and recommended that more stringent measures should be adopted. The failure of the ratchet brake remained a mystery as the tram-car's damaged state hid any evidence, but the company admitted liability and paid all claims.

Similar circumstances surrounded a tragedy on the Brooklyn Hill in Wellington on the evening of 3 May 1907, when a Palace tram hurtled backwards out of control. A smaller Palace tram grinding up the incline behind saw the runaway flying down the track on a collision course and due to hit within seconds. Fortunately for this following tram, which had 40 passengers on board, the runaway failed to negotiate the curve at right angles to the top of Nairn Street. It capsized and came to rest down an embankment. Fifty people had stared death in the face, but,

Looking down on the tramway embankment that led to the Wellington suburb of Brooklyn, showing the overturned Palace tram which ran out of control in May 1907. *A.P. Godber, Author's Collection*

although many were cut and injured, all escaped except one woman, who lay dead under the wreckage.

Open fronts in Auckland, a hangover from the horse-cars, did have their advantages on at least two occasions. In Khyber Pass Road one evening, two small children ran onto the line in front of a car driven by motorman Bach, who rang the gong and applied the emergency brake. But the children made no effort to get out of the way until the car was almost on them, when the little boy stepped out of harm's way. The other child, a little girl named Peek, did not move. It seemed that the child would be under the car before it came to a standstill. Certain death was averted by the motorman, who leaned forward over the dashboard and grasped the child by the hair, lifting her onto the car. Passengers were loud in their praise of the motorman's prompt and timely action. The following evening the father of the little girl left a gold-mounted greenstone tiepin for motorman Bach at the *Herald* office as a mark of his appreciation.

The Brooklyn tram smash of 1907. People viewing the capsized tram the following morning, while a small four-wheeled tram grinds up the hill. *Author's Collection*

Another near-miss happened in Hobson Street when a small boy ran out in front of car No. 13—not the luckiest number to tackle. There was no time to stop the car, so the motorman, a Mr Smith, leaned over the front and threw the child clear of the line, much to the astonishment and admiration of passengers.

Then there was the night a drunk went to sleep right across the rails, with no other traffic about to disturb his slumbers. Escaping a terrible death by centimetres, the prostrate man was picked up by the crew and dumped on the platform for delivery to the police station. Later that night the same tram hit the nightcart on the last trip. Depot staff who cleaned the damaged tram understandably asked for some kind of bonus.

As a rule when these bulky rail-borne vehicles tangled with other road users, their size, weight and dominating strength made them the victor in terms of damage sustained. However, an Auckland City Council steam roller evened the score one morning in Symonds Street when it collided with a packed car conveying city businessmen. Among those who received minor injuries was my grandfather, Charles Bowden. The paper reported that the tram was left in a 'serious state'! There were the foolish pranks by mischievous lads who placed stones on the lines, but on the whole boys respected the steel rails and the hero of the school in 1908 was the lad who had spotted a new tram that his mates hadn't yet seen.

Sometimes Lady Luck rode the rails. An electric car once descended a slope with the motorman watching horrified from the roadway where he had landed. It was a common practice for motormen, on changing the destination indicator, to lean outward, gripping a stanchion while they checked the sign. This rather dangerous habit had ended with the motorman falling onto the roadway. Fortunately his mate was not busy inside collecting fares, but standing on the back platform, where he viewed with astonishment his motorman sprawled on the ground as the tram trundled sedately past. A quick sprint to the front cab by the conductor saved the day.

Equally as shattering as Halley's Comet flashing across the sky in 1910 was the flight of a late tram to Onehunga in Auckland one night. Down the Khyber Pass sped No. 111, known as 'Lord Nelson' in the service. As though on a path plotted by a computer, Lord Nelson parted from the rails on reaching the curve into Broadway, Newmarket, and careered across the road. With only centimetres to spare on each side, it ran neatly into an alleyway by the Royal George Hotel without sustaining a scratch. His hotel still intact, the relieved publican opened all bars and provided drinks on the house for the shaken passengers. The motorman, it seemed, had obliged a friend early in the day by helping him to move house, and had fallen asleep passing the brewery. Old No. 111 was given a new name that night, 'Halley's Comet'. The man at the controls who had gone to sleep, was, believe it or not, named Halley!

Auckland tram No. 111, which ran out of control down Khyber Pass Road and into the alleyway by the Royal George Hotel without sustaining any damage. *Author's Collection*

Invercargill tram No. 13 after colliding with a fully loaded gravel truck on the South Invercargill line in September 1950. *Hazeledine's Studio*

Like humans, some tram-cars were prone to accidents, and others went through life without a scratch. Dunedin had an outlaw, No. 51, which was always in trouble, clocking up a record number of accidents. Two of her escapades involved serious runaways, first at Andersons Bay in 1947, and again on the Caversham Hill in 1952. After this last misdemeanour, which sent nine people to hospital, the transport department had had enough and scrapped the outlaw. The only two serious head-on collisions in Wanganui both happened at the same corner — known to the local inhabitants as Hospital Corner — and a metal truck arguing the right of the road in Invercargill wrote off the first tram to be dismantled in the Southland centre, No. 13. In many aircraft today you will notice that seat No. 13 does not exist, and most private bus companies have no No. 13 bus in their fleets. For some years all Wellington trams involved in serious accidents had numbers ending in five. The Brooklyn Hill runaway was No. 55; others were 95 in the Tinakori Road runaway, 105 in the Pirie Street accident, and the last head-on encounter between tram and bus in Courtenay Place the night before trams ceased running to Island Bay despatched No. 255 to the scrap heap.

While a crew had a meal break one afternoon, an Auckland tram left in Ponsonby Road, Three Lamps, wandered off unattended and rounded the corner into Jervois Road where, encouraged by a drop in grade, it clattered out to Herne Bay, a distance of more than a kilometre. The Curran Steet corner was taken with ease, but with no one on board to check the speed, the old car derailed at the Wallace Street corner and shot across the road into a low wall fronting a modern block of flats. An unusual twist to this story is that the tram had come to rest on a property which many years before had housed the main tramway depot. No. 133 had returned to its first home by itself.

BELOW LEFT: Runaway Auckland tram No. 133 after coming to rest at the corner of Jervois Road and Wallace Street in January 1948. BELOW: The corner of Jervois Road and Wallace Street when the Ponsonby Tramway Depot was situated on this site. *Author's Collection*

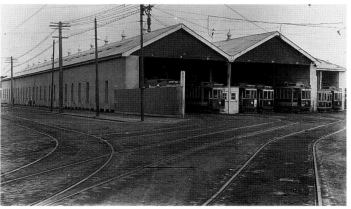

 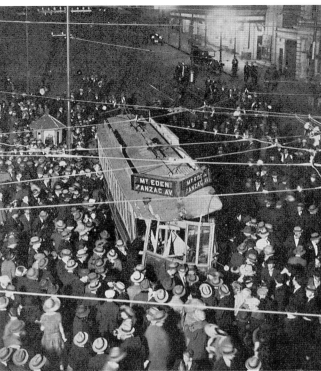

The Wellesley Street East runaway tram which finally came to a stop outside the Civic Theatre, Auckland. The photograph above shows the front of the tram with a motor car crushed by the impact. The right-hand photograph shows the back of the tram which was hit by another tram and then ran out of control. *Auckland Weekly News*

Men proved that they were made of the right material in moments of imminent catastrophe. Motorman Daniel Ferguson of Auckland, a short and stocky Scotsman, stood firmly at the controls, although he knew it was beyond his ability to stop a runaway car. He did not desert his post, but remained in his cab, sounding the foot gong strongly to warn motorists and pedestrians as the car gathered speed down the Wellesley Street East hill and plunged across Queen Street to strike a motor car outside the property on which the Civic Theatre now stands. Ferguson had stayed calmly at the front and, by a miracle, was not injured. His conductor, Bill Porteous, who was standing on the back platform, when another tram had crashed into the back, rendering all braking power useless, had his left foot jammed in the wreckage. Porteous had to stand helpless as the car careered down the hill, his foot not being released until the tram left the rails and some of the wreckage moved in the final lurch across Queen Street.

Then there was the time at a certain depot where a crew had an understanding between themselves to allow the motorman to catch the last ferryboat of the night. On entering the depot, the motorman would give the controller one notch, the slowest speed at which a tram can run, then jump off and away to catch his boat. His conductor had the routine down to a fine art. He would walk through the car, throwing over all the seat backs, nicely timing his arrival at the front to switch off and stop the tram at the end of the track. It was quite a smooth arrangement until the night the two men came face to face in the signing-off room, through some misunderstanding. A resounding crash and the tinkle of broken glass falling made them both realise it was time to sign off — completely!

Perhaps the most unlucky person ever to travel by tram was Henry Williamson of Mount Eden, who in 1911 gave up his seat to a woman and stood on the back platform, only to be killed when another tram ploughed into the rear. Other meetings with the fair sex had happy endings. In September 1925 a female leopard escaped from the Auckland Zoo, making everyone jittery, particularly after dark. Children were kept home from school and tension mounted as the missing beast was sighted all over the city. On a late tram to Grey Lynn while the scare was at its height, a young woman rang the buzzer for her stop, and was about to alight into the night, when fellow passengers started encouraging the conductor to escort the woman safely to her gate. With the approval of the motorman, who said he would take the tram down to the terminus on his own and pick him up on the way back, the conductor set off to deliver his passenger to her home without the fear of being eaten alive. From this chance encounter stemmed a romance which blossomed into marriage.

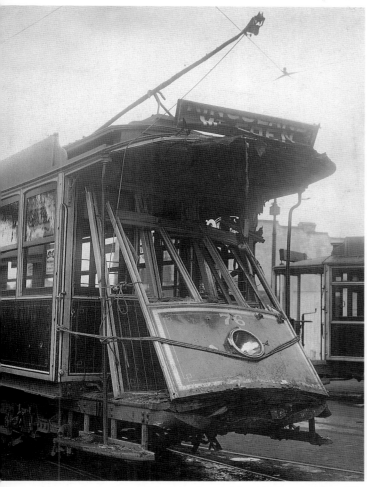
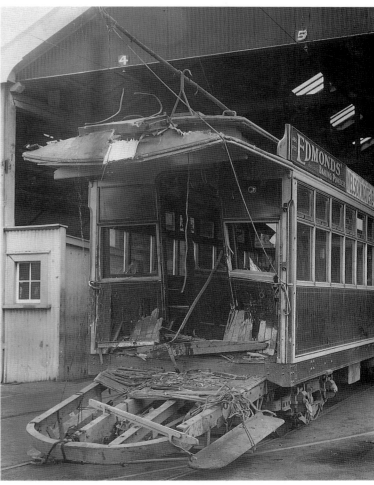

The back platform of Auckland tram No. 76 (above), where Henry Williamson lost his life in 1911. The photograph (right), of the front of the runaway tram No. 80, shows the immense impact of the collision. *Author's Collection*

'It's quite simple really — he saw me running for the tram, he stopped, I didn't.'

'If you women would wear hats that didn't blow off it'd save a heck of a lot of time!'

An illuminated tram caused as much excitement in town as did the arrival of a travelling circus. This handsome illuminated double-decker tram-car, with a New Zealand flag reproduced in electric lights on each side, celebrated the end of the war in 1918. The decker, Auckland No. 17, carried the topical destination 'Peace'. *Price, Author's Collection*

Wellingtonians use the vantage point of a combination tram in Lower Cuba Street to view a procession, c. 1918. *Press Collection, Alexander Turnbull Library*

A heavy fall of snow in Cathedral Square, Christchurch, during the peace celebrations of 1919. The Papanui-bound tram on the left is a former double-decker converted to single-deck only after an accident on the Sumner line. *Author's Collection*

160

CHAPTER EIGHT

Flivvers and Charabancs

A new age was dawning as servicemen returned from the First World War. Free spending and optimism were high, both servicemen and those who were making profits from the rising land prices investing in motor cars which were by now accepted as a reasonably cheap and reliable alternative to the horse. Petrol bowsers replaced stables, and motor-car trade names such as Oakland, Ford, Moon, Essex, Hudson, Chandler, Buick, Dodge and Chevrolet became household names. Roads built for horse-drawn transport saw increased activity with cars and charabancs ranging from expensive makes to old 'bangers'. The war had been responsible for rapid and dramatic strides in the design and manufacture of petrol engines, which could be readily adapted for passenger transport vehicles. No longer was the motor-bus a temperamental babe in napkins. It had achieved respectability and maturity, and in the cities was presenting a challenge to the smug electric streetcars of an earlier generation.

By the mid-1920s most tramway authorities had motor-buses on their establishment—Fishers, Uniteds, Guys, Grahams, Republics, Whites, Minervas, Leylands, Stewarts, AECs, Thornycrofts, Reos and Dennis's, to mention just a few of the makes available. Most consisted of modified lorry chassis fitted with ungainly box-shaped bodies, but they were flexible because they were not restricted to rails. Feeder services from tram terminals to new housing developments were their primary field and others gave service to districts hitherto completely starved of public transport. Wanganui had Vulcans, while New Plymouth possessed an Edison battery bus, both types slow and bone-jarring on their solid rubber tyres; Christchurch, apart from a mixed bag of petrol omnibuses, had two Tilling-Stevens petrol-electric vehicles and a lofty Walker storage-battery bus, known as the 'Beetle'. For the 1925-26 New Zealand and South Seas Exhibition in Dunedin—apart from a special tramline and the introduction of trailers—20 motor-buses ushered in a new era. The word 'Tramways' became a common sight on the side panels of buses.

Tramway Corporation motor-buses (below). LEFT: New Plymouth Municipal Tramways Edison battery bus. *Author's Collection* MIDDLE: Wanganui Corporation Tramways Vulcan bus. *Tesla Collection, Alexander Turnbull Library* RIGHT: No. 7 of the Dunedin City Corporation. *Russell Grigg Collection* BOTTOM: The special tramline which was laid to serve the Dunedin and South Seas Exhibition in 1925. *Hocken Library, University of Otago*

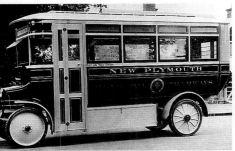

The quietest of them all. The Christchurch Tramway Board's Walker storage-battery bus is given a royal welcome on its first journey to Islington. *Press Collection, Alexander Turnbull Library*

On the domestic front the Ford Model T was rapidly superseding the family horse. One owner said his Ford should be buried with him because he had never had it in a hole it couldn't get out of! Speed, and movement ungoverned by timetables, became the object of the day as the 'Tin Lizzies' put the country on wheels.

To overcome restrictions imposed by the Wellington-Hutt Road Railway Improvement Act, the first trackless tram — today we would call it a trolley bus — came to Wellington in 1924. The act had been pushed through Parliament in 1905 by the then Minister of Railways, Sir Joseph Ward, to prevent the laying of electric tramlines on the Hutt Road and so to stifle any possibility of competition between tramways and railways. Sir Joseph had never forgiven the Auckland Electric Tramways Company for running a service in competition with the Auckland-Onehunga railway, thereby capturing practically all the passenger traffic. Since 1914 the Wellington City Council had asked for legislation to be amended to allow the city to extend its tramway service to Onslow Borough, along the Hutt Road to Kaiwarra (now Kaiwharawhara). A trackless tram running on solid rubber tyres, its twin overhead wires only 23 centimetres apart, was the loophole in the legislation which gave Onslow a connection with the city. From the tramway terminus at the north end of Thorndon Quay, wires ran along the Hutt Road to the junction with the Ngaio Gorge Road, where a loop was provided to turn the trackless trolley.

The birth of the first trackless tram-car in New Zealand. Wellington city fathers beside the forerunner of the modern trolley bus, outside the Kaiwharawhara Post Office in 1924. *Author's Collection*

The venerable ancestor of all the trolley buses to follow, this archaic vehicle was described as 'a lumberer with built-in discomfort', and was said by some unkind types to be a hybrid of a piecart. The insults may have been hurled because its

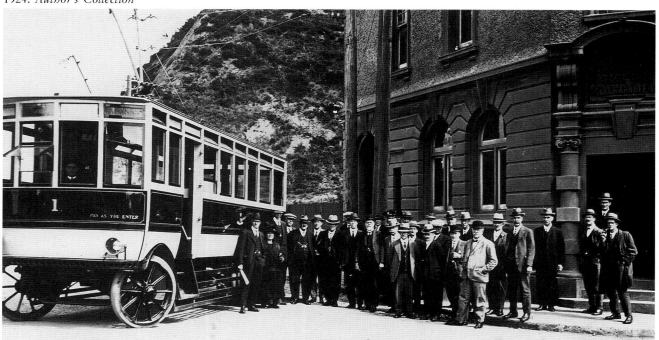

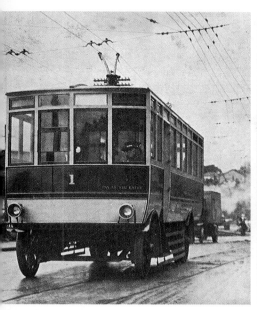

birthplace had been Auckland, where the body had been built by D.S.C. and Cousins and Cousins Limited, makers of Auckland trams. At a top speed of 27 kilometres an hour, this new pacemaker of travel inaugurated the twin-wire service in October 1924. So aware of the historical significance were the city fathers who made the maiden trip, that the first motorman, Harry Anderson, spent the rest of the day driving children under the wires at the expense of the council. On the first cash-in-hand day, even though, as one report said, 'it was washing day, and that makes quite a difference', between 500 and 600 people tried the car for comfort and convenience, every tram-car to the Thorndon terminus being met.

It was stated that the overhead wiring had cost approximately £750, whereas to lay and equip a double tramline over an equal length of roadway would have cost something like £13,000. Great ammunition for the bus promoters! Nevertheless the trackless tram was before its time. It did not possess any of the qualities associated with the trolley buses of the 1950s and bowed to competition from motor-buses from Wellington to the Hutt Valley and Khandallah in May 1932.

Although the Auckland Electric Tramways Company's contract did not expire until 1932, long negotiations leading to the purchase of the tramways by the city council ended in June 1919, when a poll of ratepayers sanctioned the raising of a loan. The changeover followed on 1 July 1919. The council had not been long in the chair when opposition from private buses running on tram routes threatened to cripple the undertaking and suspend plans to extend track mileage. All the trouble started when the city council ousted the private motor-buses from their stands in

Two views of the pioneer Wellington trackless tram-car which ran between Thorndon and Kaiwharawhara along the Hutt Road during trial runs. Auckland Weekly News and Author's Collection

The Wellington trackless tram-car on the Hutt Road. E.T. Robson, Auckland Weekly News

Gallagher's buses, which ran a service to Point Chevalier, Auckland in the 1920s before the arrival of the electric trams. *Richard Sterling, Author's Collection*

A red-letter day at Roseneath, Wellington, in June 1926, was the introduction of a bus service on the reformed Carlton Gore Road. At the opening ceremony was the Mayor of Wellington, C.J.B. (later Sir Charles) Norwood, and members of the Roseneath and Oriental Bay Ratepayers' Association. *Author's Collection*

front of the post office, where they had catered for tourists and sightseers, or to run to places not served by trams. On being relegated to a side street where custom was poor, the private buses decided to recoup some of their losses by plying for fares on the tram routes. This was the start of the famous bus versus tram war which lasted until the Motor Omnibus Traffic Act became law on 1 November 1926. 'Pirate buses', as they were called, challenged trams on most routes, racing neck and neck from stop to stop. The results surprised even the bus men. Stopping only where required to pick up and set down passengers, drawing alongside the kerb, and charging only tram fares, they were simply rushed by the public — a public tired of waiting while fully laden tram-cars passed with chains up at busy hours. In an incredibly short space of time there were dozens of buses on the roads, running everywhere, and in almost every instance well patronised. No longer did the chains go up on the trams. They loaded up to the limit; passageways, platforms and even steps were used to carry standing passengers. It seemed a far cry from company days when the council wagged its finger every time a tram was caught with even one passenger standing over the regulation limit.

BELOW: The first Auckland City Council Tramways motor-bus which started a service to Parnell in October 1924. *Author's Collection*
BELOW RIGHT: These lumbering monsters with solid tyres were later shod with inflated tyres. *Author's Collection*

Omnibus competition spread south to the other main cities. The Christchurch Tramway Board, for example, endeavoured to combat the bus menace by stepping up the acceleration rate of some trams. In Wanganui, a city slicker from Auckland placed buses in opposition to trams running to Aramoho and Wanganui East. The Wanganui Council quickly diverted some of its new buses to compete with the pirates, who had been running just ahead of the trams and scooping up all fares offering. Leap-frogging stops, the buses moved people to and from the city at high speed, but the pace could not last and Mr Private Enterprise from Auckland was off Wanganui's streets inside a month.

Early in 1925 the Christchurch Tramway Board asked the Auckland City Council to join in calling a conference to consider the control of privately owned competitive bus services throughout New Zealand. The Motor Omnibus Traffic Act resulted. All bus services in competition with publicly owned services were taken over, although private companies had the right to stay if they charged twopence more for each section above the tram fare, a clause that made economic operation out of the question. If the two opposing services had remained it could only have ended in bankruptcy for both. But, in some cases, the Auckland City Council seemed to use high-handed methods to squash all bus services within a wide radius under the act, for some had not been totally in opposition to the trams.

Sid Gallagher and Richard Sterling had been running buses to Point Chevalier since 1922 on modern lines with regular schedules and a fleet of six buses, five Reos and one Republic. Trams at this stage were not running in the district, the nearest line being Surrey Crescent, 5 kilometres away. As the pirate bus war reached its peak, the tramways suddenly extended their empire and placed three Thornycroft buses on the Point Chevalier route to skim the cream off the peak-hour loading at ridiculously low fares. Private enterprise men like Gallagher and Sterling lost heavily in 1926 because of this council opposition and were forced to sell without compensation for any goodwill they had created in the district. In an attempt to counter the act, community buses, fitted with boxes in which passengers could place a 'donation', ran in defiance until the Magistrates' Court ruled that they were omnibuses and were running illegally.

It takes two to tango. A Model T Ford and delivery truck in a close manoeuvre around the tramway centre pole in the middle of the Queen and Customs Street intersection, Auckland. On the right is a 'pirate' bus running on Dominion Road for the Atlas Bus Company. *Author's Collection*

ABOVE: Downtown Auckland in the early 1920s. The main city terminal for electric trams was in front of the post office in lower Queen Street.

RIGHT: Wanganui in the mid-1920s. A view looking up Victoria Avenue from the Ridgway Street intersection showing a tram and trailer heading for Wanganui East. The trailer had started life as an electric tram.

BELOW: This scene of Lambton Quay, Wellington, in the 1920s was starting to look busy with the increase in motor car traffic and a motor bike with a sidecar travelling at speed. *All photographs from S.C. Smith Collection, Alexander Turnbull Library*

TOP: Cathedral Square, Christchurch, in the 1920s, in the days when electric trams dominated the Square.
S.C. Smith, Author's Collection ABOVE: Tram-cars passing through Princes Street, Dunedin, bound for the suburbs.
Author's Collection

The two passenger ferries built by the Takapuna Tramways and Ferry Company for their Auckland to Bayswater service. The original ferry *Pupuke* (right) was built in 1909, and the *Lake Takapuna* (left) in 1924. *W.W. Stewart*

The cut-throat transport competition of the mid-1920s was to sound the death-knell of the Takapuna Tramways and Ferry Company, which was just recovering from the strain of rolling-stock shortages resulting from the First World War. Restrictions included running every alternate tram only as far as Minnehaha Avenue, gross overcrowding and cancelled trips.

Two powerful American Baldwin locomotives had arrived in 1919 to take over the burden while the older iron horses were given renewed life. These new Yankee steam locomotives were lifted across the harbour by the harbour board's floating crane, to be greeted by a spontaneous chorus of cheers from a workers' ferry which was pulling away from the jetty packed to the gunwales. To handle the increase in passengers, the paddle ferry *Britannia* was bought from the Devonport Steam Ferry Company and upgraded; furthermore, the company built a large ferry of majestic lines, the *Lake Takapuna*. In 1924 the final locomotive was purchased, to complete a fleet of seven locomotives and 14 carriages.

More troubles were in store. Supplies of coke became unobtainable and coal had to be substituted, giving rise to a stream of complaints about the smoke nuisance. Motorists had to stop their cars, as it was impossible to get a clear view of the road ahead. It was found that Westport coal gave off less smoke than other types.

Electric power was still on the horizon, however. The British Electric Traction Company had sent E. Parry, an electrical engineer, out from London in 1923, and London had then forwarded a definite tender to carry out the work. But the source of power was the burning question. It was not practicable for the company to electrify without supplying power for the lighting of North Shore boroughs, and the boroughs were under an agreement with the government to take a supply of Arapuni-generated power from the national grid. Intentions were to use the existing 14 trailers and to build six new cars. Ten old cars would be used as trailers and four old and six new cars would be motorised. Trams would be run comprising two

One of two Baldwin steam-tram locomotives, No. 6, imported by the Takapuna Tramways and Ferry Company in 1919, seen hauling a train of three trailers in Shakespeare Road, Milford. *Author's Collection*

motored cars and two trailers or one motored car with one trailer. The company decided not to go ahead with electrification until the motor-bus regulations were gazetted. Meanwhile the Takapuna Borough Council was granted an option to purchase, which was approved by a poll in November 1926, but which was later stalled by legal action taken by residents.

To help the company get a monopoly and electrify, the council, as licensing authority, then cancelled all bus licences between Takapuna and Devonport. This move wiped out all Devonport buses which had carried good loads and had competed severely with the trams for the past three years. Immediately war was declared by the Devonport Steam Ferry Company, which promptly put on a fleet of seven-seater Hudson limousines between Devonport and Milford. These vehicles were not omnibuses under the act and did not require licensing. The novelty of such comfortable transit at undercut fares saw the Devonport limousines well patronised, even though the tramway company met the situation with a bus service to Bayswater. Nevertheless, the limousines won the day, and in April 1927 brought the tramway company to a standstill, the debenture holders selling the ferry assets to the Devonport Steam Ferry Company.

Overnight the buff funnels of the steamers *Lake Takapuna* and *Pupuke* had been painted black like those of the Devonport company's fleet, and all passengers from Bayswater were carried by A.H. Smith's fleet of 10 yellow buses and the four vehicles formerly owned by the tramway company. A touch of humour was provided by some clever caricatures executed in white paint on the windows of a butcher's shop at Hall's Corner, Takapuna. They depicted the portly uniformed figure of the borough traffic inspector stopping a tramway locomotive, while a cow was shown singing 'Say au revoir, but not good-bye'. The Devonport ferry company was shown as a rooster crowing loudly.

TOP LEFT: The last locomotive purchased by the Takapuna Tramways and Ferry Company in 1924, a Kerr Stuart, seen with trailers in King Edward Avenue. *W.W. Stewart* LOWER LEFT: A victorious motor-bus passes a steam-tram at Hall's Corner on the last day the trams ran on the North Shore of Auckland. BELOW: A new lease of life ahead. The former Takapuna tramway trailers, which were shipped south to Wanganui, are lifted by the Auckland Harbour Board floating crane *Mahua. Author's Collection*

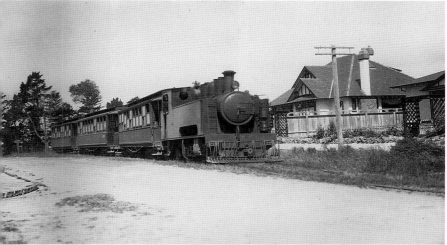

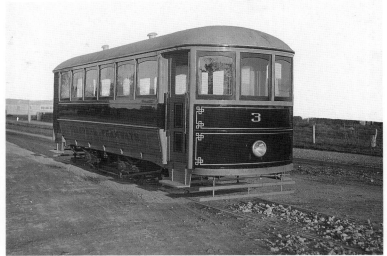

ABOVE: The first of two Gisborne battery trams built by Boon and Company, of Christchurch, at the Ormond Road terminus in 1917. *Author's Collection* ABOVE RIGHT: A Lytton Road battery tram leaving the Gisborne Post Office in Gladstone Road shortly before the system closed in 1929. *S.C. Smith, Author's Collection*

The Gisborne Borough Council was still struggling with its Edison battery trams, having just scraped through the First World War, thanks to a new tram obtained in 1917 and the arrival of the fourth and final addition to the fleet in 1919. Pitched battles had continued at Gisborne with W.D. Lysnar still contending that battery trams were winners if the tracks could be extended to the suburbs he had first proposed when mayor. Truly devoted to the cause, Lysnar in 1918 offered to supervise completion of the work and to pay any difference between the revenue and the expenses. Lytton Road, at Te Hapara, now marked the end of the line along Gladstone Road and in November 1923, with the opening of the Peel Street bridge, the last extension along Ormond Road to the borough boundary was inaugurated. Beyond the laying of rails on the Gladstone Road bridge in 1925, no further trackwork was undertaken and the little trams never reached Kaiti or Wainui Beach.

In 1922 Frederick Black, of Wellington, a noted tramway engineer who had been responsible for the Napier and New Plymouth installations and who had prepared reports on electric overhead systems for Palmerston North and Timaru, was asked to investigate the Gisborne tramways. During the following year A.R. Harris, of Christchurch, New Zealand agent for Edison Batteries, presented a report, and a third report was presented by a committee of three from the Public Works Department. Report after report was obtained in a hopeless endeavour to find some means of keeping the service running, but eventually it was decided to ask the ratepayers to sanction proposals for scrapping the system.

Lysnar put up a great fight, together with a citizens' committee formed to stop the move. Three polls were held, each giving a decision to discontinue the service. The first was annulled; luck was with the tram supporters, for on the night before the poll the Governor-General had signed the new Tramways Act and the Gisborne poll was therefore taken under the wrong act! The second poll was vetoed on a technical point, after much lobbying by the 'anti-scrap' group. Then finally, in June 1928, the third poll gave the clear mandate the council was seeking. Four buses had been taken over from L.H. Cohen under the Omnibus Act and these could be used to supplement the inefficient battery-powered tram-cars.

Within a week buses replaced the battery cars on the Ormond Road line from 7 am to 3 pm, and in November buses took over all services on this branch. July 1929 saw the tramway completely discarded in favour of motor-buses. A brave showing by the old warriors was made on the last day, when the whole fleet of four trams made a farewell procession in convoy from the Gisborne Post Office along Gladstone Road back to the depot.

The final round-up. The Gisborne battery tram fleet, which comprised only four trams, on the final day of service, 8 July 1929. *Author's Collection*

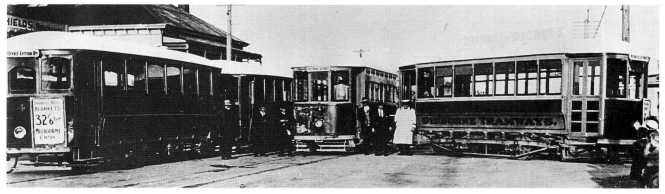

All local authorities conducting tramway services, with the exception of Napier, now maintained auxiliary motor-bus services. Motor-bus competition and the increasing use of the private motor car was troubling tramways the world over. Some car manufacturers had been able to market light cars costing little more than £200, and a vehicle only a few years old could be bought second-hand for a few pounds. In 1927 petrol cost only 1/5 for every 4 litres. Most of the smaller towns had cut the wages bill in half by introducing one-man trams, but despite the uncertainty of the decade, the need to keep pace with New Zealand's gradually increasing population saw more than 200 new trams and trailers introduced in the 1920s, as well as the extension of routes in some cities. Wellington alone built 92 trams during this period and opened the Northland branch. The ride to the top of the hill, in terms of electric tracks traversing thoroughfares in cities and boroughs throughout New Zealand, reached a peak in 1929 with over 270 route kilometres of lines. The total

This old horse was still available for hire in Christchurch during the 1920s. *Author's Collection*

Oriental Bay, Wellington, when trams were still the monarchs of the streets. *Wellington Tramways*

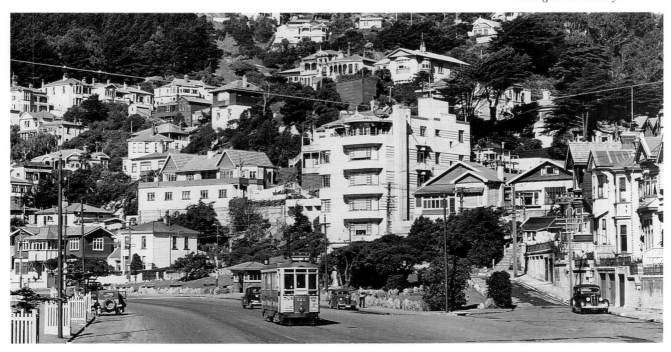

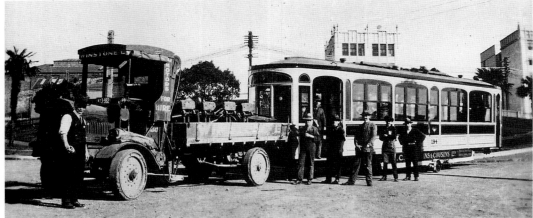

Auckland continued to build new trams throughout the 1920s and 1930s. ABOVE: The body of No. 194 being hauled on a low trailer along Princes Street from the builders, D.S.C. and Cousins and Cousins Ltd, in 1925. *Author's Collection* ABOVE RIGHT: The Auckland Transport Board started building its own tramcars in the 1930s. *Author Collection*

length of running track, including double sections and loops, was 420 kilometres, approximating the distance by road from Hamilton to Palmerston North, or Picton to Ashburton. Passengers carried on the Dominion's electric lines in 1925 reached 167,677,057, a total that was only surpassed during the Second World War.

In January 1929 all services in Auckland were taken over from the city council by the newly formed Auckland Transport Board, following a commission of inquiry into transport for the Auckland metropolitan district. During the council's regime, the unpopularity of feeder bus services had been notable and the city ratepayers had shown their disinclination to spend further money in districts not under their control. J.A.C. (later Sir John) Allum, who had been chairman of the council's tramways committee, became the first chairman of the board. Under his guidance the final major extensions of the Auckland tramways were constructed in the early 1930s and 40 new trams built, giving much needed employment to workers hit by the worldwide Depression. The only proposal not carried out was the Quay Street loop, from Queen Street around into Quay Street, and up Albert Street. The council, while operating the tramways, had purchased Gladstone Buildings, situated where Air New Zealand House now stands, and had formulated plans to make a complex tram station, with rows of tracks and platforms. This ambitious scheme, which would have been unique in New Zealand, was not destined to reach fruition.

Rail-less electric trolley buses were considered in 1929 for Point Chevalier, from Surrey Crescent and for a cross-city service to Avondale. Trolley buses to Blockhouse Bay, New Lynn, Glen Eden and Henderson were ruled out after investigation because the headways (the intervals between each bus) would be too great to justify the installation of overhead wires, electrical feeders and other equipment.

To talk of steam-propelled road vehicles may have been considered heretic in this new age of petrol, had it not been for the enterprise of A. and G. Price Limited of Thames, who built an experimental Doble steam bus in 1931 for the Auckland

The first Auckland tram to Avondale, No. 246, although still showing the destination 'Mt Albert', reached the terminus at the junction of Rosebank and Great North Roads in January 1932. *Author's Collection*

Transport Board. The feature of the steam bus which commanded attention was the entire absence of a geared transmission. The flexible steam unit provided a range of speeds from a mere crawl to 95 and more kilometres an hour by the simple process of admitting more steam to the engine, a very different matter from the handling of three or more gears in the gearbox of a vehicle powered by an internal combustion engine, especially the primitive 'crash' boxes of the pre-synchromesh era. The very compact Doble steam engine, which was the finest of its kind, was slung in the chassis just forward of the rear wheels. Under the bonnet was the steam generator (substituting for a conventional boiler), which in the main consisted of a long coil of tubing. Water was forced into one end and high-pressure steam flashed out the other end, being conducted to the two-cylinder engine which operated at a pressure of about 8275 kPa (1,200 lb per square inch). The fire which heated the generator coils used crude oil for fuel. The makers claimed that weight for weight and power for power the cost of operating a steam vehicle was about one-third the expense of a petrol-powered machine.

A report in the *New Zealand Herald* at the time said: 'The bus sped along the road to Pt Chevalier at 50 miles an hour, reckless of speed limits, and moved off from a standstill on a steep slope silently and smoothly.' High hopes were held for the establishment of a fleet of these silent, smooth-running vehicles, and for a local industry employing up to 500 men to build them. But the impressive performance on the trial did not last. The 240 metres of mild-steel tubing used in steam generation would not stand the intense heat, and to alleviate this, the temperature and pressure in the system were reduced, but the resulting performance was too poor to be suitable. Only three of these buses were built by A. and G. Price. The second bus was demonstrated in chassis form at the Auckland Winter Exhibition in 1931. About nine years later a suburban transport company fitted a body and carried out trial runs with the vehicle. However, it was never used for public transport. The third completed bus was used on the Auckland–Thames service by a private company for about three months before it was withdrawn and sent to Australia.

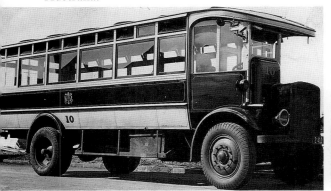

In 1922 the Napier City Council extended the tracks south along Hastings Street. A picture of the triangle junction being laid at the Dickens and Hastings Streets intersection. Telecom House now stands on this corner. *Author's Collection*

Napier now possessed an impressively large triangular tramway junction at the Dickens Street-Hastings Street intersection, and the line southward along Hastings Street had reached McGrath Street, with the ever-troublesome railway line blocking any further progress. This all happened in July 1922, when Syd Otton drove the first tram south. The burning question of how the two railway crossings at McGrath and Jull Streets were to be economically negotiated, thus facilitating completion of the southern circuit, vexed the council. Councillor W. Harvey suggested that conductors of trams carry red 'danger' flags and that they walk ahead of the tram when approaching the railway line. Crossing keepers employed by the Railways Department would cost £500 a year and the alternative was overhead bridges, both measures being prohibitive in cost. All poles were erected for the overhead, and new rails and sleepers stockpiled in Hastings Street, but the Napier South line never progressed any farther.

Extra trams for the proposed circuit had been another bugbear. First the Birney one-man safety cars were found unsuitable for the narrow 3-foot 6-inch gauge, then tenders called locally for bodies were well beyond the budget, so the solution lay in buying four second-hand bodies from Auckland for £350 each. The ex-Auckland

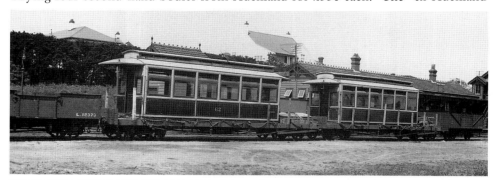

The bodies of Auckland trams 62 and 61 at the Remuera railway station, at the start of their railway journey to Napier. *W.W. Stewart*

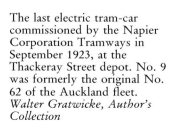

The last electric tram-car commissioned by the Napier Corporation Tramways in September 1923, at the Thackeray Street depot. No. 9 was formerly the original No. 62 of the Auckland fleet. *Walter Gratwicke, Author's Collection*

174

Passengers about to board a Napier west tram in Hastings Street at the Emerson Street intersection during the 1920s. *Author's Collection*

An elevated view of Hastings Street, Napier from the Emerson Street intersection in 1936 with the tram tracks still in the roadway, after the city had been rebuilt following the 1931 earthquake. *Charles P.S. Boyer, Author's Collection*

cars were too fat when commissioned in 1923 and restrictions had to be imposed when cars were passing on curves. On Sundays a round trip was instituted, from the depot in Thackeray Street to Hastings Street South, then to the port and back, the Auckland trams being used a lot on this shuttle run. In January 1931 a round trip by tram, ferry and bus was planned; by tram to the port, across the harbour by launch to Westshore and back along the embankment by bus. One ex-Aucklander had already been converted to a one-man car and on 2 February 1931, another was given Public Works approval to run after its conversion. At 4 pm on the afternoon of the same day, tenders closed for the reconditioning and painting of two tram-cars.

The fire which followed the Napier earthquake seen spreading along Hastings Street towards the Dickens Street junction on the afternoon of 3 February 1931. On the left is the post office, a structure which survived the earthquake and still stands today as Telecom House. ABOVE RIGHT: A view from Dickens Street looking into Hastings Street, taken within an hour of the first photograph, as buildings over the road from the post office are consumed by flames. *Author's Collection*

The next day was typical of Hawke's Bay in the summer—warm, with a clear sky and hardly a breath of wind to stir the dust. As three sailors from the visiting British naval sloop *Veronica* climbed on board a tram standing at the Port Ahuriri terminus, motorman Jim Minto checked his fob watch. The 10.48 am car from the port in the summer of 1931 was usually well patronised by women who went into town to view the bargains before luncheon at a tearoom. Motorman Minto gave a nod to his conductor, Frank Fulford, to indicate that it was time to be on their way. With the motorman's foot-gong clanging the quaint little four-wheeler started the return trip along Bridge Street. As the tram trundled across the road bridge by the Iron Pot, waterfront workers were busy loading produce into small coastal ships and schooners berthed in the basin. In the port township, several women boarded the car, choosing, as usual, to sit in the centre enclosed saloon. In Waghorne Street, Minto shut off power to reduce speed before entering the loop by Stafford Street and the car glided around the corner.

Then it struck ... The earthquake seemd to come in huge waves under the tram, lifting it, then shaking violently. At first Jim Minto thought his tram had parted company with the rails. As he said later, 'The tram was shaken like a fox terrier playing a rat.' Although shocked, passengers remained on their seats. When the second wave of earth tremors came, with the crash of falling chimneys and the agonising groan of homes fighting against the convulsions of the land, passengers and crew hurriedly left the tram. Fire broke out in a warehouse opposite, threatening to engulf the tram, now stranded without power. Minto and Fulford enlisted the help of a local motor-carrier who, with his Dennis hard-tyred lorry, managed to push the tram to safety along Waghorne Street to the Presbyterian church. Motorman and conductor made hard the brakes and decided to walk into town.

In Shakespeare Road they met the crew of an outward-bound car standing helpless by their vehicle. The sight that greeted the four tramwaymen is now history. A city in ruins, with the tramway overhead draped at crazy angles across wrecked motor cars and roadways. On the Napier South line in Hastings Street a single tram stood like an orphan, robbed of its life blood, having just left the terminus where the main south railway crosses Hastings Street when the quake unleashed its force on Napier. Back at the depot in Thackeray Street, three trams had toppled into the maintenance pits. The conductor of another tram waiting to go into service in the depot yard had taken cover under one of the seats, and would not budge. A fortnight later Jim Minto returned to his deserted tram in Waghorne Street to find his lunchbag untouched. Three weeks were to pass before tractors towed the three stranded tram-cars back home to the depot.

The earthquake of 3 February 1931 cost 256 people their lives and silenced the Napier Corporation Tramways for all time. A decision on the future of the tramway service was not immediate. The commissioners appointed to govern the

Looking south along Hastings Street at the foot of Shakespeare Road, Napier, before the earthquake. *Author's Collection*

The same scene after the Napier earthquake of 3 February 1931. *Author's Collection*

reconstruction of Napier reported that suspending the system would save about £3,000 a year. It was decided to mothball all the assets and to consider restarting the trams after an alternative system had been given a fair trial. Even trackless trams were mooted in discussion. Some considered that private enterprise should take over the system and run trams to Taradale. The Hawke's Bay Motor Company came to the rescue by converting motor lorries made redundant at Wairoa by the destruction of the railway northward from Napier. Bus bodies placed on these sturdy chassis were soon to be seen on the suburban runs.

In March 1936, five years after the earthquake, the order-in-council authorising the discontinuance of the Napier tramway service and the removal of the lines was gazetted. All the overhead installation was still intact, apart from those wires which had tumbled with the city in Hastings Street, between the post office and Brewster Street. June 1936 saw the removal of overhead lines, followed in August by the mammoth task of track removal, which took a year. In contrast with the modern machinery used after the Second World War to remove trackwork in other centres, this was a hard, laborious job undertaken with picks and shovels.

ABOVE: Former Auckland tram No. 63, purchased for service in Napier and never commissioned, was used after the Napier earthquake as an office at Beacons Aerodrome, as it was then called. *Weekly News* ABOVE RIGHT: Other Napier trams, including the two ex-Auckland trams (foreground), which saw service in Napier, were used as tourist accommodation at the Kennedy Road Motor Camp. *Weekly News*

An Overland motor car dashes past the many bicycles of Christchurch in Colombo Street. The year is 1930. On the right a trusty Model T Ford, and in the background a Boon tram approaches, heading for Fendalton. *Green & Hahn, Author's Collection*

Reminiscent of a scene from Charles Dickens' *Great Expectations*, the nine tramcars, covered in a mantle of dust after six years of lying idle, were sold. The council's camping ground purchased eight at £25 apiece for baches at the new municipal motor camp in Kennedy Road. The camp today has high-standard motel accommodation, a far cry from the converted tram bodies the council offered motorists when the grounds opened for the Easter of 1937.

When piston-engined aircraft were supreme, the air terminal at Napier, standing like a lone sentry-box on the paddock at Beacons Aerodrome, was a tram body converted for office use. The turbo-prop replaced the piston and the present spacious terminal building at the Hawke's Bay airport handles passengers with the same ease today as, in their day, did the jaunty little blue and cream trams of Napier.

In Christchurch the rot had set in with motor cars, bicycles and the Depression causing revenue to spiral downward. To offset the high cost of track renewals on lines serving sparsely populated suburbs, the Christchurch Tramway Board replaced the tramway to North Beach with one-man trolley buses running on pneumatic tyres. The first six buses with coachwork by Boon and Company were something new for New Zealand. Wellington's experimental 'trackless tram' was an antique compared with these vehicles which had smooth acceleration and good riding qualities.

Christchurch folk took kindly to the handsome vehicles which sped quietly out of noisy Cathedral Square without fuss or bother. This was remarkable, as the city had a reputation for being conservative. Yet the transition on several important routes from tram-car to trolley bus was accomplished with little adverse criticism.

The absence of noise was most noticeable, and the trolley buses earned the nickname 'silent death' because of their ability to sneak up on people without being heard. Compared with petrol and diesel buses, the trolley buses gave off no fumes, and therefore did not contribute to atmospheric pollution. For a while the authorities did have second thoughts as to their virtues, brought about mainly by a stiff road tax, which led to an abortive attempt to cancel the last four chassis from the English contractors and the abandonment of the New Brighton Esplanade service in 1933. Lack of confidence in the ability of the trolley buses to carry heavy race traffic saw the tram line left as far as Bassett Street for servicing trotting meetings at North New Brighton.

Trolley buses did not conquer Christchurch, but one did get to the top of the Cashmere Hills while on test, using the overhead tramway wire and trailing a steel skate on the tram rail for the earth return, but that was the first and last time. Petrol and diesel buses were used to provide a modest service on poorly patronised routes and conversion to one-man trams gave the system's economy a lift.

Trolley buses were first introduced to Christchurch in 1931 when electric trams were withdrawn from the North Beach service. No. 210 is now preserved at the Ferrymead Museum in Christchurch. *Green & Hahn, Author's Collection*

In 1933 the Christchurch Tramway Board used a trolley bus and 16 tram trailers placed at different points around the city and suburbs as polling booths for the board elections. BELOW LEFT: Voters seen boarding the trolley bus by the emergency door in Madras Street. *Press, Author's Collection* BELOW: The double-decker trailers ready to move out to the suburbs in Moorhouse Avenue. *Press, Bruce Maffey Collection*

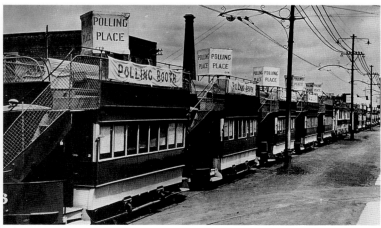

Regardless of the weather the trams kept rolling. ABOVE: Christchurch trams during a heavy fall of snow in the central city in 1952. *New Zealand Free Lance* and *Green & Hahn* LOWER LEFT: Dunedin had an extremely heavy fall of snow in 1939. LOWER RIGHT: In the deep south sleet conditions made changing the trolley-pole and points a messy job. Motorman Jack Garthwaite has difficulty with points outside the post office in Dee Street, Invercargill, in 1952. *Hazledine's Studio*

CHAPTER NINE

From Rails to Rubber

The relative merits of electric trolley buses and diesel-engined buses for municipal passenger transport were keenly discussed by local authorities in the years preceding the Second World War. It was generally agreed that tram-cars had outlived their usefulness, but with over 700 of them still in operation throughout New Zealand, it was clear that many years would elapse before trams disappeared. Nevertheless, the steady deterioration of the economic position of tramways would in time force first the smaller then the larger authorities completely to abandon their trams.

For the smaller towns, trams had been from the outset a costly amenity. The capital cost of track and overhead wires proved such a burden that by rights the trams would have had to be kept filled to pay their way at any reasonable fare structure. But although the trams may have been an expensive problem for city council financiers, perhaps, they nevertheless provided an essential service that was considered to be a prerequisite of any town long before it could aspire to become a city. The late development of many secondary towns, some of which did not begin to grow until the era of the internal combustion engine, undoubtedly accounted for the comparatively small number of electric tramways in this country.

The trolley bus was generally acknowledged to possess certain advantages over the petrol or diesel bus. It was much quieter and possibly afforded smoother travel, it had faster acceleration and deceleration and it was probably less prone to mechanical failure. But the diesel omnibus with pre-selective gearbox, hydraulic transmission and freedom from overhead wires did not lag far behind in reliability and ease of handling. Indeed, no factor weighed against the trolley bus more heavily than the fact that, although it was more flexible in traffic than the tram-car, it was also less mobile than the diesel bus.

By 1933 the success of the motor omnibus was growing healthily, and there were 522 such vehicles in the country. Of these, 372 were owned by private operators, working in and around almost every township and village throughout both main islands; 101 were owned by local bodies and 48 were operated by the Railways Department.

But trams were by no means defeated yet and streamlining, slowly being adopted by ocean liners and limousines, made its impact on tram-car design in the same year. The debut took place during a Queen Carnival procession in Wellington to raise money for the mayor's distress fund. It was a week of festivities, fireworks,

The original *Fiducia* tram, No. 232, which first graced the streets of Wellington in 1933. *W.W. Stewart*

The pride of Wellington streets in the 1930s. The prototype *Fiducia* tram, No. 232, emerging from the Seatoun tunnel. *A.C. Bellamy*

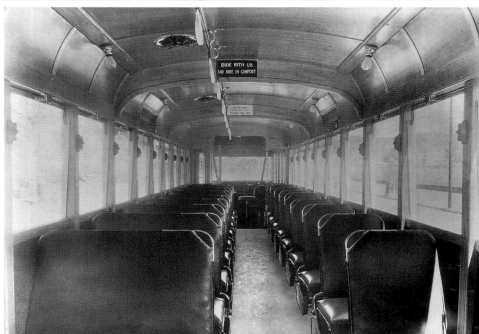

The interior of *Fiducia* No. 232, showing the red upholstered bus-style seats of the 1930s. *Wellington Studios, Author's Collection*

displays and community singing, with songs expressing the theme 'Prosperity will soon be here again'. In this gay, if artificial, atmosphere the National Confidence carnival was staged with princesses and floats. As families flocked into the city and watched the procession, a spectacular new tram appeared with the name *Fiducia* emblazoned in gold leaf on the end saloon windows. 'Fiducia' is the Latin for trust, confidence, reliance and assurance—everything people in those dark days of economic depression needed so much. The name *Fiducia* subsequently became linked with all Wellington trams of this type.

The original *Fiducia*, No. 232, was designed as a one-man car, but this form of operation was not practical in the congested streets of Wellington because traffic was held at bay while motormen collected fares. Howard Leah, Superintendent of

'I think it means "you've got to be strong to get a seat."'

One of the special lines which was laid in Wellington to carry visitors to the New Zealand Centennial Exhibition of 1939—40. This picture was taken in Resolution Street, Lyall Bay. *Wellington Tramways*

Rolling Stock, designed the tram in conjunction with Matthew Cable, the Tramways General Manager. Leah said No. 232 was well on the way to being just another standard type of the era, with its framing already in position. He and Cable decided to experiment, and the design just evolved as construction proceeded, with new ideas from overseas being added until *Fiducia* was born. *Fiducia* was the first radical departure from the old double-saloon type and, with certain modifications, was used as a pattern for the fleet of new rolling stock built to cope with the increased volume of traffic expected during the New Zealand Centennial Exhibition of 1939-40. The aesthetically pleasing appearance of bodywork painted scarlet, cream and green, the interior panelling of a light natural colour and the dark red upholstery on the seats, together with the comparatively silent running, made the Fiducia type princes among trams in Wellington, and their popularity with the public never waned.

A standard streamlined *Fiducia* type tram, No. 237, inward bound from Oriental Bay, Wellington, in the late 1930s. *Wellington Tramways*

Not to be outdone, Auckland produced a prototype 'streamliner' in 1935, which was quickly dubbed the 'Biscuit Box' because of its colour scheme. The car was painted all-over cream with mouldings and window-sash frames picked out in red, and a striking 'bow tie' in red on each of the end apron panels. Within a year, the Biscuit Box had exchanged its distinctive livery for the standard red, which was more serviceable for combating the dust and grit of a city. The last trams built in Auckland were sleek, improved versions of this prototype, always identifiable by their curved sides and their modern bogies with small wheels, imported from the Electro Mechanical Brake Company of England. The revolutionary English power units made for comparative silence, and comfortable riding was ensured by improved springing. All points of spring suspension had been equipped with rubber blocks, in conformity with modern motor-car manufacturing practice, to absorb shock and noise.

An ironical twist to the story of the streamlined trams of the 1930s was that the prototype in Auckland was built from the charred remains of the original No. 86, destroyed in a depot fire, and Wellington's experimental *Fiducia*, No. 232, was gutted by fire after 17 years of commuting.

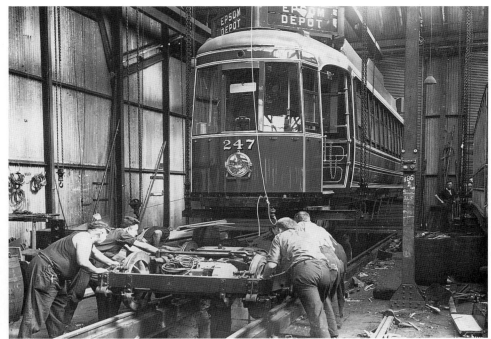

Revolutionary English bogies being fitted to the first Auckland 'streamliner' with curved sides in 1938. *Author's Collection*

Auckland 'streamliner' tram, No. 248, at the Three Kings terminus in 1938. Richard Sterling was the motorman. This tram is now restored in running order at the Museum of Transport and Technology, Auckland. *W.W. Stewart*

Interior and exterior views of the burnt-out shell of the prototype *Fiducia* No. 232, after the Kilbirnie depot fire in March 1951. *Graham Stewart*

The pioneer Dunedin Roslyn-Maori Hill electric tramway was replaced by buses in 1936. The above photographs show ex-city trams which were used to run the service in the latter years. Tram No. 87 was originally No. 9 on the city system. *A.P. Godber* and *Author's Collection*

Already in the 1930s diesel buses were challenging the trams in the southern strongholds and during 1936 replaced the Roslyn-Maori Hill service. One old-timer, writing to the newspapers, expressed the sentiment of many who did not like a change in daily habits:

When the rails are taken up the tram and I shall have had our last ride together; for, unlike a prima donna, a tram may give only one farewell performance. The first ride in an electric tram was an experience, a new rapture, unforgettable. The first ride in a bus is merely a ride in an outsize motor car, less intimate and less smooth riding. The bus looks like a beetle, sidles like a crab, and does not pursue the steady monogamous life of a tram. Bus drivers whatever their individual and personal charms are too new as a race to have acquired the instinctive urbanity of tram drivers, who, perched on their little stools, present to their passengers a width of shoulder that inspires confidence. Tram drivers eat in public with the magnificent unselfconsciousness of royalty; and if their diet strikes interested travellers as having too much cake, it may be that exposed to the weather as they are, they need the fuel supplied by carbohydrates. Busmen, beardless boys, slouching in their seats, have not attained the dignity of children who run up with bottles of tea ... Yet, when in a few days the last tram is driven into the shed there will be some rejoicing. Though the noise of the electric tram, a steady legitimate noise, is not offensive, bus addicts like to think the streets will be quieter. And greatest boon of all, wireless fans will be able to get Japan on week days as well as Sundays.

An old Dunedin 'toast rack' tram, No. 35, about to leave the Market Street depot on its final journey after being sold to a private buyer in July 1939. *Author's Collection*

Seventy years apart. The Exchange Building in Princes Street, Dunedin. In the upper photograph a steam tram thunders past. *Author's Collection* In the lower photograph, a view from Rattray Street in 1951, with one of the popular 'Takapuna' trams passing in the foreground. *Graham Stewart*

The first tram proceeding up Bowen Street, Wellington in August 1940. This *Fiducia*-type tram, No. 244, is now stored pending restoration at the Museum of Transport and Technology in Auckland. *Author's Collection*

Other centres were mooting the replacement of their trams. Christchurch announced that three routes would go to petrol buses; Dunedin wanted to change from the fixed rail; Invercargill decided in 1938 to scrap trams; and New Plymouth viewed trolley buses as the answer. The coming of import restrictions and war shortages were to give tramways a new lease of life, even if many were to live on borrowed time.

In Wellington and Auckland, the respective managers, Matthew Cable and A.E. Ford, were to be the last great advocates of the tram-car. Ford said in the mid-1930s:

> Where a tramway system has been maintained in good condition and operates profitably on streets of suitable width, it would undoubtedly be unwise, if not absurd, to scrap it. The steel wheel on the steel rail principle is still the most economical in power consumption per passenger mile. As the Auckland Transport Board possesses a thoroughly modern tramway system we will continue on the present lines.

OPPOSITE PAGE: Free transport for shoppers. Customers patronised the Farmers' Trading Company store on the corner of Hobson and Wyndham Streets, Auckland, aided by a free tram service which ran between the store and the top of Pitt Street between 1936 and 1954. Special tramway sidings were provided for the service in Beresford and Wyndham Streets. *Graham Stewart*

But war and changing social habits, with the motor car reaching a new peak in the post-war years, were to change all patterns of transport thinking, even for systems that were in good financial and mechanical health at the close of 1939.

In 1940 Matthew Cable brought to fruition 30 years of effort and public agitation with the opening of a shorter route up Bowen Street to Wellington's western suburbs. When a commission of engineers was formed in 1910 to examine possible routes, they were told that the then Prime Minister, Sir Joseph Ward, was absolutely and openly opposed to Bowen Street, so this route was never considered. This left the choice to either a new route via Hill Street or one involving an extension of the Aro Street line up Norway Street, with a tunnel to Karori Road. Hill Street was favoured but the Prime Minister of the day, W.F. Massey, was opposed to any interference with Hill Street by a tramway, because of the noise the cars would make passing close to the House of Representatives and General Assembly Library (the present Parliament Buildings had not then been constructed). Nothing was done and the report and plans were pigeon-holed. In 1924 a plan to route the line up Bowen Street to the Bolton Street cemetery, then by tunnel coming out in Sydney Street was also shelved. In March 1935, *Fiducia* No. 232 came to the rescue by demonstrating the silent running of a modern tram to the Speaker of the Legislative Council, Sir Walter Carncross, and 14 members, who were taken for a trip to Oriental Bay. This convinced the council that any objection on the grounds of noise would fade with new cars and so Karori and Northland residents were given the direct route to the city they had been seeking since 1907.

FREE TRAM SERVICE
FOR FARMERS' CUSTOMERS
KARANGAHAPE ROAD TO OUR WAREHOUSE

STARTS
TO-DAY!

QUEEN STREET BUS SERVICE
RUNS AS USUAL

FARMERS' TRADING Co. Ltd. Hobson and Wyndham Streets

Deferred maintenance on tracks during the Second World War was a major problem for permanent way staff in the post-war years, who had the task of keeping the tracks to a safe standard. ABOVE: Symonds Street, Auckland. The Sheraton Hotel is now situated on the right. ABOVE RIGHT: Queen Street, Auckland, by the town hall. *Graham Stewart*

For blackout emergencies and power failures during the Second World War, Auckland trams carried old buggy lamps at each end as a safety measure. *Author's Collection*

During the 1939-45 war, petrol rationing and tyre shortages restricted the mobility of private motor cars, bringing electric trams into demand as more and more motorists put their cars up on blocks and returned to public transport. Overcrowding, which in pre-war days was only expected at rush hours, now prevailed for a large part of each day, and at peak periods the trams and buses were unable, even when packed to their doorsteps, to accept the numbers of passengers waiting. It was impossible for conductors to pass through the cars and collect all short-distance fares and passengers were equally unable to contact the conductors. The 1943-44 figures for passengers reached the all-time high of 220,216,000. Wellington removed some centre seats to relieve overcrowding, making room for 10 additional fares, and Christchurch reconditioned three old steam trams for emergency service should the overhead wires become inoperative as a result of enemy action. This contingency was not entirely remote, because Japanese submarines had been active in New Zealand waters and enemy aircraft had flown over both Wellington and Auckland.

Blackout regulations saw cardboard shades fitted around saloon interior lights, and old buggy lamps were placed on trams for use in emergency when the power failed. As supplies of petrol dried up, feeder bus services had to be curtailed and private bus companies restricted their running to serve outer tram terminals, thus throwing a greater burden on the tramways. Dunedin and Christchurch were so embarrassed by the petrol restrictions that they were forced to reopen tram lines which had been closed in favour of petrol buses. Cinemas closed early, and late-night shopping was curtailed as strips of sticky paper appeared in criss-cross patterns on plate glass windows. Blackout trials and full-dress emergency tryouts of the EPS (Emergency Precautions Scheme) often halted all evening traffic without notice. Prominent posters with an important message 'LEST WE REGRET— DON'T TALK', illustrated by a sketch of a wartime tragedy, warned travellers not to discuss the movements of their loved ones serving in the armed forces, because enemy agents could be active.

In June 1942, to help overcome the manpower shortage, women were first employed—as tram conductors in the four main cities and later at New Plymouth. By September, 120 were at work. These women, many of them wives of tramway-men, could jack up a car and swing a trolley-pole with the best men in the service. Uniforms of navy serge, styled on the army 'battledress', were issued to the Wellington women. The slightly pouched blouse was designed so that it would not ride up when the conductresses raised their arms to pull the bell. Two breast pockets with flaps and buttons each held concession tickets and the sleeves of the

blouse had black calfskin cuffs to prevent fraying from constant dipping into the cash bag. Headgear was a smart peaked cap, proofed against rain, with a pleated crown and a chromium-plated badge. Only the Wellington women wore slacks, cuffless with a patch pocket on each thigh, and double-breasted greatcoats were issued to keep the cold at bay when riding on the open platforms, and when changing poles in driving rain.

The women had an unenviable task pushing through crowded trams, but they earned the respect of the travelling public for their ability to control obstinate passengers, herd back-platform outriders into the saloon, ease drunks off the cars and cut six o'clock wise guys down to size. Many of these 'girls', when they left the service to marry or retire, were given impromptu farewells by regular passengers as a mark of appreciation for their courtesy and care. Word would get around that a conductress was finishing duties, and at a pre-arranged spot in the suburbs, the tram would stop while an elected spokesman from the passengers made a presentation.

ABOVE LEFT: The first batch of Auckland conductresses begin training. ABOVE: An Auckland conductress changing the trolley-pole. *Author's Collection*

The first tram conductresses in Christchurch go on duty in 1942. *Green & Hahn, Author's Collection*

Prams on trams—a service that was part of the way of life in Christchurch, Dunedin and Invercargill. TOP: A period photograph at the Georgetown terminus, Invercargill. Shoppers with prams boarding a tram for the city in 1950. *W.W. Stewart* ABOVE LEFT: A Christchurch motorman obliges by hooking a pushchair safely on the front of a tram. *Coates, Bruce Maffey Collection* ABOVE CENTRE: Prams riding out front on a Christchurch Square-bound tram from Spreydon. *Graham Stewart* ABOVE RIGHT: An Exchange-bound tram from St Kilda with three wicker prams of the 1950s. *Graham Stewart*

A wartime necessity brought about by the lack of transport was the carrying of prams on the front of trams in Christchurch and Dunedin. Perambulators had always been carried, containing nothing more than a coverlet and baby clothes. Now women were packing their weekend shopping under the coverlet, and conductresses were being injured every week by the excessive strain of lifting prams loaded with parcels. 'We are not going to get to the stage where we cater for carrying baby motor-cars on our trams,' said J.S. Barr, Chairman of the Christchurch Tramway Board. 'The intention was to provide only for pushchairs, not to hold a baby, half a sack of sugar, and a roast of beef.'

With the extension of the war to the Pacific, large numbers of American forces used New Zealand as a base, adding further to the stresses and strains already being experienced by the arteries of the principal cities, but in particular those of Auckland and Wellington. Heavier axle loadings and deferred maintenance on both cars and tracks over these five years of war took their toll of the railed networks. The war had demonstrated an important point—that a country's life can be carried on almost without private transport, at a fraction of the cost.

The Second World War placed a heavy load on electric transport, as petrol supplies became short. Some motorists, like the owner of this Singer car in the Square at Christchurch, fitted inflatable gas tanks, made of treated canvas, on a roofrack. *Author's Collection*

Notwithstanding their remarkable wartime service, trams had had their day. They had a longer life than any comparable vehicle, but their robust construction and relative simplicity led to obsolescence. By the mid-1940s this obsolescence, coupled with years of wartime neglect, made their replacement a matter of urgency.

No time was lost in ringing the changes. Sir William Goodman of Adelaide recommended trolley buses for Dunedin; J.F. Fardell arrived from Reading in England to take up the appointment of general manager in Christchurch; L.B. Hutton, the General Manager of Wellington's City Corporation Tramways and Electricity Department, travelled to Australia to study developments; and in Auckland two senior executives, E.B. Foster and C.R. Gribble, sailed for England and the United States to investigate modern trends in public transportation.

Post-war shortages of steel and other vital materials made essential rejuvenation difficult. Volunteer citizen labour gangs, supervised by skilled workmen, helped to repair tram tracks on the Wellington suburban line to Lyall Bay. In the closing stages of the war, four women in Wellington had been employed as a 'pot hole gang', filling in the ragged tarseal holes beside the tram tracks. One drove a small truck, while the other three in turn, filled the holes with metal chips, poured the tar and tamped down the patches. Questions were soon asked in the House of Representatives about women being employed as labourers to repair roads in God's own country. Although the women, some former land girls, loved the job and the outdoors, the authorities bowed to political pressure and the pot holes were left to the irate motorist to dodge.

The controversial women's 'pot hole gang' in Wellington, repairing the road surface in Broadway on the Seatoun line in 1944. *C.P.S. Boyer, War Effort Collection, Alexander Turnbull Library*

In the post-war years, with motor cars in short supply, it was the trams which carried most urban commuters. These evening peak period scenes in Auckland show clearly the heavy loading. *Graham Stewart*

Conversion took years in the main cities, where fleets of 200 trams had to be gradually phased out without disrupting the flow of urban travel. As the trams disappeared from the scene, fossilised track junctions and long stretches of disused track roughly covered over with patches of tarseal made the motorist wish the whole affair, like a bad dream, would soon end.

The first city to make a complete change was Wanganui, whose citizens, in 1946, rejected a plan for trolley buses and instead voted heartily in a referendum for services operated by private enterprise. Local capital floated Greyhound Buses Limited headed by A.C. Seivewright, who gave the city's transport a new look in September 1950. Celebrations on a grand scale were held to usher in the buses, with a parade up Victoria Avenue. A shrill, high-pitched whistle heralded the approach of the veteran steam tram 'Puffing Billy', which carried a banner across its boiler reading 'I'm no greyhound, but I'm a bit of a gay dog'. The Minister of Transport, W.S. Goosman, opened the new bus service saying: 'Everyone regrets the passing of the trams, but they have been outmoded. Today is the day of rubber-tyred transport.'

This Auckland family chartered a tram to carry their returning serviceman, with all his relatives and friends, home from the railway station. *Author's Collection*

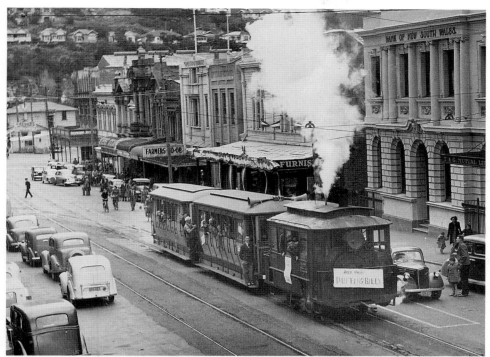

'Puffing Billy' with steam up in Victoria Avenue, Wanganui, during the farewell to trams in September 1950. Old 'Billy' came to the rescue in 1920 when no power was available to propel the electrics, owing to a threatened breakdown in the gas generating plant. For three months this Baldwin steam tramway locomotive ran an emergency service with trailers to Gonville and Castlecliff. *Graham Stewart*

'Puffing Billy' heralds the last journey into the city with a blast from her whistle in September 1950. At left is a 'Takapuna' tram. Nine of these trams were the backbone of the service in this provincial city for two decades. In the centre is No. 1, which gave Wanganui loyal service from when the service started in 1908 until the closure in 1950. *Graham Stewart*

A 'Takapuna' tram, No. 30, crossing the Dublin Street bridge. *W.W. Stewart*

Victoria Avenue, Wanganui, in the latter days of trams. A No. 2 Aramoho tram in the foreground is followed by a No. 3 tram bound for Wanganui East. *Author's Collection*

SPECIAL
ARAMOHO
CITY
WANGANUI EAST
QUICK AV.
GONVILLE
CITY
CASTLE CLIFF
DEPÔT

Wanganui destination sign. *Graham Stewart*

RIGHT: The railway line into Wanganui passed by the old tramway depot in Taupo Quay. *W.W. Stewart* BELOW: 'Takapuna' No. 32 heads into the city over the Guyton Street bridge. *W.W. Stewart*

A week later, on a Sunday night, a bonfire blazed on the beach as a crowd of 4000 paid a fitting tribute to the last tram from Castlecliff, which was farewelled to the accompaniment of a Highland pipe band, exploding fireworks and detonators and tooting car horns. Through ironsand dunes where grass grew—between the worn-out rails, rumbled the last of the stalwarts—a convoy of three faithful 'Takapunas' on their final pilgrimage, with motor cars and bicycles trailing them on their nostalgic journey into history. After the usual valedictory speeches, two little girls placed a wreath on the last tram, bearing the inscription 'You've rattled our bones and rattled our jaws and after tonight you'll rattle no more'. To the strains of 'Auld Lang Syne', motorman Jim Kidd edged No. 28 through the crowd, the interior of the car packed tightly with citizens bidding farewell to a familiar part of the city's life.

American-built Birney safety trams in Dee Street, Invercargill. *W.W. Stewart*

Two years passed before the axe fell again. This time it was Invercargill which said goodbye to its electric cars, which American servicemen had facetiously claimed would have been more profitable had they run across the streets instead of along them. This was a compliment, perhaps, to the broad streets, ably planned by men of vision. Invercargill had seen nothing like the tramway closure since VE and VJ days. Souvenir hunters had a field day as the last veteran, No. 2, driven by the sole remaining original employee, Archie Waters, made its slow, sad trip. The old tram's mileage 1,041,000 (1,675,280 kilometres) — was proudly written with chalk on its end panels. No valedictory speeches had been made in the previous year for the very last tram to run on Invercargill's Georgetown route, for two months after the buses had taken over no building could be found for a general election polling booth. So, towed by a truck, a tram returned along the old line, by now bare of overhead wires, to be used by voters. Surely this must have been a 'first' in last trips!

Birney safety tram No. 14 at the southernmost tram terminus in the world, South Invercargill, 1951. *Graham Stewart*

BELOW LEFT: Invercargill citizens said goodbye to their trams in September 1952. No. 2 about to leave the North Invercargill terminus for the last time, packed to the doors.
BELOW: Birney No. 14 suffered at the hands of the overenthusiastic crowds who gathered to farewell the Invercargill trams. *Hazledine's Studios*

PREVIOUS PAGE: Fifty years of service to Auckland. The tram in both pictures is No. 11, the first tram to be assembled in 1902. *Author's Collection* In the lower picture, No. 11 is shown decorated when Auckland celebrated 50 years of tramways in 1952. *Graham Stewart* Both views are of Queen Street from the junction of Customs Street, with the same tramway centre pole featuring on the right. No. 11 is now an exhibit at the Museum of Transport and Technology, Auckland.

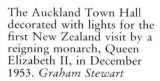

The Auckland Town Hall decorated with lights for the first New Zealand visit by a reigning monarch, Queen Elizabeth II, in December 1953. *Graham Stewart*

Dunedin No. 4 decorated for the visit of the Queen and the Duke of Edinburgh in January 1954. *Gerald C. Ditchfield*

Trams served many railway stations. OPPOSITE PAGE, TOP: A special loop line delivered passengers right to the front entrance of the Auckland Railway Station. MIDDLE LEFT: An inward-bound tram crosses over the railway line in Mount Eden Road. MIDDLE RIGHT: A tram and steam locomotive, both now memories, in Newmarket, Auckland. BELOW: This tram is crossing the bridge in Blockhouse Bay Road, Auckland. *Graham Stewart*

THIS PAGE, TOP: The Wellington Railway Station was always a mecca for trams. *Graham Stewart* CENTRE: Trams served the Christchurch Railway Station from opening day in 1905. *Steffano Webb Collection, Alexander Turnbull Library* BELOW: No. 22 bounces past the elegant Dunedin Railway Station. *S.R. Rockliff*

A Fitzroy tram passing a Westown trolley bus loading in Liardet Street. New Plymouth had the only provincial trolley buses to operate in New Zealand, a service that lasted 17 years, from October 1950 to October 1967. *Graham Stewart*

A carnival night with two hours of free rides saw the last provincial line close at New Plymouth in July 1954. Decorations, slogans and puns covered the trams. 'I'm being rubbered,' read one. 'You heard me coming, but you'll never smell me going' and 'You'll never miss me again,' read others. All the billboards back and front carried the information 'I am for sale by auction, Friday next at 2 pm'.

In the same year, their funeral procession preceded by floats, balloons, bands and marching girls, the trams of Christchurch entered the Valhalla of all old tram-cars. Fifty years of electric traction came to an end as a double-decker trailer trundled into the Square for the funeral rites with the Christchurch Municipal Band on the top deck playing 'Bravest of the Brave'.

One by one the suburban lines disappeared, and each last trip manifested a sentiment out of character with the cynical outlook on life now displayed by the average person in the street. Usually at an antisocial hour, as the local Cinderellas were hurrying home, the last cumbersome tram would be mobbed as it lumbered back to the depot along the corrugated rails. There would be a boisterous farewell with good-humoured crowds singing and dancing around the tram, showers of streamers and confetti being thrown as former strap-hangers joined hands and spontaneously sang the popular Maori farewell song 'Now is the Hour'. As the tram trundled homeward the cheering, whistling and hooters would awaken the

The last night of trams in New Plymouth. 'Farewell Tin Hare', a tribute to the fast little Birney safety trams which served the city for 33 years. No. 8 is seen turning out of Devon Street, bound for the port. *Graham Stewart*

On Friday, 23 July 1954 the citizens of New Plymouth gathered in large numbers to farewell their trams with two hours of free rides. UPPER RIGHT: No. 3 made the last trip to the port. LOWER RIGHT: The last official tram loading guests at the railway station for the ceremonial last journey through the city back to the depot at Fitzroy. *Graham Stewart*

Christchurch in the early 1950s. TOP: A Riccarton tram in Worcester Street. RIGHT: The terminus at the Sign of the Takahe on the Cashmere Hills. 'Hills' tram No. 162, as they were known because of their ability to climb the only hill line in Christchurch. BELOW RIGHT: Vehicles from another age were still being used to carry crowds to and from race meetings in the 1950s. Post-war conversion to diesel buses was only a few years away when these veterans of 70 years carried punters from the Addington Racecourse in January 1950. LOWER RIGHT: A trolley bus of 1931 vintage passing an electric tram and trailer leaving the Square depot in 1950. All trolley bus services in Christchurch ceased in November 1956. *Graham Stewart*

BELOW: A Cathedral Square sign. *Graham Stewart*

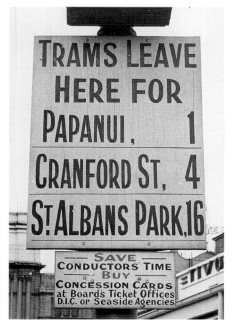

ABOVE LEFT: Inspector W.J. Patterson with women conductors on the day trams said their farewell in Christchurch in September 1954. *Green & Hahn* TOP: The last tram and trailer arriving at New Brighton in October 1952. *Green & Hahn* ABOVE: The last tram and trailer arriving at Sumner in December 1952. *Roy Gay*

LEFT: Farewell Cathedral Square! The last Christchurch trams leave the city behind, 11 September 1954. *Green & Hahn*

A busy tramway scene in Dunedin outside the Stock Exchange at the intersection of Princes Street and High Street with the post office in the background in the late 1940s. *C.J. Leeden, Author's Collection*

sleepy suburb. Doors of houses along the route would open as occupants waved handkerchiefs and torches to the tram clanging its way at the head of a procession of cars. And after it was all over the well-worn rails would lie silent, their surface already beginning to dull. Each suburb in its turn would see its citizens, like pagan worshippers, gather in the middle of the night for the farewell ritual. Although cursed and often missed by passengers on their way to school, to work and, in some cases, to fame, the electric trams had assumed a personality that was peculiarly their own and despite all criticism had endeared themselves to their users.

A minister of the church from the pulpit once compared a religious person with a tram-car. The latter, he said, travelled its appointed way, doing useful service. It was propelled, lighted within and was able to cast light in front of and all about it 'by the power of the uplifted arm'. The Christian could do likewise. The down-to-earth popularity of the tram-car may well have been summed up in this paragraph published in the *Dominion*, covering a conversation in broken English overheard on a crowded tram: 'Trams is better than bus, no?' 'Why you say so?' 'On bus you pay every time. When get in.' 'Sure.' 'On tram, big crowd — no pay!'

Decorated with fernery, flags and streamers by conductresses, the last scheduled tram in the South Island left the Stock Exchange in Dunedin in March 1956 for St Clair. Motorman Barney Plunket drove and Mrs L. Berland wedged her way through the crowd collecting fares, unperturbed by the large placard 'Do kiss the conductress — it is fare'. Powerful floodlights gave the crowds at St Clair a never-to-be-forgotten spectacle.

Dunedin University students gave the last tram to Opoho a rowdy send-off in September 1950. *Otago Daily Times*

Dunedin said farewell to its cable cars after 76 years of service in March 1957. The last Mornington cable car climbs the High Street gradient for the last time. Dunedin residents certainly had confidence in the strength of the cable on this historic occasion. *Evening Star*

The last tram-car to run a suburban public service in the South Island, leaving St Clair terminus, Dunedin, in March 1956. *Tom Lloyd, Author's Collection*

Auckland in the 1950s. RIGHT: Late afternoon tram traffic crossing the Queen and Victoria Streets intersection. The tram in the centre, No. 253, is now an exhibit at the Museum of Transport and Technology, Auckland. BELOW: Jervois Road, Herne Bay, before the trees were removed for the advent of the first suburban trolley bus service in Auckland. BOTTOM: A familiar scene during the 54 years of electric trams. The Queen and Customs Streets intersection with a traffic officer on point duty. *Graham Stewart*

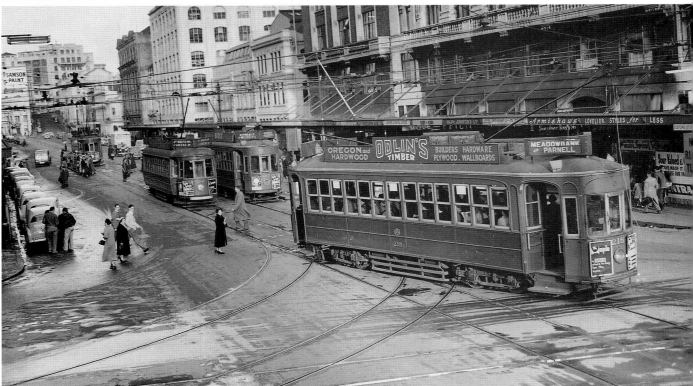

ABOVE: Auckland streamliner No. 248 in Anzac Avenue with St Andrew's Presbyterian Church in the background.
ABOVE LEFT The same tram, now preserved at the Museum of Transport and Technology, Auckland, in Queen Street during a morning peak period. *Graham Stewart*

LEFT: Pedestrians in Queen Street, Auckland, during the last week of the trams. *Graham Stewart*

When steam trains and electric trams mixed with motor traffic in downtown Auckland. The intersection of Quay Street and Queen Street. Air New Zealand House now stands on the right. *Graham Stewart*

The Epsom tram barns in Manukau Road in the final years of trams in Auckland. *Graham Stewart*

Safety zones were a haven for pedestrians waiting for a tram in the heart of Auckland city. This photograph of Queen Street was taken from Vulcan Lane. *Graham Stewart*

In the December of the same year it was Auckland's turn to rid the streets of the vehicles which for so many years had held undisputed right of the road over all other traffic. Across this narrow neck of land separating the Waitemata and Manukau Harbours ran the Onehunga tram, which Aucklanders boasted was the only tramway in the world to cross a country from one side to the other and the only ocean-to-ocean line, linking as it did the Pacific ocean and the Tasman Sea. Onehunga trams had survived until the last — a fitting end for a Maori place name meaning 'the place of burial'. Ships' sirens sounded a farewell salute during the closing ceremony on 29 December. The *New Zealand Herald* said: 'A golden chariot drawn by ten white horses could scarcely have attracted more attention than the last Auckland tramcar.' Even the bars of hotels on the route partly emptied, and there was many a raised glass as the end of an era was toasted. The tram stopped outside the Captain Cook Hotel in Khyber Pass Road, and one patron with more feeling than his compatriots left the footpath and handed the motorman, C. Berridge, a frothing glass. No longer would the big red trams surge through Queen Street; the last battle between motorists and safety zones had been fought.

Auckland's last tram, No. 242, turning out of Queen Street for the final time on 29 December 1956. *Graham Stewart*

The end of the line: Auckland's large flat-top freight tram, No. 304, making the final journey under power on 5 July 1957. No. 304 was towing No. 248 within the Epsom Tramway Workshops grounds in readiness for transportation to Matakohe for preservation. The overhead wires in Manukau Road had all been removed and the freight tram had to take a speedy 'running jump' up the grade in the workshop grounds to clear the points where the overhead ended. *Graham Stewart*

Wellington in the 1950s.
Lambton Quay, showing a
tram waiting on the single-
track loop line which ran from
Customhouse Quay down
Johnston Street, outside
Kirkcaldie and Stains. *Graham
Stewart*

Stewart Dawson's Corner at
the junction of Willis Street,
Lambton Quay and
Customhouse Quay, when the
tram-car dominated
Wellington Streets. *Graham
Stewart*

Where the Michael Fowler
Centre now stands, a tram and
a recently introduced trolley
bus in lower Cuba Street. The
Wellington Town Hall is on
the right. *Graham Stewart*

The intersection of Willis and Manners Street is still known by older Wellingtonians as Perrett's Corner after a pharmacy which was once situated at this junction. Then most streets were two-way for motor traffic. *Graham Stewart*

The junction of Jervois Quay (left) and Customhouse Quay, Wellington. The Park Royal Hotel now stands on the right. *Graham Stewart*

James Smith's corner at the intersection of Manners and Cuba Streets, Wellington. The Royal Oak Hotel building is at right in the background. *Graham Stewart*

ABOVE: Wellington double-decker trams of 1906 vintage were still used for school specials and peak-hour traffic in the early 1950s. Double-decker No. 47 (left) is now at the Museum of Transport and Technology, Auckland. *George Heron* ABOVE RIGHT: The tramway tunnel through Mount Victoria, Wellington, which was used exclusively by tram-cars from 1907 to 1962. The tram pictured, No. 257, is now at the Museum of Transport and Technology, Auckland. The tunnel is now used by buses. *Graham Stewart*

Wellington was now the last stronghold of the tram-car. The capital city appeared reluctant to make the change; indeed proposals to replace the trams were a civic issue that became a lively topic as 'Save the Trams' campaigners argued the merits of retaining the profitable 'Golden Mile' line from Courtenay Place to the railway station. The last word in tram-car sophistication, the Fiducias, now fought for survival in the concrete canyons with lumbering trolley and diesel buses, but the contest was unequal and the trams — first the double saloons and then the Fiducias — faded from the scene, taking with them part of the character of Wellington.

A ceremonial farewell was held when the final journey was made from Thorndon to Newtown on 2 May 1964. Thousands took a last sentimental ride as cheers and tears followed the electric cars into obscurity. The passing was an event of joy for the young and a matter of regret for the older folk. Two trams dressed in red, white and blue wore placards identifying them as the third-last and second-last trams in the country. Wellington's — and New Zealand's — last tram was decorated with bunting of black and gold, the colours of Wellington, and embellished on the front panel at each end, an arc of flags. The last crews were motormen D. McDonald, G. Charterus and W.G.A. McIvor, and conductors A.R. Thompson, Mrs A.R. Phillips and Mrs S. Leventi. An honorary motorman for the occasion was the Mayor of Wellington, F.J. (later Sir Francis) Kitts, who slowly but surely covered the few

Football crowds leaving Athletic Park, Wellington, after an international rugby test. *Graeme Bennett*

Wellingtonians acknowledge the last suburban trips. TOP LEFT: To the strains of 'Now is the Hour' the last Northland tram, No. 255, slowly approaches the Northland tunnel in September 1954. *Evening Post* TOP RIGHT: About 500 people farewelled the last Oriental Bay tram, No. 218, in May 1950. *Dominion* LOWER LEFT: Pipes and a lantern lead the way for the ceremonial last tram from Aro Street in August 1957. *Evening Post* LOWER RIGHT: On the last night of the public service in May 1964—typical of the friendly trams—a passenger changes the points for the motorman at the Cuba and Vivian Streets intersection. This was the last tram to run via the Vivian Street, Basin Reserve, Adelaide Road line. No. 244 is now stored by the Museum of Transport and Technology, Auckland. *Graham Stewart*

remaining kilometres through cheering, waving, clapping crowds, some perched on buildings and hoardings, others hanging out of windows. The Onslow Silver Band (formerly the Wellington Municipal Tramways Band), led the last car from Thorndon, playing 'It's a Long Way to Tipperary', to Parliament Buildings where its final salute was 'Auld Lang Syne'. After the last clang, a sad little girl painstakingly addressed a letter in big, square printing to the mayor: 'Dear Mayor, We are going to miss the trams. I like them. If they are not too dear, please keep me one, Anna.'

Nostalgically, when the cry of 'fez plez', the hiss of releasing air brakes, the throbbing of air compressors beneath the cars, the piercing ring of steel wheels rounding a bend and the clang of the motorman's gong ceased to drown out a newspaper boy's cry, a strange silence crept over the city. The last memory of elegance in public transport had vanished, said one newspaper report.

Wellington's No. 1 trolley bus being tested in April 1949 at the Oriental Bay tram terminus in Oriental Parade. *Author's Collection*

ABOVE: The Wellington destination roll reference which was in the cabs of all trams for crews. ABOVE RIGHT: Victoria University students turned out in large numbers to cheer the Wellington trams into retirement on Saturday, 2 May 1964. *Graham Stewart*

With these memories also vanished a proud vocation, that of the tramwayman. Thousands of such men gave a lifetime of service to transporting their fellow citizens to their homes, to places of employment and out to the bright lights. From the humble apprentices and skilled craftsmen at the workshops, with ability to keep the wheels turning, to the track staff, the operating personnel and the administrators, there were always men with the vision and personality to win popular esteem — managers and engineers such as Sir William Goodman, who built the first electric line; C.F. Alexander and W.H. MacKenzie of Dunedin; Frank Thompson, H.E. Jarman and J.F. Fardell of Christchurch; Stuart Richardson and Matthew Cable of Wellington; and C.R. Gribble, who administered Auckland's post-war modernisation from start to finish. Transport administration was linked with Gribble's family for over 70 years, his father-in-law being J.J. Walklate, General Manager of the Auckland Electric Tramways and City Council Tramways. Walklate began his career on a steam tramway in Birmingham, England, in the 1880s, came out to Australia in 1896 to take charge of an electrical installation, and was General Manager of the Potteries Electric Traction Company, at Stoke-on-Trent, when he resigned to come to New Zealand.

A father and son link was that of J.W.F. Welch, who first specialised in electric traction with the Railways Department before becoming Tramways Engineer for the Wellington City Corporation Tramways from 1941 to 1951, when he moved to Auckland as Chief Engineer of the Auckland Transport Board (later to become the Transport Division of the Auckland Regional Authority). His father, J. Francis Welch, was Manager of the Takapuna Tramways and Ferry Company for a number

Wellington's third-to-last tram (foreground), followed by the second-to-last tram, proceeding into the city along Webb Street for the closing ceremony on Saturday, 2 May 1964. *Graham Stewart*

216

ABOVE: New Zealand's last tram, No. 252, making the last historic journey through the streets of Wellington, in Lambton Quay (left) and in Manners Street (right). *Graham Stewart*

'Auld Lang Syne'—the Onslow Silver Band (formerly the Wellington Municipal Tramways Band) playing a final tribute to the last tram to run in New Zealand, 2 May 1964. *Graham Stewart*

FROM RAILS TO RUBBER 217

New Zealand Herald

of years, joining the company when electrification was in the air. He had trained as an electrical engineer in England and America, and returned to his native country to install the electrical sub-station and associated equipment when Christchcurch electrified its tramways in 1905.

Smaller centres had men who virtually gave 24 hours of each day to their work; men such as W.H. Huggett of New Plymouth, and F.P. Talboys and G.R. Holmes of Wanganui. Holmes, who was Superintendent of Tramways, was appointed general manager of the bus company which succeeded the trams. A man of principle, he gained great respect from the public in his 49 years of service to the community, having been associated with Wanganui's tramways since he conducted on the first tram to Castlecliff in 1912.

On our streets today, buses—trolley and diesel—now hold the stage, but they are finding their patronage threatened by the relentless onslaught of the privately owned motor car. New Zealanders have had a traditional and ongoing love affair with their cars and nobody, it seems, wishes to revert to the Victorian and Edwardian concept of mass movement.

Cities have slowly been demolished and reshaped to accommodate motor transport, and large areas laid waste as motorways were provided to bring more and more vehicles into city streets already congested to the point of thrombosis, merely to satisfy the selfishness of so many who believe it beneath their dignity to ride any form of public transport.

The ideal form of transport today is one over which we can exercise a complete personal control in both ownership and operation. But, as we are discovering only too quickly, there are limits to which we can take our ideals.

'Transportation is civilisation,' said Rudyard Kipling, and an efficient public transport system constitutes the arterial networks through which the lifeblood of any city must continue to flow.

The modern generation of tram-cars never disappeared from the major cities of Europe, and in 1992 railed vehicles started running again through the streets of the British city of Manchester. The second generation tram now has a new name, 'light rail', Manchester being the first of many new light rail schemes now being planned for cities throughout Britain. In France, where the first generation of trams was banished almost as completely as from Britain, the 'light rail' trams are returning to Paris after more than 50 years. Throughout the United States, the acme of motorisation, there is a return in the 1990s to modern forms of the tram-car.

Rust in peace. Wellington tram bodies awaiting scrapping.
Graham Stewart

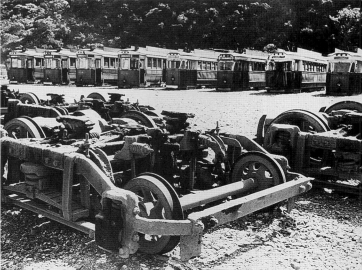

New Zealand Herald

New Zealand, with a population of only 3.4 million, does have a problem. We lack the population density to afford both an adequate, affordable public transport system in our cities and road systems to give complete freedom to the private motorist unless governments maintain adequate subsidies in the future. The scarcity of government funding will certainly be a threat to keeping the country moving in the 21st century if these warnings are not heeded.

Perhaps a quote from Henry Ford II, whose grandfather played a major role in putting the world on wheels, is a stark illustration of what may happen to our cities in the future: 'There may come a time when people will get so sore because they can't park and can't get where they want to go in a reasonable amount of time that they'll refuse to drive cars.'

BELOW: Out to new pastures — former Auckland trams awaiting buyers in a paddock at Kopu, near Thames. These veterans of Auckland commuting were used along the Coromandel Coast as seaside holiday homes. *Graham Stewart*

BOTTOM: A Christchurch tram showing the truly final destination for both morals and vehicles! *Graham Stewart*

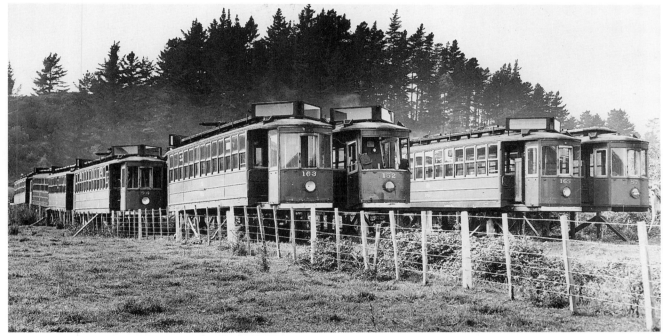

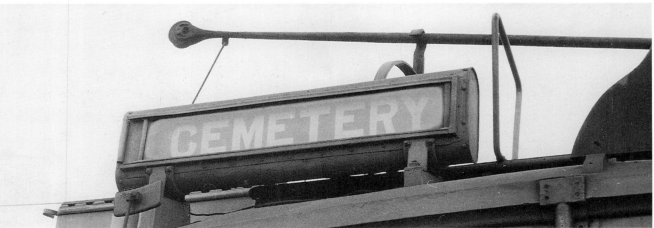

Auckland tram No. 253 being transported north to Matakohe in 1957. Orewa Beach is in the background. The Old Time Transport Preservation League of Matakohe was the first organisation in New Zealand to be established with the prime object of preserving trams. The League obtained old tramway rolling stock from Auckland, Wanganui, Wellington, Dunedin, and even approached the Christchurch Transport Board in their quest to save historic vehicles that were rotting away during the late 1950s. *Graham Stewart*

Auckland trams Nos 253 and 248 seen on their arrival at the 186-square-metre tram barn which was built at Matakohe, 153 kilometres north of Auckland, on the main highway to Dargaville, in 1958. Standing by the trams are (from left) Richard Sterling, Mervyn Sterling, Graham Stewart (author) and Ian Stewart.

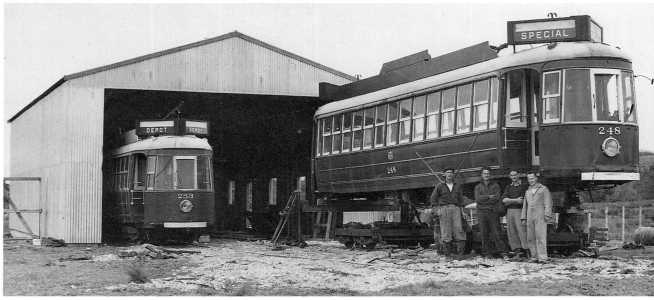

CHAPTER TEN

Preserved for Future Generations

Although the horse-tram, the steam-tram, the cable car and the electric tram are now forgotten in a purely commercial sense, future generations of New Zealanders will still have ample opportunity to experience the thrills of a mode of travel once taken for granted. Thanks to the valiant efforts of tramway museum organisations throughout the country, representative vehicles have been saved from destruction and restored to working order, even though the majority will never again rumble through the streets of their native cities.

The first serious attempt to preserve tramway vehicles in New Zealand did not become a reality until after the Auckland trams had made their final journeys.

In John Cresswell's 1976 book about the Museum of Transport and Technology, he wrote:

> Tram preservation did not start in earnest until the Auckland system was giving way to trolley and diesel buses in 1956 and a tramway historian, G.C. Stewart [the author], suggested to the Auckland Transport Board that, as tram No. 11 was preserved, it would be logical to preserve for posterity the most modern tramcar, No. 253. When nobody was willing to take care of this item, Mr Stewart formed a trust to preserve it, and this developed in 1957 into a society called the Old-Time Transport Preservation League.

T.A. McGavin and D.L.A. Turner, in their book *Rail Museums in New Zealand*, published in 1980, had this to say:

> The origins of the extensive collection of rail transport equipment at the Museum of Transport and Technology at Western Springs, Auckland, must be credited to the enterprise and perseverance of a small group of enthusiasts who formed the Old Time Transport Preservation League in 1957. Early that year the Auckland Transport Board had presented Graham C. Stewart [the author] with tram 253 for preservation, following the closure of their tramway system. The chairman of the league, Mervyn D. Sterling, donated land for the project at Matakohe, south of Dargaville. In 1958 the collection began to grow with the acquisition of a steam tram from Wanganui and a cable-car trailer (of horse-tram design) from Dunedin. The Wellington City Corporation Transport Department donated a double-deck tram (No. 47), a double-saloon tram of 1920 vintage (No. 135), and an early freight car (No. 301).

The league's plans to preserve historic public transport vehicles at Matakohe, Northland, received much opposition, as their thinking was well ahead of the times in the 1950s. These were the years before New Zealanders came to understand and appreciate their heritage and the need to save examples of a past way of life.

The success of the scheme was in many ways due to the support and backing of the then General Manager of the Auckland Transport Board, C.R. Gribble, and the Chief Engineer, J.W.F. Welch.

Mervyn Sterling was the powerhouse behind the organisation in those early days, a man who dedicated his life to the museum cause and was responsible for the establishment of several pioneer museums in North Auckland. The Otamatea Kauri and Pioneer Museum at Matakohe in Northland will forever stand as a monument to his life's work. In 1976 he received the QSM award for his services to museums. Other founding members of the league were Ian Stewart, Dick Sterling and Peter Mellor.

Wellington trams arriving at the Museum of Transport and Technology in Auckland after the long road journey from the capital in 1964. ABOVE: *Fiducias* Nos 244 and 257 which were donated by the Shell Oil Company of New Zealand. ABOVE RIGHT: Double saloon No. 135 and freight tram No. 301, which were donated by the Wellington City Council to the Old Time Transport Preservation League. *M.D. Sterling*

The league, together with the Royal Aeronautical Society (New Zealand Division) and the Historic Auckland Society, were responsible for a public meeting held in June 1960 which brought about the establishment of the Museum of Transport and Technology (MOTAT) at Western Springs, Auckland.

My brother, Ian Stewart, had been enlisted when the league was formed for his professional electrical qualifications. He went on to manage and oversee, on a voluntary basis, the restoration of the historic tram fleet and the construction of the now extensive Western Springs tramway owned and operated by the Museum of Transport and Technology New Zealand Trust in Auckland. His dedication to creating a working tramway has spanned more than 30 years and although he has been supported over the years by an enthusiastic team of hard-working volunteers, I know they would all agree that full credit must go to him for the success of this venture. This electric tramway now carries an average of 80,000 passengers a year between the museum and the Auckland Zoological Park.

Keen supporters and workers at Western Springs in the early days included Kerry Bennett, Alan Curtis, 'Jeep' Halling, Wally Hudson, Ian Mison, Barry Phillips, Roger Stanton, Kevin Swann and John Wolf.

The electric tramway at the Museum of Transport and Technology was officially opened in December 1967 by Auckland tram No. 253 and Wellington tram No. 257. Guests of honour with the museum director, John Hogan (fourth from left) and Ian Stewart (second from right), who was responsible for the building of the tramway, were, from left: Graham Stewart (author), Mervyn Sterling, Sir John Allum, Norman Spencer, Ray Gribble and Jack Welch.

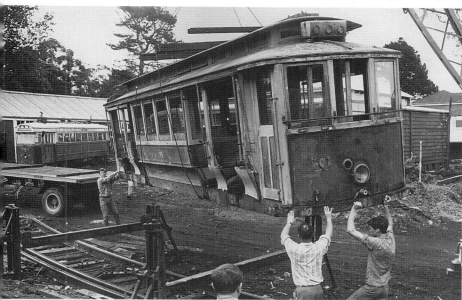

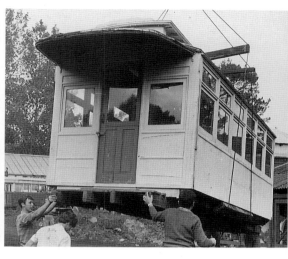

ABOVE LEFT: The body of No. 10, an old Wanganui Californian combination tram, being unloaded at MOTAT in Auckland. In the background is Wellington *Fiducia* No. 252, New Zealand's last tram. *Graham Stewart* ABOVE: No. 44, a pioneer Auckland electric tram arriving at MOTAT for restoration. *Graham Stewart* LEFT: Wellington double-decker No. 47 which was donated to the Old Time Transport Preservation League, seen about to leave the Newtown tram sheds for Auckland on the back of a transporter. *W.W. Stewart* BELOW: A tramway gala occasion at MOTAT, Auckland. An impressive line of restored tramway vehicles. Leading is Auckland No. 11 of 1902, followed by Wanganui Baldwin steam-tram No. 100 of 1891, Auckland No. 248 of 1938, Wellington No. 257 of 1950, Wellington No. 135 of 1921 and Melbourne W2 class, No. 321 of 1925. *New Zealand Herald*

Two views of Great North Road, Auckland, from the intersection of Motions Road, looking towards the city. The upper photograph was taken in 1953 shortly before the tram service to Point Chevalier was replaced by trolley buses. The lower photograph shows the tram tracks being removed. Today, the Museum of Transport and Technology of New Zealand runs restored historic electric trams on the now developed parkland area, on the left in the photographs. A tramway passing loop is situated on the corner of Motions Road. *Graham Stewart*

Further south, the desire to save tram-cars for posterity had led to the formation of the Wellington and Christchurch branches of the Tramway Preservation Association in 1960.

In Christchurch a small group of enthusiasts, led by John Shanks, campaigned to ensure the preservation of two historic trams, an 1881 Kitson steam-tram and an 1887 horse-tram, which the Christchurch Transport Board had placed in the care of W.A. Clapham, when the Canterbury Museum refused to accept them for its collection.

As the vehicles, stored without any protection from the weather, were beginning to deteriorate, the fledgling association persuaded the General Manager of the Christchurch Transport Board, John Fardell, to provide them with covered space in the board's workshop so restoration work could be carried out.

The arrangement was for six months but, thanks to the continued support of John Fardell and the board, the vehicles stayed in the workshops for five years before moving to the Ferrymead Historic Park. By then the exhibits had more than trebled, with an electric tram trailer and a double-decker trailer also under restoration, and a Christchurch and New Plymouth trolley bus in storage. Two electric tram bodies had already arrived at Ferrymead for restoration.

The Tramway Historical Society of Christchurch have restored many old tramway vehicles, the majority of which were found in an advanced state of decay. LEFT: An old Christchurch steam-tram trailer is removed from its final resting place for restoration. *Bruce Maffey* BELOW: The same trailer (left) after restoration with an open double-deck trailer of similar vintage, fully restored to working order. *Bruce Maffey* BELOW MIDDLE: A scene on the Ferrymead tramway showing restored Christchurch trams No. 152 (left) and No. 178 (middle), with Dunedin No. 22 on the right. *Bruce Maffey* BOTTOM LEFT: The body of Christchurch No. 152 being removed from a private property. *Dave Hinman* BOTTOM RIGHT: The body of Dunedin No. 22 as found at Heriot in Central Otago in 1968. *Dave Hinman*

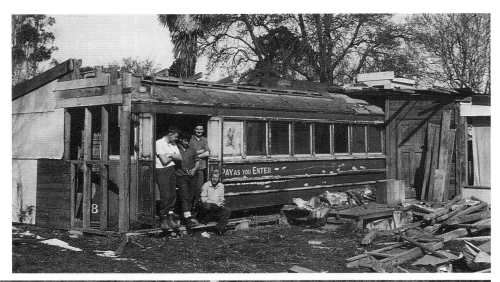

Christchurch electric tram No. 178, which had been part of a holiday cottage near Milford, Temuka, some 145 kilometres from Christchurch. Members of a work party are shown during partial demolition of the bach to remove the tram body for transportation back to Ferrymead. *L.J. Dale* BELOW: No. 178, now restored, running on the opening day of the electric tramway at Ferrymead *Graham Stewart*

The Christchurch group's first restoration task was the 19th-century horse-tram that was used to celebrate the 10th anniversary of the closing of the Papanui line during the August school holidays in 1964. Thousands of people, including children who had never ridden on a tram hauled by genuine horsepower, flocked to ride the 1887 vehicle. Fortunately, the tram rails in Papanui Road between Blighs Road and the old terminus had not then been buried beneath tarseal.

In the same year the society changed its name to the Tramway Historical Society and, with the publicity from the Papanui event, the volunteer group found they had gained a good standing in the city.

The formation of the Ferrymead Historic Park followed, where today the society operates an electric tramway service and, on special occasions, the steam- and horse-drawn trams. This priceless asset, which includes a pioneer village street along which the trams run, was started by a small number of people interested in Christchurch's transport heritage. The main tramway stalwarts in the early days included John Shanks, Russell Kent, Bruce Fleming, Gary Riggs, Chris Chaston, John Bettle and Neil Andrews. They were soon joined by Ian and Don Spicer, Neil Holder, Bruce Dale, Dave Hinman, Murray Sanders, Steve Lea, Dave Hansen, Larry Day, Alan Robb, Andy Law, Trevor Craib, and many others, too numerous to mention individually.

One of the society's major feats has been the restoration of tramway vehicles, some of which had been derelict for just on 20 years, lying in a rotting state, stripped of all equipment, in a backyard or paddock.

The Ferrymead tramway opened for steam traction in January 1968, carrying 1809 passengers on opening day. Electrification of the line followed in May 1970, with Christchurch 'Brill' No. 178 doing the honours after a restoration job that had taken two years.

At first tramway operation was limited to a 500-metre section of line near the Bridle Path Road entrance, but from the early 1970s the track was steadily extended towards the area now known as the Moorhouse Township and Museum area. The line was completed in September 1984, almost exactly 30 years after the last trams had ceased to run in the streets of Christchurch.

Christchurch is now to run a tourist electric tram service, using rolling stock provided by the Tramway Historical Society, from Rolleston Avenue down Worcester Street to Cathedral Square. The first stage of street reconstruction, using a single tram track with a paving block surface, was completed between Rolleston Avenue and Montreal Street in September 1991. In early 1992 the council was investigating possible extensions to the line, first north from Cathedral Square to Victoria Square and then along Armagh Street back to Rolleston Avenue, with a possible link into Hagley Park and the Botanic Gardens. Perhaps by 1994, 40 years after the last trams ran in Christchurch, they will return?

The Wellington Tramway Museum is situated at Queen Elizabeth Park, near the main entrance at Mackay's Crossing, about 4 kilometres north of Paekakariki, on the main road north from Wellington.

The original group, led by Bill Horne, were given their first tram in 1961 by the Wellington City Council. No. 151, a typical Wellington double-saloon type, was to be kept as a stationary exhibit. The Wellington City Council had earlier donated three trams to the Old Time Transport Preservation League at Matakohe, Northland, and a double-saloon tram to an American museum. The council felt they had fulfilled their obligation to posterity and announced a policy whereby any further trams would have to be purchased at the scrap value of £22 10s each, a lot of money in 1964.

The first £22 10s tram was No. 207, the only double saloon of this class to be preserved, thanks to the Vintage Car Club of Wellington, who donated the money. The group were determined to buy some *Fiducia*, trams and settled for four, Nos 235, 238, 239 and 260, the last tram to be built in New Zealand. A fifth *Fiducia*, No. 250, was purchased and dismantled for spare parts; the frame and bogies are still used to carry construction materials.

An early scene in 1965 of the Wellington Tramway Museum's site at Queen Elizabeth Park, showing the original track being laid in the foreground and former Wellington trams, some covered with tarpaulins as a protection against the weather, in the background, where the depot area is now situated.
Graham Stewart

The official opening of the Wellington Tramway Museum's electric tramway at Queen Elizabeth Park, Paekakariki, on 19 December 1965. *Alan Smith* RIGHT: The first official tram, Wellington *Fiducia* No. 235, about to drive through the ribbon. *Alan Smith*

The group not only had to raise the purchase price of these trams, but also had to remove them from the Newtown tram barn, an expensive exercise in itself. It was a make or break time and fortunately the museum group survived. The financial and physical demands of saving these trams resulted in them all being stored out in the open at Seaview, Petone, and at the Queen Elizabeth Park Museum site for 10 years before they could be housed.

Once arrangements for a working tramway museum had been finalised with the Queen Elizabeth Park Board in 1964, construction began, led by Ian Little, whose determination and drive in those early years saw the first section opened for the

ABOVE LEFT: The terminal area in the late 1960s, 100 metres inside the Memorial Gates at the entrance to Queen Elizabeth Park at Mackay's Crossing, 4 kilometres north of Paekakariki on State Highway One north of Wellington. ABOVE: Wellington trams Nos 238 and 207 passing on the short loop line on the Wellington Tramway Museum's electric tramway at Queen Elizabeth Park. *Graham Stewart*

public by December 1965. Ian Little has since become a personality in the world of transport preservation and in December 1988 established a working trolley bus museum at Foxton.

On open parkland exposed at times to severe weather, the construction of the first buildings and the laying of track involved heavy manual labour, much sweat and long hours. Full credit must go to the mainstays of this scheme, who included Keith McGavin, Mike Flinn, Ray Shand, Colin Perfect, Barry Ollerenshaw, Harry Berry, Charles Gibson and many others.

Now, thanks to their endeavours over many years, the tramway runs adjacent to the park road, winding up and over rolling hills and down through sand dunes to the beach on the coast. This picturesque museum tramway, operated by the Wellington Tramway Museum, has a lovely rural atmosphere which is reminiscent of travelling by tram from Wanganui to Castlecliff in the late 1940s.

Further south, in the Early Settlers' Museum at Dunedin, a cable car stands in retired splendour, and a collection of old Dunedin tram bodies has been stored at Seacliff for many years, waiting for the day when finance is available to restore them. Over 60 exhibits dating from the 1880s are being restored by these various organisations, largely on a voluntary basis, so New Zealanders yet unborn will be able to experience the forms of transport that once made our cities mobile.

A 1970s scene at the Museum of Transport and Technology of New Zealand showing Auckland tram No. 253 carrying visitors on the internal tram line. The destination sign on the tram was advertising the first edition of this book. *Graham Stewart*

MUSEUM & ARTS CENTRE

Drawings of the tourist electric tramway for Christchurch at present under construction in Worcester Street. The lower drawing shows the position of the tram track on the Worcester Street Bridge. The north side of the bridge is on the right. *Upper drawing by Elizabeth Briggs, Lower drawing by Andrew Craig, Environmental Policy and Planning, Christchurch City Council.*

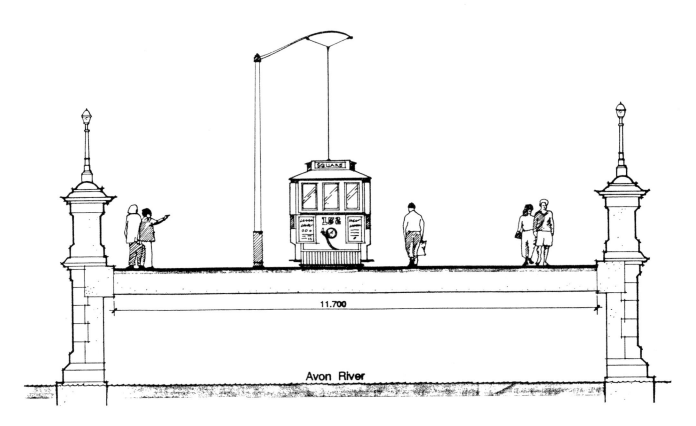

Urban Transport Milestones During the Tramway Era

7 May 1862	First horse-drawn passenger street tramway service started between Nelson and the Port of Nelson.
1860s	Horse-drawn tramways running on wooden rails used extensively on the West Coast of the South Island during the goldrush.
9 November 1867	First suburban railway line between Christchurch and Lyttelton opened.
2 December 1871	First steam tramway opened between Grahamstown and Tararu on the Coromandel Peninsula.
31 December 1872	Dunedin to Port Chalmers railway line opened.
24 December 1873	Opening of the Auckland to Onehunga railway line.
14 April 1874	Wellington's first railway was opened for traffic to Lower Hutt.
24 August 1878	Steam tramways inaugurated at Wellington by the Governor, the Marquis of Normanby.
7 July 1879	David Proudfoot started steam- and horse-tram services in Dunedin.
9 March 1880	Canterbury Tramway Company commenced the first steam-tram service in Christchurch, between the Square and the Railway Station.
24 February 1881	First cable tramway south of the equator began running up Rattray Street, Dunedin.
4 August 1881	The Devonport Steam Ferry Company was registered at Auckland.
3 December 1881	Southernmost horse-trams in the world started running from Invercargill to the suburb of Gladstone.
1882	Horse traction replaced steam in the streets of Wellington.
16 March 1883	Mornington cable trams commenced running from the Exchange in Dunedin.
11 August 1884	Horse-trams started a service from Queen Street to Ponsonby in Auckland.
18 March 1885	In Dunedin the Maryhill cable line opened—reputed to be the steepest cable tramway in the world at the time.
25 September 1886	A horse tramway from Devonport to Cheltenham Beach, on the North Shore of Auckland, started a service meeting all ferryboats.
1896	Wooden-railed horse tramway operating at Paeroa.
22 February 1900	The Kelburn cable tramway started running in Wellington.
1 August 1900	Wellington City Council took over horse-tram services.
22 October 1900	A cable car service from the Octagon in Dunedin, up Stuart and Albert Streets and down into the Kaikorai Valley commenced.
23 October 1900	First electric tram-cars started running at Maori Hill, Dunedin.
21 March 1901	Dunedin City Council took over the running of horse-tram services.
17 November 1902	Electric tramways at Auckland officially opened by Sir John Logan Campbell—the public service did not start until 24 November.
August 1903	The Hawke's Bay Motor Company placed a steam-driven bus on the Napier-to-Taradale service.
27 September 1903	Electric tramway opened to the wharf at Onehunga in Auckland.
24 December 1903	Municipal electric tramway service opened for the public in Dunedin.
April 1904	The first motor-bus service started in Christchurch between the Railway Station and Cathedral Square.
2 June 1904	A motor-bus service from Auckland to Howick was inaugurated by Sir Maurice O'Rourke.
30 June 1904	The first Wellington electric trams started running from the Newtown Sheds to the gates of St Patrick's College.
5 June 1905	Christchurch inaugurated an electric tram service, the first suburb served being Papanui.
15 March 1908	Horse-trams ceased running in Invercargill.
11 December 1908	First provincial tramway service started at Wanganui to the suburb of Aramoho.
22 December 1910	Steam-trams in Auckland commenced a service from Bayswater to Takapuna and Milford, with a connecting ferry service between Bayswater and Auckland.
12 March 1912	Electric trams introduced to the streets of Invercargill.
1913	Private bus services in Timaru taken over by the council.
13 April 1913	Edison battery tramway service opened at Gisborne.
1 September 1913	Eastbourne Borough Council purchased the ferries from the Harbour Ferry Company.
8 September 1913	Municipal electric tramway service started at Napier to Port Ahuriri.
November 1913	The Tramways Amendment Bill was passed, requiring all trams to be equipped with a centre passageway.
10 March 1916	Electric trams started running at New Plymouth—the last city in the country to install electric tramways.
1916	The first woman conductor in New Zealand employed on Searle's motor-bus at Oamaru.
1 July 1919	The Auckland City Council purchased the electric tramway system from the Auckland Electric Tramways Company Ltd.
September 1920	A free bus service opened in Auckland to the Farmers' Trading Co.

8 September 1921	Municipal bus service started at Palmerston North with four Commer vehicles.
26 October 1921	The first one-man trams, dispensing with conductors, placed in service at New Plymouth.
October 1924	The first trackless tram (trolley bus) inaugurated a service in Wellington, from Thorndon to Kaiwarra (Kaiwharawhara).
1 November 1926	The Motor Omnibus Traffic Act came into force, making it illegal for private buses to run in competition with tram-cars.
November 1926	First suburban road service to be operated by the Railways Department started between Napier and Hastings.
1 April 1927	Eastbourne Borough Council acquired omnibus service for £8,000.
27 April 1927	The steam-tram service from Bayswater to Milford came to a standstill, motor-buses taking over.
May 1927	Motor-bus competition on the new waterfront road at Auckland caused the closure of the ferry service to St Helier's Bay.
1929	Peak for tramway tracks in suburban streets—with 273 route kilometres of lines. The total length of running track, including double sections and loops, was 420 kilometres.
16 January 1929	Tramway and motor-bus services operated by the Auckland City Council taken over by the newly formed Auckland Transport Board.
14 February 1929	First suburban electric railway service inaugurated between the port of Lyttelton and Christchurch.
8 July 1929	Motor-buses replaced battery trams at Gisborne.
3 February 1931	Earthquake closed the Napier Corporation Tramways service.
1 April 1931	Trolley buses introduced to Christchurch—from the Square to Shirley.
30 May 1932	Pioneer trackless tram in Wellington withdrawn from service.
22 November 1933	Tram No. 232 Fiducia introduced to the Wellington public, marking a new style of tram travel in the capital.
6 May 1936	Free tram service for shoppers started in Auckland from Beresford Street to the Farmers' Trading Co. in Wyndham Street.
1 July 1936	The first electric tramway line at Maori Hill, Dunedin, closed.
4 July 1938	Opening of the first suburban multiple-unit electric railway service at Wellington, to the suburb of Johnsonville.
19 December 1938	First trolley bus service in Auckland started between Wyndham Street and Hobson Street as a free shoppers service for the Farmers' Trading Co.
June 1942	Women conductors first employed on tram-cars.
1943–1944	Petrol rationing during the Second World War saw passenger totals for electric tramways reach the all-time high of 220,216,000.
31 July 1947	Stuart Street cable line in Dunedin closed without prior public notice.
2 July 1948	Eastbourne-Days Bay ferries ceased running across Wellington Harbour.
5 September 1949	Multiple-unit electric railway coaches introduced on the Wellington to Paekakariki suburban service.
24 September 1949	Trolley buses replaced trams on the Herne Bay route in Auckland—the start of the conversion from trams to trolley buses.
29 May 1950	Trolley buses introduced on the first suburban route in Wellington to Oriental Bay—replacing trams.
24 September 1950	Greyhound Buses Limited took over all services formerly operated by the Wanganui Corporation Tramways.
27 October 1950	The only provincial trolley bus service to run in New Zealand inaugurated at New Plymouth—to the suburb of Westown.
24 December 1950	The first trolley bus service in Dunedin started to Opoho—formerly served by electric trams.
26 October 1951	The pioneer Roslyn cable car line built in 1881 closed with full ceremony in Dunedin.
10 September 1952	Celebrations marked the change from municipal trams to buses at Invercargill.
14 September 1953	First section of Hutt Valley suburban railway electrification opened to Taita Station.
23 July 1954	Last provincial tramway system closed at New Plymouth.
11 September 1954	Christchurch farewelled its electric trams in Cathedral Square.
24 July 1955	Completion of electrification of suburban railway services in Wellington—with multiple-unit electric coaches reaching Upper Hutt.
29 October 1955	Last day of the Maryhill cable tram in Dunedin.
29 March 1956	The last tram-car in the South Island at Dunedin made the final journey from the Exchange to St Clair.
8 November 1956	Diesel buses replaced trolley buses in Christchurch—bringing to an end the use of electric transport in the streets of Christchurch.
29 December 1956	The last tramline at Auckland from Queen Street to Onehunga closed with full ceremony.
2 March 1957	The last Dunedin cable car line at Mornington closed.
30 May 1959	Opening of the Auckland Harbour Bridge—vehicular ferry services to Birkenhead and Devonport ceased during the afternoon. Passenger ferry services to Chelsea, Birkenhead, Northcote and Bayswater finished at midnight.
31 May 1959	North Shore bus services at Auckland started running across the Harbour Bridge into the central city area.
2 May 1964	Wellington's and New Zealand's last tram made a ceremonial journey from Thorndon to Newtown car sheds.

Suburbs Once Served by Street Tramways

NELSON (Horse tramway) 3-foot gauge. From corner Hardy and Trafalgar Streets to port of Nelson, Via Haven Road. Opened May 1862.
(closed 1901)

THAMES (Steam tramway) 3-foot 6-inch gauge. From Curtis' Wharf, in Albert Street, around the foreshore to Tararu Point. Opened December 1871.
(closed November 1874)

WELLINGTON (Steam and horse tramways) steam withdrawn 1882, 3-foot 6-inch gauge.
Along Lambton Quay, Willis Street, Manners Street, Cuba Street, Vivian Street, Cambridge Terrace, around Basin Reserve, to terminus in Adelaide Road, at corner of King Street. Opened August 1878.
Branch line from Lambton Quay, along Grey Street to entrance of Queen's Wharf. Opened August 1878.
Thorndon Quay to Pipitea Point (just south of Davis Street). Opened September 1878. Via Courtenay Place line. Opened March 1881.
Loop line along Featherston Street. Opened September 1881.
(replaced by electric service 1904)

DUNEDIN (Steam and horse tramways) steam withdrawn 1884, 3-foot 6-inch gauge.
From Cargill's Monument to Water of the Leith via High and Castle Streets and Princes and George Streets. Opened July 1879.
Branch from Exchange down Rattray Street to car barn. Opened July 1879.
to Bethunes Gully (North-east Valley). Opened 1880s.
to Cargill's Corner—with branch along Cargill Road and David Street to Playfair Street, Caversham. Opened 1880.
— the other branch along King Edward Street and Prince Albert Road to St Kilda, with a short extension along Richardson Street to Forbury Park. Opened 1880.
From Forbury Corner (cnr David Street and Cargill Road), along Forbury Road to St Clair. Opened 1880.
(replaced by electric service 1903/05)

MAORI HILL—Dunedin (Horse tramway) 3-foot 6-inch gauge.
From Roslyn cable tramway terminus in Ross Street (Town Belt), to Bishopscourt, via City Road and Highgate. Opened December 1882.
(replaced by electric service 1900)

DUNEDIN (Cable tramways) 3-foot 6-inch gauge.
Roslyn Line
From cnr Rattray and Maclaggen Streets, up Rattray Street, through private right-of-way in Town Belt, to foot of the present Ross Street. Opened February 1881.
City extension along Rattray Street to Princes Street. Opened 1900.
Extension into Kaikorai Valley to Frasers Road. Opened August 1906.
(replaced by buses 26 October 1951)

Mornington Line
From Princes Street, up High Street, Queens Drive, to Mornington. Opened March 1883.
(replaced by buses 2 March 1957)
Maryhill Extension
From Mornington cable tram depot, down private right-of-way and along Glenpark Avenue to Mitchell Avenue. Opened March 1885.
— service suspended between 1916 and 1919.
(replaced by bus 29 October 1955)
Kaikorai Line
From Octagon, up Stuart and Albert Streets, through private right-of-way in Town Belt, and into Kaikorai Valley, to Nairn Street. Opened October 1900.
(replaced by buses 1 August 1947)
Elgin Road Line
From Mornington township, up Mailer Street, left into Lawrence Street, right into Havelock Street, left into Elgin Road, to terminus at Mitchell Avenue. Opened October 1906.
— service suspended 9/10/07 to 10/12/07 and again from 7/7/08 to 10/11/08.
(replaced by bus 22 January 1910)

WELLINGTON (Kelburn cable tramway) Original system 3-foot 6-inch gauge, double track.
From Cable Car Lane, off Lambton Quay, to Upland Road. Opened February 1902. Closed 22/9/78.
New system. Opened 20/10/79.
Single-track metre gauge with a crossing loop at mid-point, Talavera Station.
— tramway runs on private right-of-way.

CHRISTCHURCH (Steam and horse tramways) 4-foot 8½-inch gauge. Horse operation started 1882.
Cathedral Square to Railway Station via Colombo Street. Opened March 1880.
Cathedral Square to Railway Station via High and Manchester Street. Opened July 1880.
Cathedral Square to St Albans. Opened June 1880. To Papanui, opened July 1880.
Cathedral Square to Sydenham Park. Opened August 1880. To Devon Street, opened December 1880; to Cashmere (Dyers Pass Road), opened December 1898.
From Manchester Street, along High Street, Ferry Road to Olliviers Road. Opened April 1882. To Heathcote Bridge, opened December 1882; to Sumner via McCormacks Bay, Redcliffs and over a wooden bridge at Clifton Bay, opened 1888; Nayland Street to Herberden Avenue, opened January 1890.
Cathedral Square to Addington Railway Station, via Colombo Street, Tuam Street, Hagley Avenue, Lincoln Road. Opened January 1882. To Showgrounds October 1887. To Sunnyside (Hoon Hay Road), opened January 1896.
From Worcester Street, through Cathedral Square, along Worcester Street, Linwood Avenue, Buckleys Road, Slaughterhouse Road (now Rudds Road). Opened March 1886. Branch line for hearse tram ran down Cemetery Road (now Butterfield Avenue), to Linwood Cemetery. April 1886. Linwood to New Brighton, opened February 1887.

From Lichfield Street, via Manchester Street, Cashel Street to Stanmore Bridge. Opened September 1893. Through Richmond and Shirley to Burwood, opened October 1893; Burwood to North Beach and along Esplanade (now Marine Parade), to New Brighton, opened October 1894.

(replaced as electric services introduced 1905/14)

INVERCARGILL (Horse tramways) 3-foot 6-inch gauge.
Dee Street to Gladstone, along North Road. Opened December 1881.
Along Tay and Conon Streets, to Ettrick Street. Opened December 1883.
Extension to Biggar Street, along Conon Street. Opened February 1884.
Gladstone to Waikiwi. Opened October 1884.
Branch line along Tay Street and East Road, to Mary Street. Opened 1883.

(closed 15 March 1908)

AUCKLAND (Horse tramways) 4-foot 8½-inch gauge.
From Queen Street via Wellesley Street West, Hobson Street, Pitt Street, Karangahape Road to Ponsonby Road Opened August 1884.
Along Ponsonby Road to Three Lamps, and down Jervois Road to Wallace Street. Opened February 1885.
Along Karangahape Road from Pitt Street and up Symonds Street to Khyber Pass Road. Opened November 1885.
Wellesley Street East, Symonds Street to Karangahape Road, and Khyber Pass Road to Grafton Road. Opened December 1885.
From Grafton Road, down Khyber Pass Road into Broadway. Newmarket, to siding in Remuera Road. Opened February 1886.
Choral Hall branch—from top of Wellesley Street East, down lower Symonds Street to Grafton Road. Opened March 1886.
Manukau Road—from Remuera Road to Greenlane Road. Opened February 1888.
Onehunga—Greenlane Road to Onehunga Wharf. Opened March 1903.

(Horse-trams used electric tram rails for a temporary service until the electric trams started.)

(replaced by electric service 1902/03)

AUCKLAND—North Shore (Horse tramway) 4-foot 8½-inch gauge.
From Devonport ferry jetty, along King Edward Parade, Cheltenham Road, to Cheltenham Beach. Opened September 1886.

(closed in 1888)

MAORI HILL—*Dunedin* (Electric tramway) 3-foot 6-inch gauge.
From 23 October 1900 to 1 July 1936.
From foot of the present Ross Street, via City Road and Highgate to Maori Hill.

AUCKLAND (Electric tramways) 4-foot 8½-inch gauge.
From 24 November 1902 to 29 December 1956.
HERNE BAY: To Wallace Street via College Hill, December 1902, to Herne Bay Road, October 1903. Closed 24/9//49.
PONSONBY: via Wellesley Street West, Ponsonby Road to Three Lamps, November 1902. Closed 9/11/51.
GREY LYNN: (via Surrey Crescent) to Surrey Crescent, May 1903, to Francis Street terminus, May 1910. Castle Street section Closed 22/7/32.
RICHMOND ROAD: Via Ponsonby Road to Lincoln Street, October 1930, to Francis Street, February 1931, to Castle Street, August 1932, Closed 29/8/52.
WESTMERE: To Auckland Zoo, December 1923, to West End Road, May 1931. Closed 13/3/53.

POINT CHEVALIER: To Hall Corner, March 1930, to Point Chevalier Beach, July 1930. Balloon loop at terminus. Closed 20/11/53.
AVONDALE: To Kingsland, May 1903, to Morningside, July 1912, to Mount Albert, September 1915, to Great North Road, January 1932. Closed 13/1/56.
OWAIRAKA: To Parrish Road, February 1925, to Calgary Street, March 1925, Eden Park Loop (capacity 35 trams), September 1925, to Owairaka Avenue, February 1931, terminus extension, May 1936. Closed 6/8/54.
MT ROSKILL: To Herbert Road, August 1908, to Balmoral Road, August 1920, to Halston Road, December 1929, to Mt Albert Road, January 1930. Closed 11/9/53.
THREE KINGS: To Pencarrow Avenue, May 1908, to Rewa Road, October 1930, to Mt Albert Road, March 1931. Closed 22/5/53.
ONEHUNGA: Khyber Pass Road to Newmarket, December 1902, to Epsom Depot, March 1903 (Greenlane Road branch, April 1939), to Royal Oak, April 1903, to Captain Street, August 1903, to Onehunga Wharf, September 1903. Closed 28/12/56.
PARNELL: To Domain Drive, December 1902, to Newmarket, January 1903. Closed 29/12/56.
MEADOWBANK: Remuera Road to top of Victoria Avenue, May 1904, to Greenlane Road, August 1906, to Upland Road, May 1913, to Meadowbank Road, June 1930. Closed 17/8/56.
VICTORIA AVENUE: From Remuera Road to Shore Road, June 1913. Closed 1/4/56.
GREAT SOUTH ROAD: To Market Road, June 1923, to Campbell Road, October 1923. Closed 4/12/53. Racecourse Loop, via Woodbine Avenue and Wairakei Street, November 1923. Closed 3/1/55.
CITY LINES: Queen Street, to Wellesley Street junction, November 1902; via Town Hall to Karangahape Road, and from Pitt Street, along Karangahape Road to Symonds Street, October 1916; from Wellesley Street West, up Hobson Street and Pitt Street, along Karangahape Road to Ponsonby Road, November 1902; Customs Street West and up Hobson Street to Victoria Street West, December 1902; Hobson Street, from Victoria Street to Wellesley Street West, May 1903; Wyndham Street and Beresford Street sidings for Farmers' free service, May 1936; Wellesley Street East and branch down lower Symonds Street to Waterloo Quadrant, November 1902; Symonds Street to Khyber Pass Road, December 1902; Anzac Avenue, February 1921; Fanshawe Street, Halsey Street to Gaunt Street Depot, November 1925; Stanley Street siding, October 1929; Railway Station loop, November 1930; Fanshawe Street, along Halsey Street to Victoria Street West, November 1938.

(replaced by electric trolley bus and diesel bus services 1949/56)

DUNEDIN (Electric tramways) 4-foot 8-inch gauge.
From 24 December 1903 to 29 March 1956
NORMANBY: Along North Road to junction of Norwood Street, December 1903. Closed 25/8/51.
ST CLAIR: Along Forbury Road and Bedford Street to terminus, April 1905. Closed 29/3/54.
GARDENS: Via High Street, Castle Street and Howe Street, December 1903. Closed 24/12/50.
Via Princes Street and George Street, February 1904. Closed 7/5/55.
ANDERSONS BAY: To Ross Corner, March 1905, to Andersons Bay, March 1906, 5-chain extension to terminus, 1928. Closed 8/11/52.
ST KILDA: Along Prince Albert Road to Victoria Road, 1905. Closed 3/3/56.
TAHUNA: Along Royal Crescent, Culling Street, Victoria Road, to St Kilda tram terminus, 1906 (Three-rail track to Tahuna Park—NZR trains 3-foot 6-inch gauge,

shared track with trams during November Otago Agricultural Show for cartage of stock until 1938)—Culling Street, Victoria Road link closed 1942—to Bowen Street closed 6/10/52.

CAVERSHAM: Via Hillside Road and David Street, and Via Main South Road, 1905. Closed 28/8/54.
(David Street link closed July 1938)

OPOHO: Along Opoho Road and Signal Hill Road to Blacks Road, September 1924. Closed 30/9/50.

FORBURY PARK: Along Richardson Street, with loop line around Plunket Street, Victoria Road, and Moreau Street, December 1925. Closed 24/2/56.

LOGAN PARK: Along Albany Street, Forth Street and Union Street to Logan Park November 1925. Balloon loop at terminus. Closed 24/5/43. (Between 1939 and 1942, line temporarily closed three times.)

CARISBROOK: From Hillside Road, along McGlashan Street to Neville Street, July 1908. Closed; Unknown.

(replaced by diesel bus and electric trolley bus services 1943/56)

WELLINGTON (Electric tramways) 4-foot gauge.
From 30 June 1904 to 2 May 1964

NEWTOWN: From car shed to Basin Reserve, June 1904; to Courtenay Place, July 1904; from Newtown tram shed to Zoo, April 1914, balloon loop at terminus; Cuba Street to Wallace Street, August 1904; Wallace Street to John Street, July 1925. Closed 2/5/64.

ISLAND BAY: Rintoul Street, Luxford Street, to Adelaide Road, August 1904; Adelaide Road to Medway Street, November 1905; Medway Street to Island Bay, December 1905. Closed 2/5/63.

ORIENTAL BAY: From Courtenay Place, along Oriental Parade to terminus at Carlton Gore Road, September 1904. Closed 28/5/50.

ARO STREET: From Customhouse Quay, along Willis Street to Aro Street terminus, September 1904. Closed 17/8/57.

BROOKLYN: Upper Willis Street, Brooklyn Road, Ohiro Road to terminus in Cleveland Street, May 1906. Closed 17/8/57.

THORNDON: Lambton Quay to Thorndon terminus, November 1904. Closed 4/5/64. Siding into Thorndon Station; December 1904. Closed 1956.

HATAITAI: From Kent Terrance, along Elizabeth, Brougham, and Pirie Streets, to Austin Street, November 1906; from Austin Street, through Hataitai tramway tunnel, and Hataitai to Kilbirnie, April 1907; Waitoa Road terminus at Hataitai, about 1919. Tunnel closed 3/11/62. Hataitai to Kilbirnie Closed 30/11/57.

MIRAMAR: From Kilbirnie, along Coutts Street, Hobart Street, Park Road, Rotherham Terrace, Darlington Road, to Camperdown Road, June 1907; extended to balloon loop 1939. Closed 30/11/57.

Temporary double-track siding laid in Calabar Road, from Broadway, and balloon loop line at Tirangi Road, Kilbirnie, from Coutts Street, for Centennial Exhibition tramway traffic—1939/40.

SEATOUN: From Miramar junction, along Broadway, Ferry Street, Dundas Street to terminus at Falkirk Avenue, December 1907. Closed 3/5/58.

LYALL BAY: From Coutts Street, along Onepu Road, to Lyall Parade, December 1911, to Queens Drive loop, 1914. Closed 30/7/60.

Temporary loop line from Onepu Road, along Endeavour Street, Yule Street, and Resolution Street, for Exhibition tramway traffic, 1939/40.

CONSTABLE STREET: Up Constable Street to the top of the hill, August 1904; to Kilbirnie Post Office via Crawford Road, December 1915. Closed 31/3/61.

WADESTOWN: From Molesworth Street to Pitt Street, Wadestown, July 1911, Pitt Street to Wadestown

terminus, October 1911. (Barnard Street to Wadestown terminus mostly on private right-of-way, closed 22/1/49) Barnard Street to Lambton Quay. Closed 27/2/49.

KARORI: Lambton Quay, via Mulgrave Street, Aitken Street, Molesworth Street, and Tinakori Road, to Botanical Gardens, November 1904; to Karori Tunnel, 13 March 1907; to Nottingham Street, 26 March 1907; to Karori terminus at Karori Park, May 1911. Connection in Molesworth Street from Lambton Quay to Aitken Street, December 1911. Bowen Street Deviation from Lambton Quay to Tinakori Road, August 1940. Tinakori Road line closed 27/2/49. Karori line closed 1/10/54.

NORTHLAND: From Chaytor Street, along Northland Road to Woburn Road. June 1929. Closed 17/9/54.

CITY LINES: Courtenay Place to Harbour Board Office in Jervois Quay via Manners Street and lower Cuba Street, Cuba Street to Wallace Street, August 1904; Harbour Board Office to Lambton Station via Customhouse Quay and Ballance Street, September 1904; from Kent Terrace, along Vivian Street to Cuba Street, November 1904; from Cuba Street, along Manners Street to Willis Street, and along Willis Street and Lambton Quay to Lambton Station, December 1904; from Willis Street along Customhouse Quay to Jervois Quay, 1912; Wakefield Street and Hunter Street lines, October 1926; Johnston Street line, 1925; Ballance Street lines transferred to Whitmore Street, 1927; Stout Street, October 1937; Bunny Street, Waterloo Quay, 1938.

(replaced by electric trolley bus and diesel bus services 1949/64)

CHRISTCHURCH (Electric tramways) 4-foot 8½-inch gauge.
From 6 June 1905 to 11 September 1954

PAPANUI: From Square, via Colombo Street, Victoria Street, Papanui Road, Harewood Road, to Papanui Railway Station, June 1905. Closed 11/9/54. Railway siding closed 15/4/34.
Balloon loop, August 1922.
Temporary loop line from Victoria Street along Peterborough Street, Park Terrace, and Salisbury Street for Exhibition traffic in 1906/07.

NORTHCOTE: Main North Road from Papanui, March 1913. Closed 30/9/30.

CASHMERE: From Square to south end Colombo Street, August 1905; to foot of Hackthorne Road, December 1911; to Dyers Pass Road, February 1912; to Cashmere Hills terminus by Sign of the Takahe, May 1912. Barrington Street siding, October 1917. Cashmere Hills line to Barrington Street closed 21/6/53.
Barrington Street to Square closed 11/9/54.

SUMNER: From Square via High Street and Ferry Road to Heathcote Bridge, November 1905; to Sumner via McCormacks Bay, Redcliffs, Clifton, Nayland Street to Heberden Avenue, April 1907; balloon loop off Nayland Street; loop off Ferry Road, along Lancaster, Stevens, and Falsgrave Streets for Lancaster Park traffic. Closed 6/12/52.

CRANFORD STREET: From Square along Colombo Street, Edgeware Road, Cranford Street to Westminster Street, July 1910; terminus extension, 1922; reversing triangle extension at terminus, 1933. Closed 26/7/53.

NEW BRIGHTON: Via Worcester Street, Linwood Avenue, Buckleys Road, Pages Road, and Seaview Road, August 1906; via Cashel Street line, November 1910; balloon loop at terminus, Oram, Beresford Streets and Marine Parade, 1911. Closed 18/10/52.

LINWOOD: Via Worcester Street, March 1906; extension to Dallington; via Worcester Street, Rochester Street, Gloucester Street to Dallington Bridge, November 1912. Closed 1/11/36.

LINCOLN ROAD: From Square via Worcester Street, Oxford Terrace, Hagley Avenue, Lincoln Road to Hoon

Hay Road, February 1906; line off Lincoln Road, along Lindores, Moule, and Twigger Streets for Trotting Club traffic; balloon loop at terminus, April 1933. Closed 26/7/53.

RICCARTON: From Hagley Avenue, along Riccarton Road, to Clyde Road, November 1905; Main South Road, O'Briens Road, Racecourse Road and Yaldhurst Road—rejoining line in Riccarton Road, March 1906; branch line to Plumpton Park Racecourse (now Wigram airfield), from corner of Main South Road and Racecourse Road, December 1915; siding off Racecourse Road into Riccarton Racecourse; Clyde Road balloon loop, 1934. Closed 14/6/53.

FENDALTON: From Papanui Road, along Bealey Avenue, Carlton Mill Road, Rhodes Street, Rossall Street, Holmwood Road, November 1909; Fendalton Road and Burnside Road to terminus at Clyde Road, December 1912; extension across Clyde Road, April 1915. Closed 5/2/50.

RICHMOND, BURWOOD AND NORTH BEACH: Stanmore Road, North Avon Road, North Parade, Shirley Road, New Brighton Road, Bassett Street, Travis Road, Rookwood Avenue, Bowhill Road, to Marine Parade at North Beach.
— to Burwood, August 1910;—to North Beach and along Marine Parade to New Brighton, October 1914. (trams withdrawn between Burwood and North Beach from August 1927 to October 1928). Closed 4/7/31. Richmond closed 16/12/34.

ST MARTINS: Waltham Road, Wilsons Road, Centaurus Road, to terminus at Rapaki Road, April 1914. (Closed 6/1/41 reopened 6/7/42, because of petrol rationing) finally closed 19/5/46.

OPAWA: From Colombo Street, along Wordsworth Street, Waltham Road, Shakespeare Road, and Opawa Road to terminus at Heathcote River, November 1909. Closed 5/2/50.

SPREYDON: From Moorhouse Avenue, along Antigua Street, South Crescent Road, to Selwyn Street, August 1911; small extension into Coronation Street, September 1915; Coronation Street, Simeon Street and Athelstan Street to terminus at Barrington Street, August 1922; balloon loop 1933. Closed 21/6/53.

ST ALBANS PARK: From junction Armagh Street, along Colombo Street, Bealey Avenue, Barbadoes Street, to Edgeware Road, December 1906; to terminus at Warrington Street, July 1915; reversing triangle 1934. Closed 21/6/53.

RAILWAY STATION: Via Manchester Street, June 1905. Closed 6/4/32.
Via Colombo Street, July 1905. Closed 1/11/36.
(ballast and depot lines not listed) (replaced by bus services 1930/54)

WANGANUI (Electric tramways) 4-foot 8½-inch gauge.
From 11 December 1908 to 24 September 1950
ARAMOHO: Taupo Quay, Victoria Avenue to Aramoho Junction, via Victoria Avenue and Glasgow Street, December 1908. Closed 22/7/50.
Via Guyton, Campbell, Ingestre, Bell and Dublin Streets and Somme Parade, December 1908. Closed 14/2/35.
To Quick Avenue, April 1915; to Aramoho Cemetery, September 1923. Closed 19/5/50.
Dublin Street—from Victoria Avenue to Bell Street, February 1935. Closed 3/9/50.
WANGANUI EAST: Dublin Street, Dublin Street Bridge, Jones, Moana, Duncan, Tinirau Streets to Patapu Street, November 1914; to East Town Railway Station via Hakeke, Holyoake and Salisbury Streets, November 1915. Closed 3/9/50.
GONVILLE-CASTLECLIFF: Guyton Street and siding in Purnell Street for racecourse traffic, December 1908;

along Guyton Street, with deviation over viaduct crossing railway Heads Road, Carlton Avenue, one line branching along Koromiko Road, Tawa Street, Bignell, and Abbot Street to Gonville—the other branch via Carlton Avenue, and Alma Road to Gonville, then along Puriri, Cross, Polson, Carson, Cornfoot, and Rangiora Street to Beach, October 1912. Closed 24/9/50.
Ridgway Street—city terminal siding, September 1915.
(replaced by Greyhound Bus Company services 1950)

TAKAPUNA—Auckland (Steam tramways) 4-foot 8½-inch gauge.
From 22 December 1910 to 26 April 1927
From Bayswater Wharf, along Marine Terrace, King Edward Avenue, Lake Road, Hurstmere Road, Kitchener Road, Shakespeare Road, Taharoto Road, Anzac Street, and back into Lake Road, December 1910. Closed 26/4/27.
(replaced by a motor bus service)

INVERCARGILL (Electric tramways) 4-foot 8½-inch gauge.
From 26 March 1912 to 10 September 1952
WAIKIWI: From Dee Street, along Main North Road to Durham Street, March 1912. Closed 1947.
— line down Leet Street to depot.
(Trams used line to Holywood Terrace, Gladstone, until March 1951.)
GEORGETOWN: From Dee Street, Tay, Conon, Tweed Streets, Elles Road South, Ettrick, Nelson, Rodney, and Pomona Streets, to terminus by Centre Street, March 1912. Closed 2/7/51.
(Line used to Rugby Park until August 1951.)
SOUTH INVERCARGILL: From Dee Street, Tay, Conon, Grace Streets, Elles Road South, to Tramway Road, mid-1912. (Southernmost electric street tramline in the world.) Closed 31/5/52.
NORTH INVERCARGILL: From Dee Street, Yarrow, Mary, Sydney, King, Windsor Streets, to terminus at Herbert Street, mid-1912. Closed 10/9/52.
(replaced by bus services 1947/52)

GISBORNE (Storage battery tramways) 4-foot gauge.
From 13 April 1913 to 8 July 1929
GLADSTONE ROAD: From Post Office, along Gladstone Road, to Roebuck Road, April 1913; to Stanley Road, 1915; to Lytton Road, September 1918. Closed 8/7/29.
— branch line down Carnarvon Street to Depot.
— tracks laid across Gladstone Road Bridge, February 1925, but never used.
ORMOND ROAD: From Gladstone Road, Peel Street, over Peel Street bridge, Fitzherbert Street, Ormond Road to Whataupoko, November 1923. Closed 11/28.
(replaced by bus services 1928/29)

NAPIER (Electric tramways) 3-foot 6-inch gauge.
From 8 September 1913 to 3 February 1931
PORT AHURIRI: From Faraday Street tram sheds, along Thackeray, Dickens, and Hastings Streets, Shakespeare Road, Waghorne and Bridge Streets, to terminus at commencement of Hyderabad Road, September 1913. Closed 3/2/31.
(Duplication of Dickens Street 15/6/21—cross-over at Browning Street 21/8/22.)
RAILWAY STATION: From Dickens Street into Munro Street and Station Street to Railway Station, September 1913. Closed 3/2/31.
HASTINGS STREET: From Dickens Street, along Hastings Street to McGrath Street railway crossing, July 1922. Closed 3/2/31.
(Bus services introduced after streets cleared of earthquake damage.)

NEW PLYMOUTH (Electric tramways) 4-foot $8\frac{1}{2}$-inch gauge.

From 10 March 1916 to 23 July 1954

FITZROY: Devon Road, Egmont Street, St Aubyn Street, to Railway Station, March 1916. Closed 23/7/54.

PORT: St Aubyn Street, South Road, Breakwater Road, to port, April 1916. Closed 23/7/54.

WESTOWN: Devon Street to Morley Street, May 1916; along Morley Street, Tukapo Street, to terminus at David Street, November 1923. Closed 6/10/50.

LIARDET STREET: From Devon Street, along Liardet Street to Fillis Street, with short spur line along Gilbert Street, July 1924. Closed 1/3/37.

(replaced by electric trolley bus and diesel bus services)

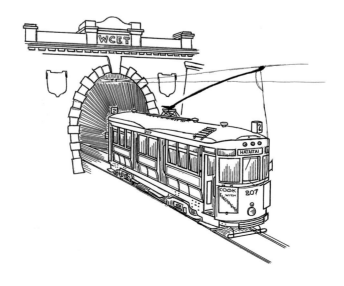

Summary of Horse, Steam and Cable Tramway Rolling Stock

HORSE TRAMWAY VEHICLES

Nelson—1862 to 1901: Three horse-trams, single-truck, double-deck, closed below, first tram built in Sydney, 1862.

Invercargill—1881 to 1908: Original trams imported from Starbuck Co., England. All single-truck, saloon—small and large, with clerestory roofs. One double-deck tram built 1887.

Maori Hill—1882 to 1889: Single-truck, small saloon, clerestory roof.

Auckland—1884 to 1902: 34 horse-trams, all single-truck, imported and local coach builders, saloon—small and large with clerestory roofs, palace and open summer cars.

STEAM AND HORSE TRAMWAY VEHICLES

Thames—1871 to 1874: Two locomotives, one built by Chaplin of Glasgow, ex-Bay of Islands Coal Company, 1871; the other Fraser and Tinnie, Auckland, 1872; one carriage was built of kauri.

Wellington—1878 to 1904: Eight tram-car engines built by Merryweather and Sons, London, 1878. Engines were named: *Florence, Hibernia, Wellington, Zealandia, Victoria, Cambria, Scotia* and *Anglia*. Withdrawn 1882. Original fleet of trailers and horse-trams consisted of 14 trailers by Stephenson Co., New York, single-truck, saloon, clerestory roof, eight large, six small, and four goods wagons. Later additions to fleet from overseas and local coach builders, included double-deckers and palace cars.

Dunedin—1879 to 1905: The fleet of tram-car engines included three from Henry Hughes and Co., England, two from Baldwin Locomotive Works, USA, and one from Kitson and Co., of England. Names given the Dunedin tram engines were: *City of Dunedin, Empress, New Zealander, Atlantic, Gordon, Washington* and *Grand Pacific*. Withdrawn 1884. Original fleet of trailers and horse-trams, a total of 32, were imported from England, USA and Norway. All single-truck, saloon—small and large, double-deck, open. Replacements made by local coach builders.

Christchurch—1880–1930s: Nine tram-car engines, eight built by Kitson and Co., England. Locomotives 1 to 5, built 1879; Locomotives 6 to 8, built 1881. CTB Locomotive No. 9, an 1884 Baldwin, was purchased second-hand from Sydney in 1906. Trailers and horse-trams: over 60 owned by three private companies, majority were double-deck, although Canterbury Tramway Co. had three types of single-deck trams. John Stephenson Co., New York, Moor and Sons, Booth McDonald and Co., and Boon and Stevens (later Boon and Co.) all of Christchurch, were the principal coach builders. Most of the private company vehicles were incorporated into the electric fleet of the Christchurch Tramway Board.

Takapuna—1910 to 1927: Seven Locomotives; Nos 1 and 2, built in 1909 by Kerr Stuart, England (named *Waitemata* and *Bayswater*); No. 3 built Kerr Stuart, 1911; No. 4, built

Baldwin Locomotive Works, USA, 1914; No. 5 and 6, built by Baldwin, 1919; No. 7, built Kerr Stuart, 1924. Fourteen trailers, double-truck, saloon, clerestory roof, coach builders, D.S.C. and Cousins and Cousins Ltd., Auckland. Cars 3 to 8, 1910; cars 1, 2 and 9, 1912; cars 10 and 11, 1915; cars 12 to 14, 1923.

Wanganui—1908: one tram-car engine, Baldwin 1891 (ex-NSWGT 100), purchased second-hand from Sydney for construction of Gonville-Castlecliff tramway in 1910. Ran emergency service hauling two trailers to Castlecliff during powerhouse failure in 1920.

CABLE TRAMWAY VEHICLES

Roslyn—1881 to 1951: Original series of 1881 imported from Cutten and Co., coach work by Stanfield and White. Four grip cars, a coal tram and a water tram. Grip cars 5 and 6, built mid-1880s, combination, closed saloons at each end, arch roof with clerestory. These six trams withdrawn 1906/08. Four grip cars, bodies only, imported from Melbourne in 1901, but found unsuitable, so never placed in service. Second series of grip cars, 1 to 7, built by Cossen and Black, Dunedin, 1906/08. Car 1 had clerestory roof, all other cars had arch roofs. Cars renumbered by City Corporation, 91 to 97 in 1921.

Mornington—1883 to 1957: Original series of 1883, open grip cars, clerestory roof, and four saloon, clerestory roof, trailers, imported from Jones Car Company, New York. Trailer No. 4, only vehicle of original stock to survive fire of 1903. Renumbered 107 by DCCT. One four-wheel open coal trailer used behind passenger grip cars. First additions to fleet were combination grip cars with large arch roofs and small clerestory. To replace burnt rolling stock, borough council had second series of grip cars 1 to 5 built in 1903, combination, saloon at each end, clerestory roof. Renumbered 101 to 105 by DCCT. Grip car 108 built by city corporation in 1925, combination, saloon at each end, arch roof. Trailers 109 and 110, saloon, built by borough council in 1904. Trailers 111 and 112, built by city corporation in 1924.

Maryhill Extension—1885 to 1955: Original grip car, No. 10, combination, saloon at each end, arch roof with clerestory, burnt 1903. Grip car No. 5 (DCCT No. 105), combination, end saloons, used on this extension until 1910. Ex-Elgin Road grip car No. 6 (DCCT No. 106), ran service from 1910 to 1955. No. 105 retained as spare tram—also used on Mornington line.

Kaikorai—1900 to 1947: Six combination grip cars. Nos 1 to 6 (renumbered 121 to 126 by DCCT). Cars 1 to 5 had clerestory roofs.

Elgin Road—1906 to 1910: Special grip car built locally for this extension, combination with saloons at each end. Renumbered 106 by DCCT.

Kelburn, Wellington—1902 to ——: Rolling stock used on the original system. Three combination grip cars: Nos 1 and 2 had an enclosed saloon at each end. No. 3 had an enclosed saloon at each end together with an open section at each end. Withdrawn 22/9/78. Three Palace type trailers, Nos 4 to 6, former Wellington horse-trams. Withdrawn 27/7/74.

Second generation rolling stock used on the new system. Nos 1 and 2, built by Habegger, Switzerland. Fully enclosed, 30 seated, 70 standing. Entered service 20/10/79. Still in service.

Roster of Electric Tramway Rolling Stock

AUCKLAND

Car Number	Coach Builders	Year Introduced	Description and General Remarks
1 to 10, 21 to 28, 44 to 49.	Brush Co., England. No. 44, Auckland Electric Tramways Company. No. 49, Cousins and Atkin, Auckland.	1902/05	Single-truck, saloon, clerestory roof, Car 44 originally a freight tram. Car 49 built as California combination, later rebuilt to single saloon. Car 24 used as rail grinder in 1916. From 1911 to 1918 these cars were gradually coupled in pairs. Series withdrawn 1931.
11 to 16, 29 to 37, 40 to 43.	Brush Co., England.	1902	Double-truck, combination, clerestory roof. Car 11, first tram assembled in Auckland. Series withdrawn 1951/53.
17 to 20, 38, 39.	Brush Co., England.	1902	Double-truck, double-deck, only double-deckers used in Auckland. Upper decks removed 1923. Car 38 used as rail grinder 1936−55. Rest of series was withdrawn 1948.
50 to 56.	Brush Co., England.	1905	Double-truck, saloon, clerestory roof. Series withdrawn 1953.
57 to 60. 64, 65, 70, 71.	Cousins and Atkin, Auckland. Car 57. A.E. Tramway Co.	1906/08	Double-truck, saloon, clerestory roof. Cars 64 and 71 retained large windows and small fanlights. Series withdrawn 1952/53.
61 to 63.	Cousins and Atkin, Auckland.	1907	Radial truck, saloon, clerestory roof. Double truck fitted later. Bodies sold to Napier in 1921. New double-truck trams took over these fleet numbers in 1921/22.
66 to 69.	Ex-Metropolitan Electric Tramways, London.	1907	Shipped to NZ complete. Radial truck, saloon, clerestory roof. Double truck fitted later. Known as the 'Lobster' Series, withdrawn 1921. One body sold to Napier, but never used. New trams took over these fleet numbers.
72 to 77.	D.S.C. and Cousins and Cousins, Auckland. Car 72, A.E. Tramway Co.	1908	Double-truck, saloon, clerestory roof. Known as 'Dreadnoughts' after famous class of battleship. Car 75 first Auckland tram fitted with air brakes in 1909. Takapuna tramway trailers built to this design. Series withdrawn 1953.
78 to 169, 61 to 63, 66 to 69.	78 to 87, 112 to 116, 122 to 126. Brush Co., England. 88 to 100, 102 to 111, 117 to 121, 127 to 169, 61 to 63, 66 to 69, D.S.C. and Cousins and Cousins Ltd., Auckland. Car 101, A.E. Tramway Co.	1908/22	Double-truck, saloon, clerestory roof. Series withdrawn 1952/55. Car 86 gutted by fire at Gaunt Street Depot 1933, Auckland Transport Board rebuilt this car as the first streamliner in 1935− scrapped 1956.
170 to 205.	D.S.C. and Cousins and Cousins Ltd, Auckland.	1923/26	Double-truck, saloon, semi-steel construction. Cars 170, 173, and 184 rebuilt to streamline design 1936−37. Series withdrawn 1955/56.
206.	Auckland City Corporation Tramways.	1926	Double-truck, saloon, same design as semi-steel cars, but timber construction. Only tram built by council during its ownership of tramway system.
207 to 246.	207 to 211, 232 to 241, Auckland Transport Board. 212 to 216, H.C. Williams Ltd. 217 to 231, 242 to 246, Henderson and Pollard.	1930/34	Double-truck, saloon, all previous cars 7 feet 6 inches wide, these were 8 feet. Similar design to semi-steels. Series withdrawn 1955−56.
247 to 256.	Auckland Transport Board.	1938/43	Streamline design, double-truck, saloon. Only six sets of EMB 27-inch diameter trucks shipped from England, owing to Second World War. Cars 252, 254, 255, and 256, equipped with locally-built 33 in trucks. Car 253 equipped as a regenerative control car 1940 to 1950. Series withdrawn 1956.
300.	Auckland Electric Tramways Co.	1908	Single-truck, freight tram. Body built in 1904 and used in traffic carrying the fleet number 44 till 1906. Later used as a revenue car between depots and ATB head office in Customs Street West until 1948.

301 to 303.	Auckland Electric Tramways Co.	1907/11	Double-truck, sprinkler trams. Car 301—3500-gallon tank. Cars 302 and 303, 3000-gallon tanks. Equipment and frames used to build passenger cars 167 to 169 in 1921.
304.	Auckland Electric Tramways Co.	1913	Double-truck, flat-top freight tram, with crane. Last tram to be dismantled in Auckland, 1957.

GISBORNE

1 & 2.	Federal Storage Battery Car Co., New Jersey, USA.	1913	Single-truck, saloon, battery powered. Withdrawn in 1929.
3 & 4.	Boon and Co. Christchurch.	1917/19	Single-truck, saloon, battery-powered. Withdrawn in 1929.

NAPIER

1 to 5.	Brush Co., England.	1913	Single-truck, California combination, clerestory roof. Withdrawn 1931.
6 & 7.	Boon and Co., Christchurch.	1915	Single-truck, California combination, clerestory roof. Withdrawn 1931.
8 & 9.	Cousins and Atkin, Auckland.	1923	Double-truck, saloon, clerestory roof. Bodies former Auckland trams Nos 61 and 62, built in 1907. Later converted to one-man control. Withdrawn 1931.

NEW PLYMOUTH

1 to 4.	Boon and Co., Christchurch.	1916	Single-truck, combination. Open compartments closed 1923. Converted to saloon, one-man operation 1930. Withdrawn 1954.
5, 6, 10.	Boon and Co., Christchurch. No. 10.	1916 1925	Double-truck, saloon. Cars 5 and 6 converted to one-man operation 1932. Car 10 converted to one-man operation 1939. Series withdrawn 1954.
7 to 9.	J.G. Brill Co., Philadelphia, USA.	1921	Single-truck, saloon, Birney Safety cars. Trams shipped from USA in sections and assembled at New Plymouth. Series withdrawn 1954.

WANGANUI

1 & 2.	Lyons and Co., Wellington.	1908	Single-truck, California combination, clerestory roof. Car 1 converted to trailer 1925, to saloon one-man tram 1928. Car 2 converted to trailer 1925, to saloon one-man tram 1928. Car 2 scrapped 1935, Car 1 scrapped 1950.
3 & 4.	Lyons and Co., Wellington.	1908	Single-truck, saloon, clerestory roof. Car 3 converted to trailer 1925, Car 4 converted to trailer 1924. Series withdrawn 1932.
5 to 12. 16 to 19, 23 to 25.	Boon and Co., Christchurch.	1909/12 1921/23	Single-truck, California combination, clerestory roof. Car 11 converted to semi-enclosed type 1925. Car 7 used as breakdown tram 1931 to 1950. Cars 5, 6, 9, 17, 18, 19, 23, 24, 25 stripped and all equipment used for Takapuna cars. Car 16 converted to saloon, one-man operation 1935, scrapped 1950. Cars 8, 10, 11, and 12, stored at depot until 1950.
13 to 15. 20 to 22. 26 to 34.	Boon and Co., Christchurch. D.S.C. and Cousins and Cousins, Auckland 1910/15.	1913/16 1921/22 1929/32	Single-truck, convertible trailers with aluminium sides. Former double-truck, saloon, clerestory roof trailers used by Takapuna Tramways and Ferry Co., Auckland till 1927. Converted to one-man electric trams at Wanganui. No. 34's one-man equipment from Napier 8. No. 26 ex-trailer No. 10; 27 ex-9; 28 ex-2; 29 ex-8; 30 ex-1; 31 ex-7; 32 ex-4; 33 ex-5; 34 ex-6. Known as the 'Takapunas'.

WELLINGTON

1 to 12.	British Electric Car Co. Ltd., Trafford Park, Manchester.	1904	Single-truck, saloon, double-deck. Cars 2 to 12 withdrawn 1931. Car 1 scrapped 1941.
13 to 24.	British Electric Car Co. Ltd., Trafford Park, Manchester.	1904	Single-truck, saloon, clerestory roof. In 1911 cars 13 to 20 rebuilt as double-truck combinations. Cars 21 to 24 withdrawn 1931. 13 to 20 withdrawn late 40s early 50s.
25 to 32.	British Electric Car Co. Ltd., Trafford Park, Manchester	1904	Double-truck, combination, small saloon, clerestory roof. Withdrawn 1940s/early 1950s.
33.	J.G. Brill Company, USA.	1904	Single-truck, convertible, clerestory roof. Used as a city councillors' car and as a motorman instruction car. Known as 'Aunty'. Withdrawn 1931.
34 to 36.	Dick Kerr, England.	1905	Single-truck, single-saloon, double-deck. No. 35 used as illuminated advertising tram until about 1939. Cars 34 and 36 withdrawn 1931. Car 35 scrapped 1950.
37 to 39.	Dick Kerr, England.	1905	Single-truck, open cars, clerestory roof. Known as 'Hong Kong' or 'Toastrack' trams. Ten-bench. No. 37 boarded up and used as rail grinding car. Series withdrawn 1931.

40 to 42.	Rouse and Hurrell, Wellington.	1905/06	Double-truck, combination, small saloon, clerestory roof. Series withdrawn early 1950s.
43.	Rouse and Hurrell, Wellington.	1906	Single-truck, four-compartment Palace. Rebuilt to double-saloon, centre entrance, centre aisle. Withdrawn 1931.
44, 45.	Rouse and Hurrell, Wellington.	1906	Single-truck, open cars. Nine-bench. Rebuilt to four-compartment Palace, later rebuilt to double-saloon, centre entrance, centre aisle. Series withdrawn 1931.
46.	Wellington City Tramways Department.	1906	Single-truck, four-compartment Palace. Rebuilt to double-saloon, centre entrance, centre aisle. Withdrawn 1931.
47 to 52.	Rouse and Black, Wellington.	1906/07	Double-truck, double-deck, with five Palace compartments on lower deck. Rebuilt later with two lower saloons, centre entrance, centre aisle. Known as 'Big Bens'. 48 to 52 withdrawn 1954. No. 47 retained at Depot for maintenance in Hataitai Tramway Tunnel and depots until 1962.
53 to 80.	Rouse and Black, Rouse and Hurrell. Wellington City Tramways Department.	1906/08	Double-truck, six-compartment Palace. Rebuilt to double-saloon, centre entrance, centre aisle. No. 55 altered to single-saloon as an experiment for a short period. Series withdrawn 1940s and early 1950s.
81.	Wellington City Tramways.	1909	Double-truck, five-compartment Palace. Rebuilt to double-saloon, centre entrance, centre aisle. Withdrawn 1940s.
82 to 87.	Rouse and Hurrell, Wellington.	1911	Single-truck, four-compartment Palace. Rebuilt to double-saloon, centre entrance, centre aisle. 82 used as an advertising tram. Series scrapped 1940s.
90, 91.	Wellington City Tramways.	1911	Double-truck, combination, large saloon. Series withdrawn 1954/55.
92 to 160.	Wellington City Corporation Tramways.	1913/25	Double-truck, double-saloon, open centre compartment. Open compartments closed 1931/35. No. 116 first car altered. Car 103 renumbered 119, April 1955, original 119 broken up. Car 92 used as cement-carrying tram by contractors rebuilding Kilbirnie Sheds 1955–57. Series withdrawn 1955/60.
161 to 231.	Wellington City Corporation Tramways.	1924/35	Double-truck, double-saloon, Cars 161 to 225 built with open centre compartments, which were closed 1931/35. Car 225, first car fitted with upholstered seats. Series withdrawn 1955/63.
232.	Wellington City Corporation Tramways.	1933	'Fiducia' double-truck, saloon. One-man equipment from Napier No. 9. Gutted by fire, Kilbirnie Depot, March 1951.
233 to 260.	Wellington City Corporation Tramways.	1937/40	Double-truck, saloon, 'Fiducia' type, construction on Cars 257 to 260 stopped by Second World War, cars completed 1950/52. No. 260 last tram to be built in NZ. Series withdrawn 1964.
300, 301.	Wellington City Corporation Tramways.	1911 1915	Single-truck, freight trams. Original fleet Nos 200 and 201. Renumbered 300 and 301 in August 1928. No. 300 converted to breakdown emergency tram and No. 301 to a track grinding car in 1920s. No. 300 scrapped 1955. No. 301 withdrawn 1964.
Sprinkler	Hursthouse & Co.	1907	Single-truck, street sprinkler, 1780-gallon tank.

CHRISTCHURCH

1 to 5.	John Stephenson Co., New Jersey.	1905	Single-truck, California combination, clerestory roof. Converted to single-saloon, multiple-unit running cars 1919/20. Car 1 converted to trailer 1944; Car 2 staff lunch car at Square Depot 1946, converted to rail grinding car 1950; Car 4 used as Art Union advertising tram from 1946. Series withdrawn 1948/54.
31 to 35.	Boon and Company. Christchurch.	1905	Single-truck, California combination, clerestory roof. Cars 31 and 32 coupled as an experiment May 1918. Series converted to single-saloon, multiple-unit running 1920/21. Later used as motorman training trams. Series scrapped 1949/52. No. 34 used as paint-drying room at workshops scrapped October 1947.
21 to 23.	John Stephenson Co., New Jersey.	1905	Single-truck, saloon, clerestory roof. Fitted for multiple-unit running 1920. Car 23 converted to rail grinding car 1946. Series scrapped 1950/52.
11 to 20.	John Stephenson Co., New Jersey.	1905	Double-truck, combination, small saloon at one end, large open section, clerestory roof. Open sections closed 1929. Known as the 'Yanks'. Series withdrawn 1952/54.
24 to 26.	John Stephenson Co., New Jersey. (143 to 145 in 1920/21)	1905	Double-truck, double-deck, closed below. Converted to single-deck trams 1918. Converted to radial truck, four-wheel trailers and renumbered 143 to 145 in 1920/21. Known as 'Facing Mother' trailers. Series withdrawn 1952.
30.	John Stephenson Co., New Jersey.	1905	Double-truck, combination baggage and passenger car, clerestory roof. Later used as staff bicycle tram. Withdrawn 1947.
6 to 9. 36 to 47. 150 to 161.	Boon and Co., Christchurch.	1909 1906/07 1910	Double-truck, drop centre section, open, clerestory roof, closed saloon at each end. Centre sections closed 1929/32. Known as 'Boon' cars. Withdrawn 1950/54.
24 to 26. 162 to 171.	Boon and Co., Christchurch.	1920 1912	Double-truck, combination, large convertible section, small saloon. Fronts of Cars 162 and 165 rebuilt with sloping windows.

172 to 196.	Boon and Co., Christchurch. Cars 195 and 196 built by Christchurch Tramway Board.	1921/26	Car 165 in April 1944 and Car 162 in June 1945. This class mainly used on Cashmere Hills route, became known as the 'Hills' cars. Withdrawn 1952/54. Double-truck, saloon, equipped for multiple-unit running. Converted to one-man operation 1932/36. Series withdrawn 1953.
203 to 205.	Boon and Co., Christchurch.	1927	Built as single-truck, saloon trailers in 1921/23. Converted to one-man trams 1927. Car 205, the first one-man tram in Christchurch — used on St Martins line. Car 203 converted into bicycle tram 1947. Car 205 reverted to trailer 1945. Series withdrawn 1949/54.
Sprinklers. No. 1.	John Stephenson Co., New Jersey.	1905	Single truck, street sprinkler. 1850-gallon tank. Known as 'Wet Willie'. Used as a track cleaner until system closed in 1954.
No. 2.	McGuire Cummings, USA.	1908	Double-truck, street sprinkler. 4000-gallon tank.
No. 3.	Cooper and Duncan, Christchurch.	1909	Double-truck, street sprinkler. 4000-gallon tank. Both cars equipped for use as snow ploughs 1926/30 — scrapped 1940 — tanks used for petrol and fuel oil at Sockburn during Second World War.
Overhead Tram.	Christchurch Tramway Board.	1906	Single-truck, workshop tram with tower platform for overhead wire maintenance. Withdrawn 1950s. Known as 'Gentle Annie'.

TRAILER CARS — CHRISTCHURCH

50.	John Stephenson Co., New York.	1887	Former horse-tram, single-truck, California combination, clerestory roof. Since 1920s used only on special occasions as a horse-tram.
51.	Christchurch Tramway Board.	1905	Rebuilt from two single-truck, double-deck, steam trailers into a double-truck, centre entrance, double-deck trailer. Had two nicknames, 'Jumbo' and 'Rotomahana', after well-known steamer of the day. Withdrawn late 1930s.
52 to 70, 84 to 100,	Former horse- and steam-tram trailers from the 1880/90s taken over from original companies.		Single-truck, double-deck, closed below Single-truck, double-deck, closed below. Scrapped 1919/51.
71 to 83.	" "		Single-truck, double-deck, open on both decks. Known as 'Cages'. Trailers 71, 75, 77, 78, and 79, had lower deck closed in 1923. Series withdrawn 1943/51.
101 to 104.	Former horse- and steam-tream trailers from the 1890s taken over from original companies.		Single-truck, double-deck, open on both decks, straight staircases. Trailer 103 had top deck removed and sides closed for use with tram 30 carrying staff bicycles in 1946. Series withdrawn 1947/54.
105 to 109.	Former horse- and steam-tram trailers from the 1880s taken over from original companies.		Single-truck, open trailers, five bench, known as the 'Punts'. Series withdrawn 1930s.
110 to 115.	Boon and Co., Christchurch.	1908	Single-truck, Palace, four compartments. Rebuilt to single-saloon, centre aisle in 1919/20. Known as 'Duckhouse' trailers. Series withdrawn 1952.
116 to 119.	Boon and Co., Christchurch.	1911	Double-truck, open, later made convertible saloon, 13-bench. Centre aisle added later. Known as the 'Dreadnought' series. Withdrawn 1952/53.
120 to 123.	Boon and Co., Christchurch.	1913	Double-truck, convertible saloon, 12-bench. Series withdrawn 1953/54.
124, 125.	Boon and Co., Christchurch.	1915	Single-truck, radial axle, convertible saloon. Known as 'Big Berthas'. Series withdrawn 1952.
126 to 142, 146 to 149, 201 to 206.	Boon and Co., Christchurch.	1917/18 1921 1921/23	Single-truck, radial axle, single-saloon. Known as the 'Standard' trailers. Mainstay of the trailer fleet. Series withdrawn 1952/54.

DUNEDIN

1 to 14.	J.G. Brill Co., Philadelphia, USA	1903	Single-truck, saloon, clerestory roof. Car 5 converted to grinder and breakdown car 1914, transferred to Maori Hill branch and reverted to passenger car, 1933; Car 1 rebuilt to double-truck, combination, to test suitability of Dunedin for double-truck trams in 1917, known as 'Big Lizzie'; Car 8 transferred to Maori Hill in 1924 and renumbered 86; Car 9 transferred to Maori Hill in 1923 and renumbered 87; Cars 10 and 11 coupled in 1922 — reverted to single units in 1926; Cars 2 and 12, and 6 and 7, coupled in 1925. Series withdrawn 1936/54.
15 to 28.	J.G. Brill Co., Philadelphia, USA.	1903	Single-truck, California combination, clerestory roof. No. 27 transferred to Maori Hill branch for a brief period as a trial. Series withdrawn 1953/55.

29 to 43.	J.G. Brill Co., Philadelphia, USA	1903/05	Single-truck, open, 10-bench, clerestory roof. Cars 29 to 34 (original series), converted to California combination in 1926/27. Three of these open cars ran briefly as trailers in 1927. Known as the 'High Steppers'. Series withdrawn 1927/52.
44 to 49.	Dunedin City Corporation Tramways.	1913/14	Single-truck, California combination, clerestory roof. Known as the 'Bobtails'. Series withdrawn 1953/55.
50.	J.G. Brill Co., Philadelphia, USA.	1903	Single-truck, street sprinkler, 2500-gallon tank and dust-suction equipment. The Quertier patent track cleaner. Suction equipment removed about 1906. Withdrawn 1930s.
51 to 62.	Meadowbank Manufacturing Co., Sydney, Australia.	1921/22	Double-truck, double-saloon, drop centre, convertible centre section. Known as 'Sydney Bogies'. Series withdrawn 1953/56.
63 to 66.	D.S.C. and Cousins and Cousins, Auckland.	1930	Former double-truck, saloon, clerestory roof, trailer cars 11, 12, 13, and 14, built in 1915–23 for the Takapuna Tramways and Ferry Co., Auckland. Used as such until 1927. Converted at Dunedin to electric trams. Known as the 'Takapunas'. Series withdrawn 1956.
75 to 80.	Dunedin City Corporation Tramways.	1923/25	Single-truck, saloon trailers, built to handle traffic to NZ and South Seas Exhibition, 1925/26. Toastrack cars 29 to 43 hauled these trailers. Converted to electric trams in 1926/27. Mainly used on Caversham line. Series withdrawn 1952/54.
	Former horse-tram trailers.	1903	Six trailers, selected from old horse-cars, were renovated and mounted on new Brill trucks—no documents or pictorial record of these trailers in service with electric trams.

MAORI HILL—DUNEDIN

1 to 3.	J.G. Brill Co., Philadelphia, USA.	1900	Single-truck, saloon, clerestory roof. First electric trams in NZ. Cars renumbered after city corporation took over line in 1921. Car 1 became 88 and No. 2, 89. Car 3 renumbered 81 and transferred to city system and converted to track grinder and breakdown car. Last used 1948. Series withdrawn 1936/48.

INVERCARGILL

1 to 10.	Boon and Co., Christchurch.	1912	Single-truck, California combination, clerestory roof. Converted to saloon, one-man operation 1922/28. Series withdrawn 1951/52.
11 to 16.	J.G. Brill Co., Philadelphia, USA.	1921	Single-truck, saloon, Birney Safety cars. Trams shipped from USA in sections and assembled at Invercargill. Series withdrawn 1950/52.

MAPS

Public Works Department records at National Archives, Wellington, and the author's private archives, show that each of the tramway systems experienced continual changes to its permanent way over the decades, in response to many factors. A definitive record of such alterations giving the details of all co-existing loops, junctions, and single and double track sections would require several maps for each system. Hence within the space available, the editorial decision to show only the streets once traversed by trams.

The maps show the electric and cable systems at their maximum extent. Not all sections of track were in operation simultaneously or continuously. Section opening and closing dates are shown in Appendix II.

Buildings are not drawn to scale and geographic features, most particularly shorelines, are shown essentially as they exist in 1993.

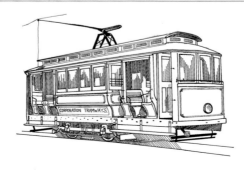

Route Maps of Tramway Systems

Street Tramways of New Zealand

Opening and Closing Dates of Horse, Steam, Cable, Battery and Electric Tramway Systems

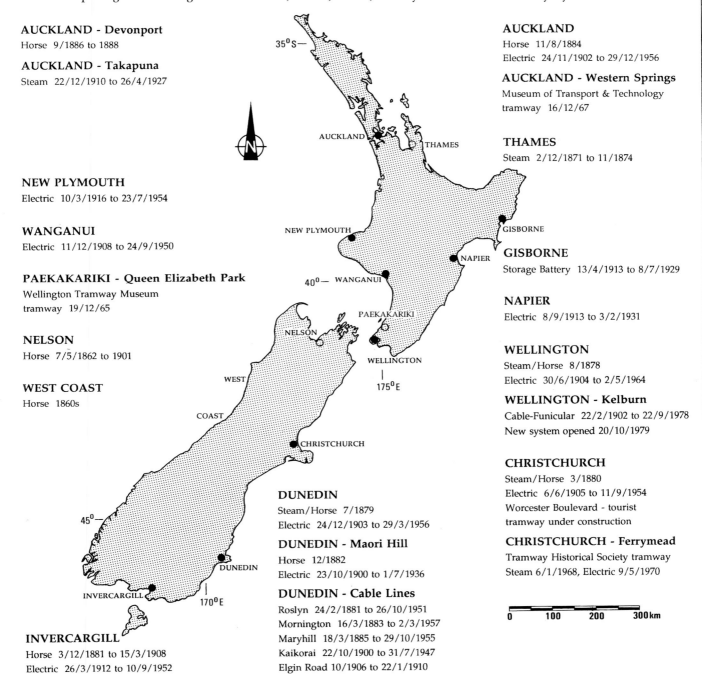

AUCKLAND - Devonport
Horse 9/1886 to 1888

AUCKLAND - Takapuna
Steam 22/12/1910 to 26/4/1927

NEW PLYMOUTH
Electric 10/3/1916 to 23/7/1954

WANGANUI
Electric 11/12/1908 to 24/9/1950

PAEKAKARIKI - Queen Elizabeth Park
Wellington Tramway Museum
tramway 19/12/65

NELSON
Horse 7/5/1862 to 1901

WEST COAST
Horse 1860s

INVERCARGILL
Horse 3/12/1881 to 15/3/1908
Electric 26/3/1912 to 10/9/1952

AUCKLAND
Horse 11/8/1884
Electric 24/11/1902 to 29/12/1956

AUCKLAND - Western Springs
Museum of Transport & Technology
tramway 16/12/67

THAMES
Steam 2/12/1871 to 11/1874

GISBORNE
Storage Battery 13/4/1913 to 8/7/1929

NAPIER
Electric 8/9/1913 to 3/2/1931

WELLINGTON
Steam/Horse 8/1878
Electric 30/6/1904 to 2/5/1964

WELLINGTON - Kelburn
Cable-Funicular 22/2/1902 to 22/9/1978
New system opened 20/10/1979

CHRISTCHURCH
Steam/Horse 3/1880
Electric 6/6/1905 to 11/9/1954
Worcester Boulevard - tourist
tramway under construction

CHRISTCHURCH - Ferrymead
Tramway Historical Society tramway
Steam 6/1/1968, Electric 9/5/1970

DUNEDIN
Steam/Horse 7/1879
Electric 24/12/1903 to 29/3/1956

DUNEDIN - Maori Hill
Horse 12/1882
Electric 23/10/1900 to 1/7/1936

DUNEDIN - Cable Lines
Roslyn 24/2/1881 to 26/10/1951
Mornington 16/3/1883 to 2/3/1957
Maryhill 18/3/1885 to 29/10/1955
Kaikorai 22/10/1900 to 31/7/1947
Elgin Road 10/1906 to 22/1/1910

All Maps © Bruce Gamble BE (Hons), PhD, PEng (Alberta), MASCE MIPENZ

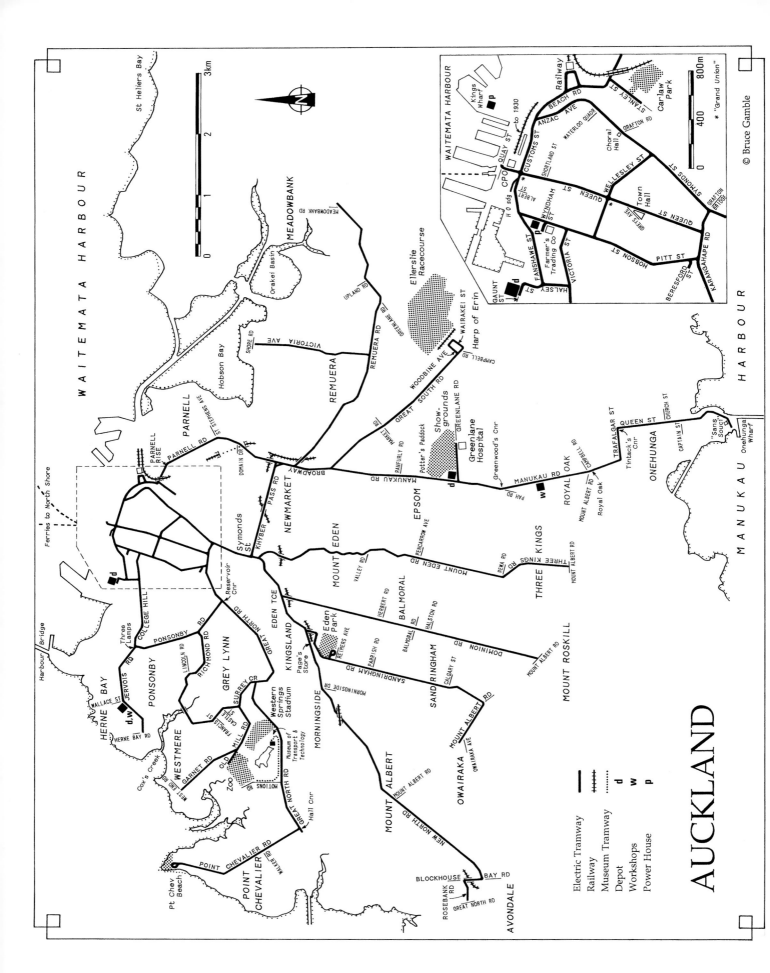

AUCKLAND

Electric Tramway
Railway
Museum Tramway
d — Depot
w — Workshops
p — Power House

© Bruce Gamble

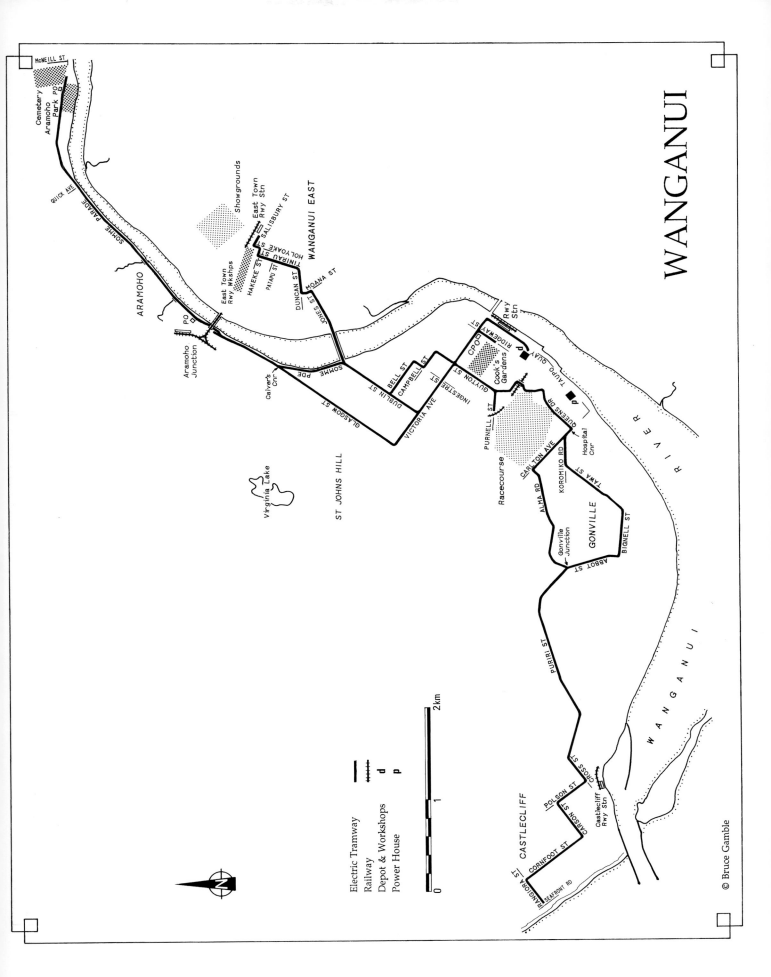

WANGANUI

McNEILL ST

Cemetery
Aramoho
Park PO

QUICK AVE

SOMME PARADE

ARAMOHO

PO

Aramoho
Junction

Calver's Cnr

SOMME PDE

GLASGOW ST

Showgrounds

East Town
Rwy Wkshps

East Town
Rwy Stn

HAKEKE ST

PATAPU ST

TINIRAU ST

SALISBURY ST

HOLYOAKE ST

WANGANUI EAST

MOANA ST

JONES ST

DUNCAN ST

BELL ST

CAMPBELL ST

DUBLIN ST

INGESTRE ST

VICTORIA AVE

GUYTON ST

Cook's
Gardens

CPO

RIDGEWAY ST

Rwy Stn

TAUPO QUA

QUEENS DR

PURNELL ST

Racecourse

CARLTON AVE

ALMA RD

KOROMIKO RD

Hospital
Cnr

TAWA ST

Gonville
Junction

GONVILLE

BIGNELL ST

ABBOT ST

PURIRI ST

CROSS ST

POLSON ST

CARSON ST

Castlecliff
Rwy Stn

CASTLECLIFF

CORNFOOT ST

RANGIORA ST

SEAFRONT RD

WANGANUI RIVER

Virginia Lake

ST JOHNS HILL

Electric Tramway
Railway
Depot & Workshops
Power House

2km

1

0

N

© Bruce Gamble

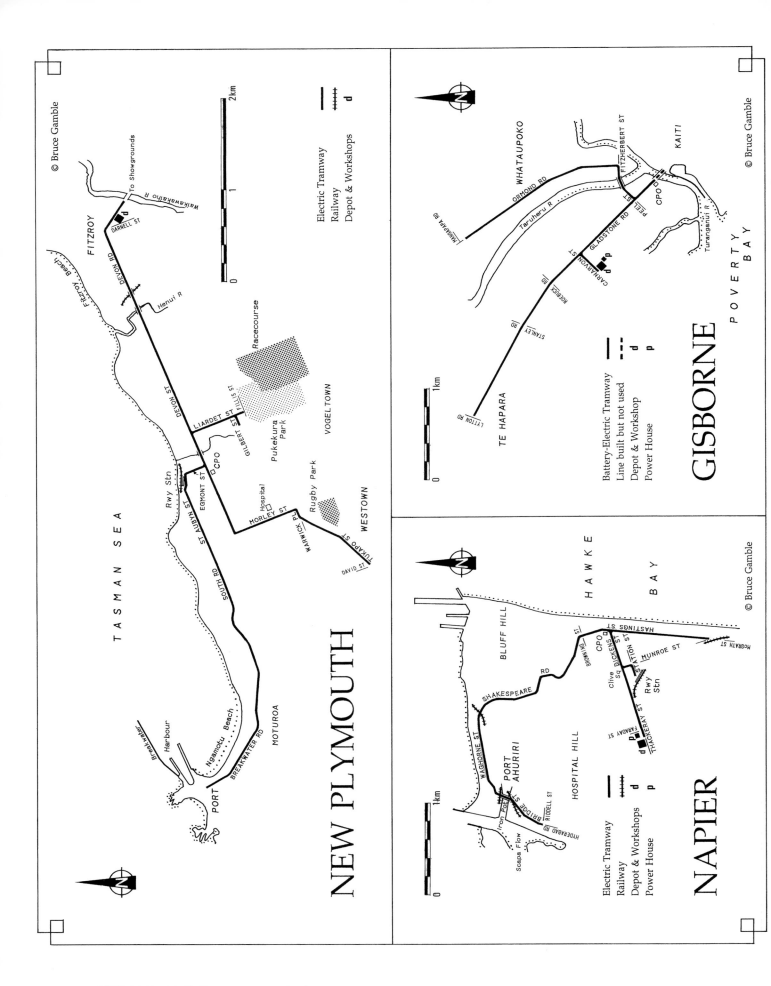

NEW PLYMOUTH

TASMAN SEA

© Bruce Gamble

2km

1

0

Electric Tramway
Railway
Depot & Workshops   d

To Showgrounds

FITZROY

Waikawakaiho R

DARNELL ST   d

DEVON RD

Fitzroy Beach

Henui R

DEVON ST

Racecourse

FITZGERALD ST

LIARDET ST

GILBERT ST

Pukekura Park

VOGELTOWN

CPO

EGMONT ST

Rwy Stn

ST AUBYN ST

Hospital

Rugby Park

MORLEY ST

WARWICK PL

WESTOWN

DAVID ST

TUKAPO ST

SOUTH RD

BREAKWATER RD

MOTUROA

PORT

Ngamotu Beach

Harbour

Breakwater

GISBORNE

POVERTY BAY

© Bruce Gamble

WHATAUPOKO

ORMOND RD

Taruheru R

FITZHERBERT ST

PEEL ST

KAITI

MANGAPAPA RD

GLADSTONE RD

CARNARVON ST   d   p

CPO

Turanganui R

ROEBUCK RD

STANLEY RD

TE HAPARA

LYTTON RD

1km

0

Battery-Electric Tramway
Line built but not used   d
Depot & Workshop   p
Power House

NAPIER

HAWKE BAY

© Bruce Gamble

BLUFF HILL

Shakespeare RD

BROWNING ST

CPO

DICKENS ST

HASTINGS ST

SHAKESPEARE RD

MCGRATH ST

MUNROE ST

Clive Sq

Rwy Stn

SALTON ST

WAGHORNE ST

PORT AHURIRI

Iron Pot

BRIDGE ST

HYDERABAD RD

RIDDELL ST

Scapa Flow

HOSPITAL HILL

THACKERAY ST

FARADAY ST   p   d

1km

0

Electric Tramway
Railway   d
Depot & Workshops   p
Power House

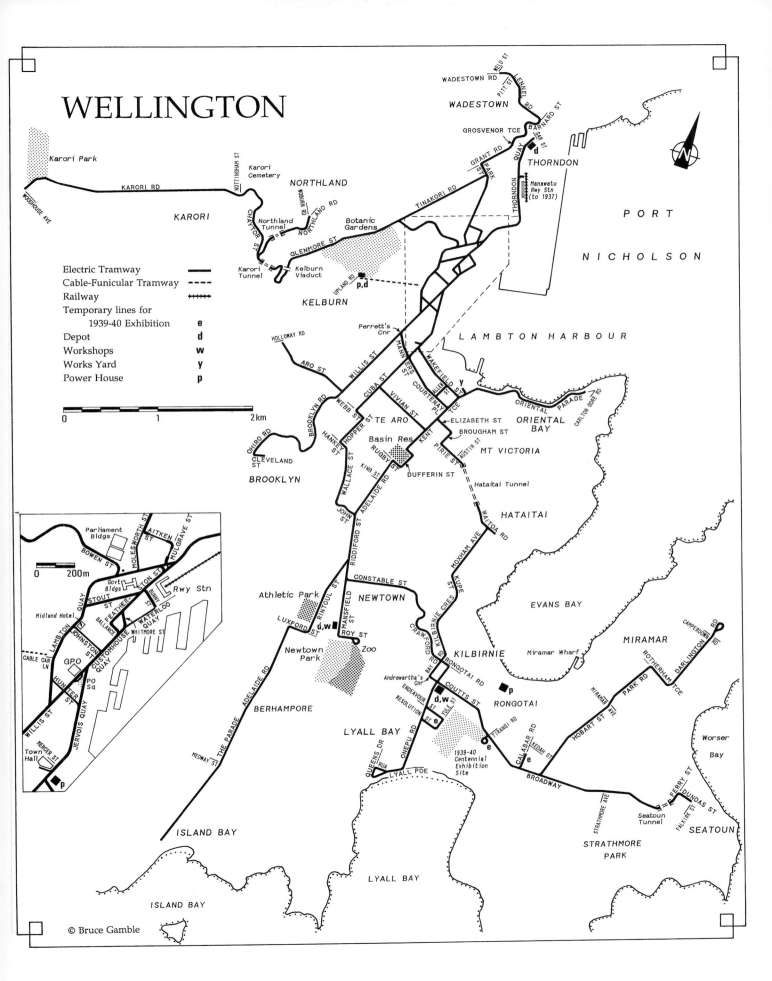

WELLINGTON

Electric Tramway ———
Cable-Funicular Tramway - - -
Railway +++++
Temporary lines for
1939-40 Exhibition e
Depot d
Workshops w
Works Yard y
Power House p

0   1   2km

Karori Park

KARORI RD

NOTTINGHAM ST

Karori Cemetery

NORTHLAND

WOBURN RD

NORTHLAND RD

CHAYTOR ST

Northland Tunnel

KARORI

WOODHOUSE AVE

TINAKORI RD

Botanic Gardens

GLENMORE ST

Karori Tunnel

Kelburn Viaduct

UPLAND RD

p,d

KELBURN

HOLLOWAY RD

Perrett's Cnr

ARO ST

WILLIS ST

BROOKLYN RD

WEBB ST

CUBA ST

HOPPER ST

VIVIAN ST

TE ARO

HANKEY ST

WALLACE ST

OHIRO RD

CLEVELAND ST

BROOKLYN

RUGBY ST

KING ST

ADELAIDE RD

JOHN ST

Basin Res

KENT

PIRIE ST

DUFFERIN ST

AUSTIN ST

ELIZABETH ST

BROUGHAM ST

Hataitai Tunnel

MANNERS ST

WAKEFIELD ST

COURTENAY PL

TORY ST

TCE

ORIENTAL PARADE

CARLTON GORE RD

ORIENTAL BAY

MT VICTORIA

y

WADESTOWN RD

WELD ST

PITT ST

LENNEL RD

BARNARD ST

WADESTOWN

GROSVENOR TCE

SAR ST

THORNDON **d**

GRANT RD

PARK ST

THORNDON QUAY

Manawatu Rwy Stn (to 1937)

PORT NICHOLSON

LAMBTON HARBOUR

RIDDIFORD ST

CONSTABLE ST

HATAITAI

WAITOA RD

MOXHAM AVE

KUPE ST

KILBIRNIE CRES

CRAWFORD RD

EVANS BAY

Miramar Wharf

CAMPERDOWN RD

MIRAMAR

ROTHERHAM TCE

DARLINGTON RD

PARK RD

MIRAMAR AVE

HOBART ST

Worser Bay

Athletic Park

MANSFIELD ST

RINTOUL ST

NEWTOWN

LUXFORD ST

d,w

ROY ST

Newtown Park

Zoo

BERHAMPORE

ADELAIDE RD

THE PARADE

MEDWAY ST

Andrewartha's Cnr

RONGOTAI RD

COUTTS ST

ENDEAVOUR ST

RESOLUTION ST

e

d,w

YULE ST

p

RONGOTAI

KILBIRNIE

BROADWAY

TIRANGI RD

CALABAR RD

KEDAH ST

e

e

LYALL BAY

QUEENS DR

ONEPU RD

RUA

LYALL PDE

1939-40 Centennial Exhibition Site

STRATHMORE AVE

FERRY ST

DUNDAS ST

FALKIRK ST

Seatoun Tunnel

SEATOUN

STRATHMORE PARK

ISLAND BAY

LYALL BAY

ISLAND BAY

Parliament Bldgs

AITKEN ST

MULGRAVE ST

MOLESWORTH ST

BOWEN ST

STOUT ST

BUNN ST

Govt Bldgs

Rwy Stn

FEATHERSTON ST

BALLANCE ST

WHITMORE ST

WATERLOO QUAY

CUSTOMHOUSE QUAY

JOHNSTON ST

LAMBTON QUAY

Midland Hotel

CABLE CAR LN

GPO

PO Sq

JERVOIS QUAY

WILLIS ST

MERCER ST

Town Hall

HUNTER ST

p

0   200m

© Bruce Gamble

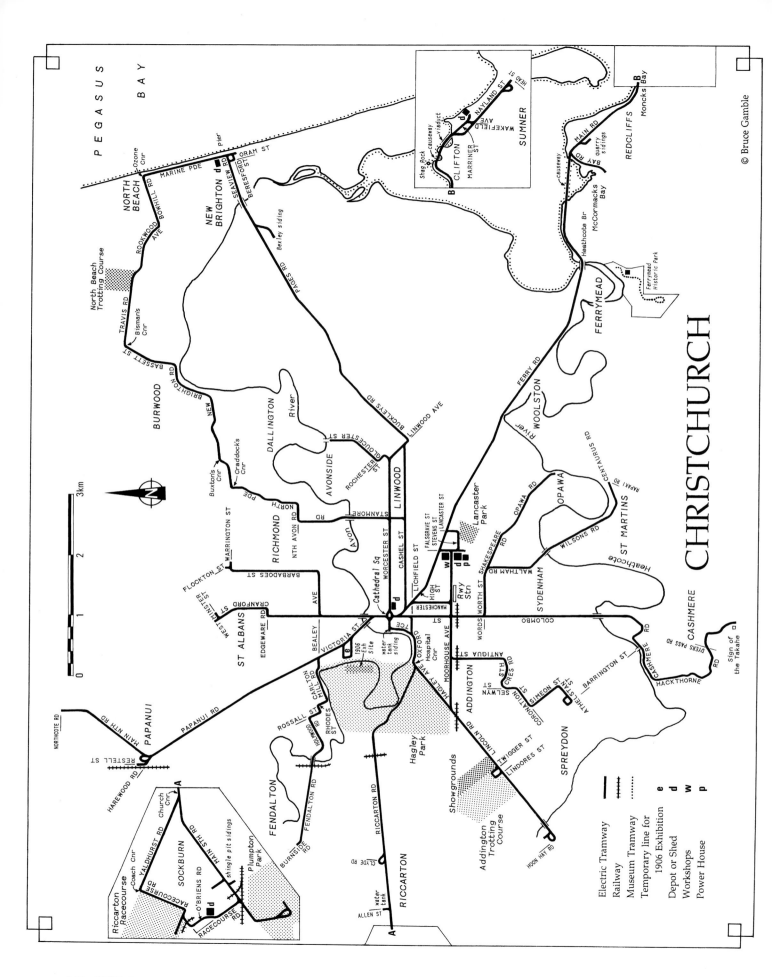

© Bruce Gamble

CHRISTCHURCH

Legend:
- Electric Tramway
- Railway
- Museum Tramway
- Temporary line for 1906 Exhibition
- e
- d — Depot or Shed
- w — Workshops
- p — Power House

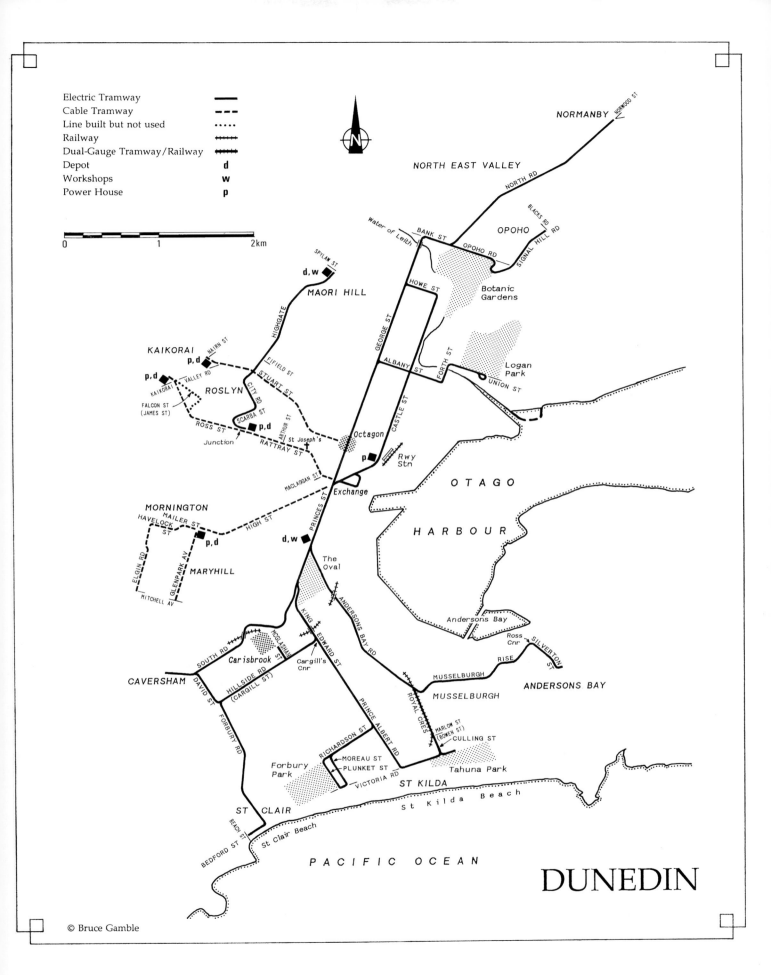

Electric Tramway
Cable Tramway
Line built but not used
Railway
Dual-Gauge Tramway/Railway
Depot   d
Workshops   w
Power House   p

0   1   2km

© Bruce Gamble

DUNEDIN

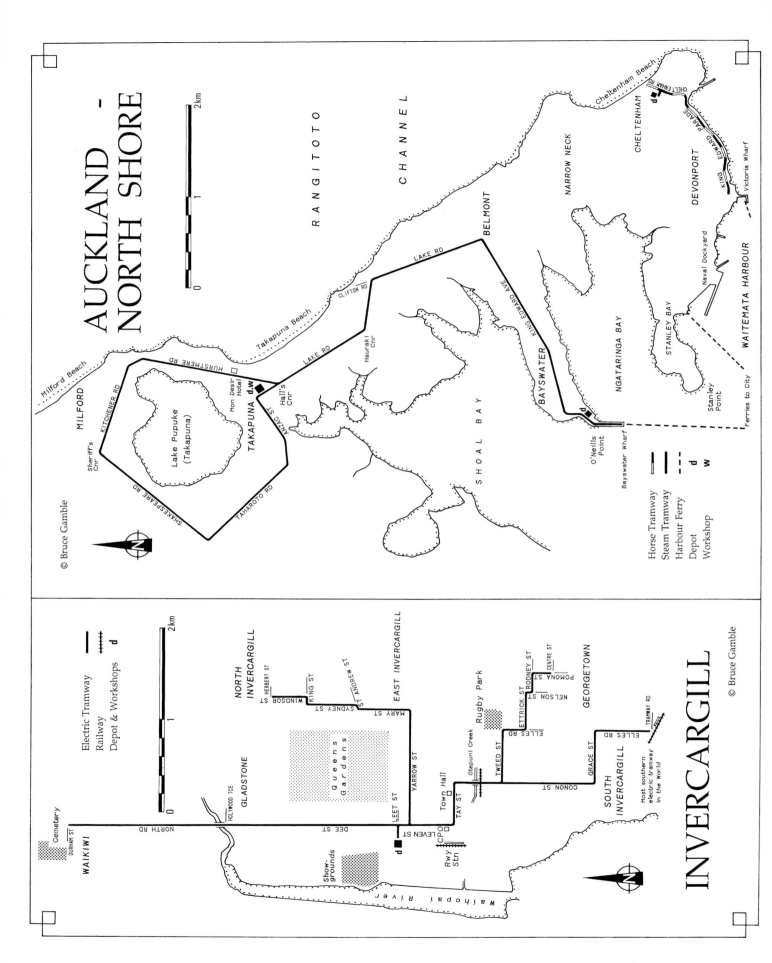

AUCKLAND - NORTH SHORE

© Bruce Gamble

2 km
0 1

RANGITOTO CHANNEL

Cheltenham Beach

CHELTENHAM
d

CHELTENHAM RD

NARROW NECK

DEVONPORT

KING EDWARD PARADE

Victoria Wharf

Naval Dockyard

STANLEY BAY

Stanley Point

WAITEMATA HARBOUR

Ferries to City

NGATARINGA BAY

BAYSWATER

KING EDWARD AVE

O'Neills Point
d

Bayswater Wharf

SHOAL BAY

BELMONT

LAKE RD

CLIFTON RD

LAKE RD

Hauraki Cnr

Hall's Cnr

TAKAPUNA d,w

ANZAC ST

Mon Desir Hotel

HURSTMERE RD

Takapuna Beach

Lake Pupuke (Takapuna)

KITCHENER RD

Sheriff's Cnr

SHAKESPEARE RD

TAHAROTO RD

MILFORD

Milford Beach

N

Horse Tramway
Steam Tramway
Harbour Ferry
d Depot
w Workshop

INVERCARGILL

© Bruce Gamble

Electric Tramway
Railway
d Depot & Workshops

2 km
0 1

WAIKIWI

Cemetery

DURHAM ST

NORTH RD

HOLYWOOD TCE

GLADSTONE

Showgrounds

Waihopai River

DEE ST

LEET ST

Queens Gardens

HERBERT ST

WINDSOR ST

KING ST

ST ANDREW ST

SYDNEY ST

NORTH INVERCARGILL

MARY ST

EAST INVERCARGILL

YARROW ST

Town Hall

TAY ST

ELEVEN ST
d

CPO

Rwy Stn

Otepuni Creek

Rugby Park

TWEED ST

ELLES RD

ETTRICK ST

NELSON ST

RODNEY ST

POMONA ST

CENTRE ST

GEORGETOWN

CONON ST

GRACE ST

ELLES RD

SOUTH INVERCARGILL

TRAMWAY RD

Most southern electric tramway in the World

N

Tramway Museums

MUSEUM OF TRANSPORT AND TECHNOLOGY, Auckland (Motat)

Layout

The track layout consists of approx. 300 metres within the museum complex and approx. 1.1 kilometres external to the museum laid along the roadside boundaries of the adjacent Western Springs Park to the Auckland Zoo. The external line begins with a passing loop outside the Motat entrance gates at Western Springs then continues as a single track along the park/footpath boundary of Great North Road to a passing loop on the corner of Motions Road. It then continues as a single line along the park/footpath boundary of Motions Road to a double-track terminus adjacent to the zoo entrance. The line has still to be completed with an extension across and along Motions Road to within the Motat II site at Meola Road, a distance of 700 metres.

Opening Dates

Museum internal line	16 December 1967
Museum gates to Motions Road corner	19 December 1980
Motions Road corner to zoo terminus	18 December 1981

Permanent Way

The track is dual gauge. It is 1219 millimetres for the Wellington cars and 1435 millimetres for the Auckland and other cars. The majority of the track is laid in mass concrete using 85-pound and 91-pound T rail with 112-pound grooved tramway girder rail on the curves. Rail joints consist of sole plates welded to the rail foot. All points have fabricated open mates on the dual rail side and cast tongue switches on the common rail. Crossings are also fabricated.

Overhead

The overhead is both span wire and side arm bracket construction using steel poles.

Power Supply

A 675 kW Hewittic mercury arc rectifier supplied from the local power supply authorities. HT network provides the 550 volt DC traction power. The rectifier was one of the many that supplied Auckland's former trolley bus system.

Workshops, Barns

A double-track workshop with a maintenance pit and a display and storage barn is provided within the museum complex.

Service Details

The tramway service operates approx. every 30 minutes during the weekdays and is popular with school children when their schools visit the Motat Education Centre. During weekends and holidays the headway is varied between 20 and six minutes with the necessary increase in cars to suit passenger loading.

WELLINGTON TRAMWAY MUSEUM, Paekakariki

Layout

The tramline begins from the depot, which is located about 100 metres inside the Memorial Gates at the entrance to Queen Elizabeth Park at MacKays Crossing, 4 kilometres north of Paekakariki on State Highway One north of Wellington. An island platform tram station within a terminus passing loop is the departure point. The single-track main line follows MacKays Road on the right-hand side of the road through Elizabeth Park for 1.85 kilometres where it terminates at Whareroa Beach. There is a passing loop at the midway point. Approaching Whareroa Beach, the line climbs steeply over sand dunes, the gradient increasing to a maximum of 1 in 18 for the final 100 metres to the summit, then descends, passing a short spur siding, before swinging away from the road and down an embankment to the picnic area at Whareroa Beach. The tramway, running through rolling sand-dune terrain, offers passengers extensive scenic views ranging from the Tararua Ranges at the depot end to coastal scenery including panoramic views of Kapiti Island.

Opening Dates

First 200 metres	19 December 1965
Various extensions including the loop, gave a total route length of 1 kilometre	by 1967
Other small extensions over the next 20 years gave a total route mileage of 1.2 kilometres	
Over the hill to the spur siding— total length of 1.65 kilometres	31 March 1985
To the beach and picnic area— total length of 1.85 kilometres	10 December 1988

Permanent Way

The track is laid to Wellington's 1219-millimetre (4-foot) gauge. The majority of the track is tramway girder rail from the former Wellington tramway system. More recent extensions and re-lays where the track is reasonably straight, 50-pound T rail from the original Wellington cable car system has been used.

Overhead

On the single-track main line the overhead is side arm bracket construction off wooden poles. In the depot area and at the passing loop, span wire construction from steel poles is employed.

Power Supply

The 550 volt DC traction power is provided from a 400 kW Hewittic mercury arc rectifier which is supplied from the local power authority's 11 kv high-tension supply. The rectifier set formerly supplied power to the New Plymouth trolley bus system and was commissioned in 1970. Before this power was supplied from a diesel generator.

Buildings

The main tram barn is capable of housing up to 12 trams (four rows of three), and was officially opened on 15 October 1978. A double-track workshop building of 300 square metres is currently in the planning stage and, when built, will enable the main barn building to be developed into the main museum display building. The maintenance pit has been completed for the workshop building. A large storage building at the rear of the site houses vehicles for restoration in the long term.

Service Details

Trams operate every 30 minutes from 11 am to 5 pm during the weekends, public holidays and every day from Boxing Day to Wellington Anniversary Day in the summer. On busy days, the headway is reduced to 15 minutes.

TRAMWAY HISTORICAL SOCIETY, Ferrymead, Christchurch

Layout
The total length of operating track is approx. 1.5 kilometres and involves a mainly single-tracked line commencing at the Bridle Path Road car park and connecting with the Truscotts Road Museum site. A now little used branch travels in a northerly direction to the end of the Ferrymead Reserve with a passing loop at the end. The track layout at the Bridle Path Road Depot area, where there are two tram sheds, includes a triangle around the former Cathedral Square tram shelter, a former CTB workshop traverser linking the two buildings and a passing loop at the commencement of the line to Truscotts Road. The sharpest curves on the system are in this area (15-metre radius), but elsewhere these are of greater radius, eg 20 metres at Church Corner, 25–30 metres elsewhere. The line proceeds south and then in a westerly direction past the former Heathcote rubbish tip, crosses Truscotts Road and over a small bridge into double track, around Church Corner and through the created historic Bowman Street in double track with bracket arm construction. At Moorhouse Square the track branches providing a loop system around to the Exhibition Area (Hall of Wheels etc). A set of points has been provided for a future 'town' shed, yet to be built, and there is also a branch line into the Hall of Wheels to allow rolling stock to be displayed there.

Opening Dates

Tram barn to boundary with Ferrymead Reserve (steam only)	6 January 1968
Electrified line to reserve	9 May 1970
Completion of reserve line	11 December 1971
Extension to paddock loop	23 March 1974
Extension to Truscotts Road	1 August 1976
Completion of township, including loop	17 September 1984

Permanent Way
The track is standard gauge (1435-millimetre). Most of the track as far as Truscotts Road is 55-pound T rail, lifted by the society from the former Blackball branch line on the West Coast and using a lighter rail as a check rail on curves. This track is of sleeper construction, but once into the township area, mass concrete has been used using mainly 70-pound rail with some grooved tram rail on some curves. Point work includes ex-Christchurch and ex-Wellington tramway points and also in some areas railway blades and point levers with fabricated crossing. Overhead style includes span wires, side arm brackets and centre poles. Former CTB steel poles and wooden poles are used, the overhead wire is 30 and 40 gauge from the former New Plymouth and Dunedin trolley bus systems.

Power Supply
A small 75 kW Hewittic mercury arc rectifier acquired from the Timaru Harbour Board is located in the tram barn at Bridle Path Road and a larger 375 kW system obtained from Dunedin and using ex-Auckland trolley bus system switchgear has been installed in a specially designed sub-station at the Truscotts Road site.

Workshops, Barns
Tram barn No. 1 (recently extended) contains five roads and is used for storage of unrestored and restored vehicles and as a restoration workshop. Tram barn No. 2, which has two roads, holds restored vehicles and also a maintenance pit.

Service Details
The tramway service operates approximately every 30 minutes during weekdays and every 20 minutes at weekends and holidays. The track layout is such that, on very busy weekends, with several vehicles operating, a headway of less than five minutes is possible.

Rolling Stock Preserved by Museums

(b) denotes body only   (f) denotes frame and bogies only
(r) under restoration in 1992

MUSEUM OF TRANSPORT AND TECHNOLOGY,
Auckland
Auckland electric trams: 17 (b), 11 (restored to c1912
    condition), 44 (b) , 89 (b), 203 (b), 248, 253.
Wellington electric trams: 47 (r), 135 (restored to original
    condition), 252, 244, 257, 301.
Wanganui electric trams: 10 (b), 21 (b) trailer, Baldwin
    steam tram 100.
Kelburn Cable Tramway: 3 Grip car.
Dunedin Cable Tramway, Mornington: 107 trailer.
Melbourne electric tram, Australia: 321.

WELLINGTON TRAMWAY MUSEUM, Paekakariki
Wellington electric trams: 17 (b), 82 (b), 151 (restored to
    c1940), 159 (restored to c1940), 185 (b), 207, 235, 238,
    239, 250 (f), 260.
Kelburn Cable Tramway: 2 Grip car and 6 trailer.
Wanganui electric tram: 8 (b).
New Plymouth electric tram: 8 (b)
Brisbane electric tram, Australia: 133.

WELLINGTON CITY COUNCIL
Kelburn Cable Tramway: 1 Grip car and 4 trailer.

TRAMWAY HISTORICAL SOCIETY, Ferrymead,
    Christchurch.
Christchurch electric trams: 1 (b), 20 (b), 24 (b), 26 (r),
    152 (restored to c1915 condition), 178 (restored to c1938
    condition).
Christchurch trailer cars: 10 (restored to c1890 condition),
    43 (restored to Californian style), 64 (b), 74 (restored to
    latter CTB style), 84 (b), 115 (restored to 1919/20 style),
    118 (b), 202 (b).
Kitson steam-tram No. 7 (restored to c1900).
Dunedin electric trams: 11 (restored to c1915 condition),
    22 (restored to c1925 condition), 37 (b).
Roslyn electric tram: 3 (b).
Dunedin horse-tram: 18 (r).
Roslyn cable line: 95 (grip car restored to c1940 condition)
Mornington cable line: 103 grip car (b), 110 (r) trailer,
    111 (b) trailer.
Invercargill electric trams: 5 (b), 15 (b).
Brisbane electric tram: 236 (restored to late c1930 condition
    —on lease from the Wellington Tramway Museum).

YALDHURST TRANSPORT MUSEUM, Christchurch
Christchurch electric tram: 6 (b).

OTAGO EARLY SETTLERS' MUSEUM, Dunedin
Maryhill cable car 106.

DUNEDIN MUSEUM OF TRANSPORT AND
    TECHNOLOGY
Roslyn electric tram: 1 (b).
Roslyn cable line: 93 (b).
Kaikorai cable line: 125 (b).
Dunedin electric trams: 2 (b), 6 (b), 7 (b), 12 (b), 17 (b),
    33 (b), 35 (b), 43 (b), 52 (b).

SEASHORE TROLLEY MUSEUM
Kennebunkport, Maine, USA
Mornington/Maryhill cable car 105.

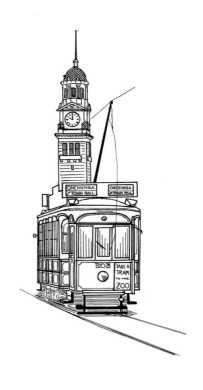

Bibliography

BOOKS

Arnold, Ian. *Locomotive, Trolley, and Rail Car Builders*, Trans-Anglo Books, 1965.
Auckland Electric Tramways Company Limited. *Rules and Regulations for the Officers & Employees*, 1907.
Gibbs, T.A. *The Metropolitan Electric Tramways*, The Tramway and Light Railway Society, 1962.
McDonald, K.C. *City of Dunedin*, Dunedin City Corporation, 1965.
Keating, John D. *Mind the Curve!* Melbourne University Press, 1970.
McLintock, A.H. (editor). *An Encyclopaedia of New Zealand* (3 vols.), Government Printer, 1966.
Palmer, A.N. *New Zealand's First Railway*, NZ Railway and Locomotive Society, 1962.
Reed, A.W. *Maori Place Names*, A.H. & A.W. Reed, 1962.
Walsh, T. *From Wherry to Steam Ferry on the Waitemata*, Walsh Printing Company, 1932.
Whitcombe, H.A. *History of the Steam Tram*, The Oakwood Press, Surrey, England.
Wilson, Frank E. *The British Tram*, Percival Marshall, 1961.

PERIODICALS AND NEWSPAPERS

NZ Railway Observer, NZ Railway and Locomotive
    Society Inc., Wellington.
Modern Tramway, Ian Allan and Light Railway Transport
    League, England.
Tramway Topics, Wellington Tramway Museum, Tramway
    Historical Society, Tramway Division, Museum of
    Transport and Technology.
The Controller, Auckland Transport Club.
Tramway Journal, Wellington Corporation Tramways.
Air Brake, Christchurch Tramway Employees' Social and
    Welfare Club.
Transport Magazine, Dunedin City Corporation Transport
    staff magazine.
Weekly News, Auckland.
New Zealand Herald, Auckland.
Auckland Star, Auckland.
The Zealander, Auckland.
Thames Star, Thames.
Wanganui Chronicle, Wanganui.
Wanganui Herald, Wanganui.
Taranaki Herald, New Plymouth.
New Zealand Times, Wellington.
Dominion, Wellington.
Evening Post, Wellington.
Daily Telegraph, Napier.
Gisborne Herald, Gisborne.
Nelson Examiner, Nelson.
Lyttelton Times, Christchurch.
Press, Christchurch.
Canterbury Times, Christchurch.
Otago Daily Times, Dunedin.
Evening Star, Dunedin.
Southland Times, Invercargill.

OTHER SOURCES

General Assembly Library, Wellington.
National Archives, Wellington.
First-hand interviews with former employees throughout New Zealand.

REFERENCES

The author will make available to students of transportation any references and source material from the text of this book by writing to Grantham House Publishing.

Index

WHEN TRAMS WERE TRUMPS IN NEW ZEALAND
Graham Stewart

Suburban travel before the motorcar. New Zealanders rode them to school, to work, to sports and many to fame. A pictorial parade of these classic vehicles through the changing facades of streets in our cities, spanning more than 100 years.

NEW ZEALAND TRAGEDIES
Tangiwai and other Railway Accidents
Geoff Conly and Graham Stewart

Notable railway accidents since 1880. The miraculous escapes and the tragedies — of human failings and the force of the elements against man-made structures. The complete story of Tangiwai — Christmas Eve 1953 — when 151 people lost their lives through forces and circumstances beyond man's control.

NEW ZEALAND TRAGEDIES
Shipwrecks and Maritime Disasters
Gavin McLean

Stories of terrifying storms, of inhospitable coastlines, of human error, of the malicious hand of fate. Also testimonies to tremendous courage and endurance. More than 200 superb photographs help bring alive the dramatic events of New Zealand's seafaring past.

NEW ZEALAND TRAGEDIES
Fires and Firefighting
Gavin McLean

Fires that shocked the nation, Colonial City Catastrophies, Ballantyne's 1947, Fire Service Unit histories, 300 photographs.

PORTRAIT OF THE ROYAL NEW ZEALAND NAVY
A Fiftieth Anniversary Celebration
Grant Howard. Paintings by Colin Wynn

Fifty colour plates of the naval ships which have served New Zealand. The book traces the part played by the Navy since the arrival of Lieutenant James Cook, RN, in HMS *Endeavour* in 1769. Black and white photographs of human interest complete the story.

PORTRAIT OF AN AIR FORCE
The Royal New Zealand Air Force
Geoffrey Bentley and Maurice Conly

A celebration of RNZAF aircraft, squadrons and personnel — a timely tribute to our Air Force. 28 full-colour oil paintings, 73 charcoal drawings and over 200 photographs.

CITY OF AUCKLAND TRAMWAYS

AND

Suburban Land Company, Limited,

47, 55, QUEEN STREET,

Auckland

Wellington City Tramways.

Wanganui Corporation Tramways

Gonville & Castlecliff Tramway Board.

(Wanganui,

Wellington City Corporation

Tramways Dept.
Harris Street,
Wellington, N.Z.

The Auckland Electric Tramway

TELEPHONE NO. 318.
P.O. Box 549.

(Head Office: DONINGTON HOUSE, NORFOLK ST

CABLE ADDRESS
"TRAMWAYS" AUCKLAND.
Telephone :— 45-900.

Auckland C

The Kelburne & Karori

Napier Muni

Tramways & Electricity

Faraday Stree

PLEASE ADDRESS ALL LE
"TRAMWAYS MANAG

Telephone No. 2134
Cable Address : "GENERATOR."
Code : WESTERN UNION (Universal Edition)

\. NES,
NORTH ROUTE:
..edin to North-East Valley
and Normanby.
SOUTH ROUTE:
Dunedin to Caversham, St.
Clair, and Ocean Beach.

TELEPHONE Nos:
OFFICE, 354.
STABLES, 361.

The Dunedin City & Suburban Tramways Co. Ltd.

Offices : CORNER OF MANSE & STAFFORD STREETS.

Dunedin, N.Z.

Christchur

Morningto

The Dunedin & Roslyn Tramway Company, Limited.

OFFICE: KAIKORAI VALLEY.

Dunedin.

The Dunedin and Kaikorai

LIMITED.

TRAMWAY TERMINUS, KAIKO

Dunedin City Corporation Electric Tramways.
Manager's Office,
CAR HOUSE, MARKET ST

Dunedin, N.Z.